RANDOM HOUSE

LARGE
PRINT

*How to Know God: The Soul's Journey
Into the Mystery of Mysteries*

ENDORSEMENTS

"I congratulate Dr. Deepak Chopra for this wonderful book, reaching out to many, many readers, on the subject of spirituality, but with a scientific approach. And I absolutely agree with Dr. Chopra's view that 'if we want to change the world, we have to begin by changing ourselves.' This is the same message that I have always been conveying."

The Dalai Lama

"The most important book about God for our times. Deepak Chopra is an amazing combination of William James and Shankara. In this book he has built for us a magical stairway to ascend to life-changing experience of the sacred, keeping our scientific outlook and an ever more open heart and mind."

Robert Thurman, Ph.D.,
professor of religion,
Columbia University

"Deepak Chopra has introduced literally millions of people to the spiritual path, and for this we should all be profoundly grateful. In *How to Know God*, Deepak continues his pioneering outreach, showing that God consciousness unfolds in a series of stages, each important and remarkable in itself, yet each getting closer to Source. This is at once a map of Spirit, and a map of your own deepest Self, for in the last analysis, they are one and the same."

Ken Wilber, author of
Integral Psychology

"Spiritual health and moral responsibility are two of the most precious gifts that any leader can offer. Few thinkers have done as much as Deepak Chopra to allow millions to embrace the project of personal and social transformation. I agree completely with Dr. Chopra's insight that 'if we want to change the world, we have to begin by changing ourselves.' In a world where overcoming poverty, inequality, greed, and cynicism will be the great human challenges of the twenty-first century, Deepak Chopra offers life-affirming suggestions for developing a more just and peaceful society."

Oscar Arias, president of
Costa Rica (1986–1990),
1987 Nobel Peace Prize
Laureate

"Deepak Chopra has blessed the world by spreading the light of vedic knowledge and the timeless teachings on nonduality. Vedanta has inspired and transformed the lives of seekers for thousands of years. However, every age needs a voice that can articulate ancient Wisdom in a contemporary framework. Dr. Chopra has given the seekers of self-knowledge a clear and scientific road map to understand and realize the ultimate reality. I congratulate him for his brilliant work."

> His Holiness Vasudevanand
> Saraswati, Jagad Guru
> Shankracharya of Jyotirmath
> World Headquarters
> established by Adi Shankara
> (sage-philosopher of India
> A.D. 686–718)

"This is a profound and accessible exploration of the experience of God, including an understanding of it in biological and scientific terms. *How to Know God* is both fascinating and uplifting."

> Andrew Weil, M.D., director
> of the Program in Integrative
> Medicine at the University
> of Arizona

"One of the best books ever written about a subject that more people think about than anything else."

> Larry King,
> host of *Larry King Live*,
> CNN

"A renowned physician and author, Deepak Chopra is undoubtedly one of the most lucid and inspired philosophers of our times."

> Mikhail Gorbachev, president,
> Citation of the Medal of the
> Presidency of the Italian
> Republic awarded by the
> Pio Manzu International
> Scientific Committee

"Deepak Chopra has really done it this time—a brilliant, scholarly yet lyrical synthesis of neuroscience, quantum physics, personal reminiscence, Eastern, Western, and spiritual thinking. Dr. Chopra's new theory of seven stages of understanding God is extremely relevant to the ongoing transformation in medicine today from the old soul-less paradigm to the new one with spirituality and emotions occupying center stage. This will be the Bible of the New Medicine, the scientifically accurate medicine that will replace the dying reductionist old thinking."

> Candace B. Pert, Ph.D.,
> research professor at George-
> town University School of
> Medicine, department of
> physiology and biophysics,
> Washington, D.C., and author of
> *Molecules of Emotion: The Science
> Behind Mind-Body Medicine*

"*How to Know God* should be on the night table of every seeker of truth and Spirit. Even better, every seeker should keep it with them at all times as they travel on their soul's journey."

Shirley MacLaine, actress and author of *The Camino* and *Out on a Limb*

"In the tradition not only of William James but especially Carl Gustav Jung, Deepak Chopra finds the soul where it belongs, an essential element of being and links spirituality to human needs. In the spirit of Abraham Maslow's *The Farther Reaches of Human Nature*, he carries stages of development/potentiality even beyond self-actualization and peak experience. Chopra sees the soul as the culmination of an evolution that enables man to find God. Most importantly, he puts ways of experiencing God in a development sequence, ontogeny recapitulating phylogeny spiritually as well as biologically. 'God is a process.' It is appropriate that Deepak Chopra, who previously dealt with physical health, now approaches spirituality in 'a similarly inspired way, since growing evidence suggests the two may be linked."

George Freeman Solomon, M.D., Professor of Psychiatry and Biobehavioral Sciences, Emeritus, University of California, Los Angeles

"Deepak continues to lead us even deeper into the mysteries and joys of true spirituality."

James Redfield, author of
The Celestine Prophecy and
The Secret of Shambhala

"For the thousand years which preceded modernity, the world was G-d intoxicated. Theology was man's greatest pursuit embraced by the earth's leading minds. Then along came mind-numbing sound bites about the deity—'G-d is love,' 'May the Force be with you'—which propelled the knowledge of G-d back to its infancy. Deepak Chopra's profound and insightful book inspires us once again to apprehend G-d in all His majesty and all His glory. Hats off to Deepak for restoring awe and mystery to the grandest of all subjects."

Rabbi Shmuley Boteach,
author of *Kosher Sex* and
*An Intelligent Person's Guide
to Judaism*

"Deepak Chopra takes a scientific as well as spiritual approach to the ultimate mystery of life, giving us a breathtaking and awe-inspiring version of Divinity and ourselves. After reading *How to Know God*, you'll have a much deeper understanding of who you are and your role in the universe."

Joan Borysenko, Ph.D., author
of *Seven Paths to God* and *A
Woman's Journey to God*

"Just when I think he can't go any deeper, he does. With *How to Know God*, Deepak Chopra makes it clear: we have in our midst a spiritual genius."

Marianne Williamson, author of *Return to Love* and *Enchanted Love*

"This book will be a very challenging book for those who read it as it was for the adventurous author who wrote it. The philosophical and theological differences raised by scholars from other traditions make the book even more inviting for reflection and discussion. I personally found the book both rewarding and exciting and have enjoyed immensely the serious discussion it provoked. With this work Dr. Chopra moves his many talents from the arena of the medical to the realm of the spiritual, and in so doing 'awakens' our consciousness, which is what spirituality is all about in the first place."

Father J. Francis Stroud, S.J.,
executive director of
DeMello Spirituality Center,
Fordham University

"A brilliant mind has created a book which should be read by believers and nonbelievers. It is a treasure chest of knowledge that everyone should open and explore regardless of one's belief or faith. The knowledge presented can change your life."

Bernie S. Siegel, M.D., author
of *Love, Medicine and Miracles*
and *Prescriptions for Living*

"Deepak offers a fresh, gorgeous, and illuminating approach to the perennial quest to know God. This work of wisdom beautifully weaves religion, quantum physics, and neuroscience in practical, powerful ways to awaken the reader."

Harold H. Bloomfield, M.D., best-selling author of *Healing Anxiety Naturally* and *Making Peace with Your Past*

"This is a very wise book about consciousness and our connection with the Divine. It is a marvelous advance beyond the morbid, godless messages of materialistic science. Above all, it is about waking up to who we really are: infinite, immortal, eternal. No matter what your religious inclinations may be, you can find affirmation, joy, and fulfillment in these pages."

Larry Dossey, M.D., author of *Reinventing Medicine* and *Healing Words*

"There is a paradigm shift going on, and Deepak Chopra, M.D., is one of its most popular and eloquent spokespersons. In this new paradigm, consciousness, popularly called God, is the ground of all being. Opponents often ask, So how do I know this consciousness? Certainly my ego is nothing like you describe! Now Chopra has given a very readable response in *How to Know God*. It is not easy to know God, says Chopra correctly, because God is separated from us by a discontinuity. Chopra explains this beautifully using quantum physics and relativity theory. But you can know God with God's Grace, assures Chopra, as he gives many steps to follow. If you want to investigate Reality or God, especially if you are a beginner, this book will be of real help."

> Amit Goswami, professor, department of physics, University of Oregon, and author of *The Self-Aware Universe* and *Quantum Creativity*

"The ultimate how-to book! Brilliant!"

> Dean Ornish, M.D., founder and president of the Preventive Medicine Research Institute; clinical professor of medicine, UCSF School of Medicine, and author of *Love & Survival* and *Dr. Dean Ornish's Program for Reversing Heart Disease*

"Very simply, the most profoundly enlightening book I have ever read. I am in awe at the depth of feeling on these pages—Astounding—Brilliant—A course in knowing God, rather than knowing about God."

Wayne W. Dyer

"This book opens the door to the new millennium with a quantum leap into the world of Infinite creativity. Who is God? Are you God? Can you experience God directly? In this groundbreaking road map to the ultimate awakening, Deepak Chopra emerges as *the* scientist of the inner world. He shows us step by step how we can meet God face-to-face. This book is a must for those who are ready to enter the new millennium as blissful, creative, multi-dimensional beings."

Margot Anand, author of
The Art of Everyday Ecstasy

"In his personal search for spiritual truths, Deepak has discovered definitions so simple and pure that they can change a life in the blink of an eye. I promise that there are readers who will need to do nothing more than open this book at a random page and read any line on which their eye lights—and that line will rewrite their lives. An extraordinary claim? Try it for yourself."

Uri Geller, author/
paranormalist,
Sonning, England

"It is a cri de coeur by one of the most brilliant minds of our time."

Rustum Roy, Evan Pugh Professor of the Solid State; professor of science, technology and society; and professor of geochemistry; Pennsylvania State University

"The true gift of *How to Know God* is that it is about getting to know ourselves. God is the mirror in which we reveal ourselves to ourselves. Deepak Chopra shows that we cannot have an angry righteous god without being governed inwardly and unconsciously by fear. Likewise if we have a loving god we ourselves have a visionary sense of our own infinite potential. The legacy of this book is the true legacy of every human life: the depths to which we have made God in our own hearts."

Richard Moss, M.D., author of *Words That Shine Both Ways*, *The Second Miracle*, *The Black Butterfly*, and *The I That Is We*

"In *How to Know God*, Deepak Chopra teaches us to recognize our everyday lives as the raw material of our spiritual evolution. By reclaiming science as a thread through our spiritual labyrinth, he connects the big questions of meaning, God, and immortality—once the exclusive province of theologians and philosophers—with our daily existence. And he does it all with his infectious sense of awe and wonder."

> Arianna Huffington, syndicated columnist and author of
> *The Fourth Instinct*

"With astonishing insight and breathtaking clarity, Deepak Chopra has here answered the only question that has ever really mattered. The human race will remember this time in our history as the moment when the final veil was lifted from the face of God."

> Neale Donald Walsch, author of
> *Conversations with God*

"With childlike awe and wonder, in words of elegant simplicity, Deepak Chopra invites us to effortlessly discover the mystery of life. Embracing the challenge in gratitude for every grace-filled moment, readers are irresistibly drawn to enjoy the fulfillment of Life's all-encompassing purpose: 'To know, love, and serve God with our whole mind, our whole soul, our whole heart, and to love our neighbor as ourself.' This work of love offers an 'in-the-body' transformative experience assessible to all who choose to accept it."

Sister Judian Breitenbach,
Catholic Order of the Poor
Handmaid of Jesus Christ, The
Healing Arts Center on the
River, Mishawaka, Indiana

"This remarkable book, called *How to Know God*, expresses so profoundly a universal message of the unity of spiritual ideals. It also generously offers a glimpse of the 'Divine' which becomes more and more accessible to readers of all beliefs as the words gradually disclose magic nourishment to mind, heart and soul. While turning the pages, one by one, cascades of revelation come flowing out, washing away all preconceived ideas and dogmatic hindrances which have dominated religious thinking all down the ages. As all barriers between the material and the spiritual worlds crumble through the power of the all-pervading light shining into the heart, the reader is placed face to face with the greatest of all mysteries, losing thereby the illusion of the self, a process which Deepak Chopra illustrates with sublime inspiration."

Hidayat Inayat-Khan
Pir-o-Murshid, Spiritual Head
and Representative General,
International Sufi Movement

Also by Deepak Chopra

Creating Health
Return of the Rishi
Quantum Healing
Perfect Health
Unconditional Life
Ageless Body, Timeless Mind
Journey into Healing
Creating Affluence
Perfect Weight
Restful Sleep
The Seven Spiritual Laws of Success
The Return of Merlin
Boundless Energy
Perfect Digestion
The Way of the Wizard
Overcoming Addictions
Raid on the Inarticulate
The Path to Love
The Seven Spiritual Laws for Parents
The Love Poems of Rumi
*(edited by Deepak Chopra; translated by
Deepak Chopra and Fereydoun Kia)*
Healing the Heart
Everyday Immortality
The Lords of the Light
On the Shores of Eternity

HOW TO KNOW GOD

The Soul's Journey into the Mystery of Mysteries

DEEPAK
CHOPRA

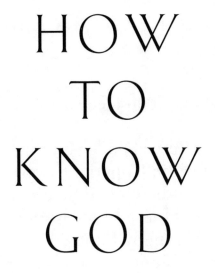

RANDOM HOUSE
LARGE PRINT

A Division of Random House, Inc.
Published in Association with
Harmony Books
New York 2000

FOR HERMS ROMIJN

Copyright © 2000 Deepak Chopra, M.D.

All rights reserved under International and Pan-American Copyright Conventions. Published in the United States of America by Random House Large Print in association with Harmony Books, Member of the Crown Publishing Group, New York, and simultaneously in Canada by Random House of Canada Limited, Toronto. Distributed by Random House, Inc., New York.

The Library of Congress has established a cataloging-in-publication record for this title.

ISBN 0-375-40869-X

Random House Web Address:
http://www.randomhouse.com/
Printed in the United States of America
FIRST LARGE PRINT EDITION

This Large Print Book carries the
Seal of Approval of N.A.V.H.

CONTENTS

In what concerns divine things,
belief is not appropriate.
Only certainty will do.
Anything less than certainty is unworthy of God.
—SIMONE WEIL

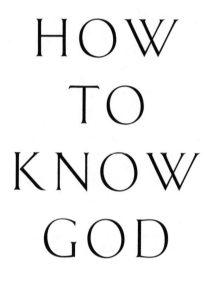

HOW
TO
KNOW
GOD

One

A REAL AND
USEFUL GOD

God has managed the amazing feat of being worshiped and invisible at the same time. Millions of people might describe him as a white-bearded father figure sitting on a throne in the sky, but none could claim to be an eyewitness. Although it doesn't seem possible to offer a single fact about the Almighty that would hold up in a court of law, somehow the vast majority of people believe in God—as many as 96 percent, according to some polls. This reveals a huge gap between belief and what we call everyday reality. We need to heal this gap.

What would the facts be like if we had them? They would be as follows. Everything that we experience as material reality is born in an invisible realm beyond space and time, a realm revealed by science to consist of energy and information. This invisible source of all that exists is not an empty void but the womb of creation itself. Something creates and organizes this energy. It turns the chaos of quantum soup into stars, galaxies, rain forests, human beings, and our own thoughts, emotions, memories, and desires. In the pages that lie ahead we will see that it is not only possible to know this source of existence on an abstract level but to become intimate and at one with it. When this happens, our horizons open to new realities. We will have the experience of God.

After centuries of knowing God through faith, we are now ready to understand divine intelligence directly. In many ways this new knowledge reinforces what spiritual traditions have already promised. God is invisible and yet performs all miracles. He is the source of every impulse of love. Beauty and truth are both children of this God. In the absence of knowing the infinite source of energy and creativity, life's miseries come into being. Getting close to God through a true knowing heals the fear of death, confirms the existence of the soul, and gives ultimate meaning to life.

Our whole notion of reality has actually been topsy-turvy. Instead of God being a vast, imaginary projection, he turns out to be the only thing that is real, and the whole universe, despite its immensity and solidity, is a projection of God's nature. Those astonishing events we call miracles give us clues to the workings of this ineffable intelligence. Consider the following story.

In 1924 an old French villager is walking home. With one eye lost in the Great War and the other severely damaged by mustard gas in the trenches, he can barely see. The setting sun is bright, so the old man is completely unaware of the two youths on bicycles who have wheeled around the corner and are barreling down on him.

At the moment of impact an angel appears. He takes the lead bicycle by its two wheels, lifts it a few feet in the air, and sets it down safely on the grass beside the road. The second bicycle stops short, and the youths become tremendously excited. "There are two! There are two!" one of them shouts, meaning that instead of just the old man alone, two figures are standing in the road. The entire village becomes very worked up, claiming afterward that the youths were drunk or else they made up this fantastic tale. As for the old man, when he is asked about it, he says he doesn't understand the question.

Could we ever come to an answer ourselves? As it happens, the old man was a priest, Père Jean Lamy, and the appearance of the angel has come down to us through his own testimony before his death. Lamy, who was saintly and beloved, seems to be credited with many instances where God sent angels or other forms of divine aid. Although reluctant to talk about them, his attitude was matter-of-fact and modest. Because of Lamy's religious vocation, it is easy to dismiss this incident as a story for the devout. Skeptics would not be moved.

Yet I am fascinated simply by whether it could have happened, whether we can open the door and allow helpful angels into our reality, along with miracles, visions, prophecy, and ultimately that great outsider, God himself.

We all know that a person can learn about life without religion. If I took a hundred newborn babies and filmed every moment of their lives from beginning to end, it wouldn't be possible to predict that the believers in God will turn out to be happier, wiser, or more successful than the nonbelievers. Yet the video camera cannot record what is happening below the surface. Someone who has experienced God may be looking on the entire world with wonder and joy. Is this experience real? Is it useful to our lives or just a subjective event, full of meaning to the person having it but otherwise no more practical than a dream?

One bald fact stands at the beginning of any search for God. He leaves no footprints in the material world. From the very beginning of religion in the West, it was obvious that God had some kind of presence, known in Hebrew as *Shekhinah*. Sometimes this word is simply translated as "light" or radiance. Shekhinah formed the halos around angels and the luminous joy in the face of a saint. It was feminine, even though God, as interpreted in the Judeo-Christian tradition, is masculine. The significant fact about Shekhinah was not its gender, however. Since God is infinite, calling the deity He or She is just a human convention.* Much more important was the notion that if God has a presence, that means he can be experienced. He can be known. This is a huge point, because in every other way God

* A note on gender: Finding a pronoun for God is not easy. In keeping with common tradition, this book uses *he*. But surely God transcends all gender. I could have rotated three different pronouns—*he, she,* and *it*—but that would not have gotten any nearer to the truth, and it would have made for very clumsy reading.

is understood to be invisible and untouchable. And unless some small part of God touches the material world, he will remain inaccessible forever.

We personify God as a convenient way of making him more like ourselves. He would be a very perverse and cruel human, however, to remain so hidden from us while demanding our love. What could possibly give us confidence in any kind of benevolent spiritual Being when thousands of years of religion have been so stained by bloodshed?

We need a model that is both part of religion yet not bounded by it. The following simple, three-part scheme fits our commonsense view of God. Shaped like a reality sandwich, this scheme can be pictured as follows:

God

————— TRANSITION ZONE —————
Material world

The picture is not new in its top and bottom layers, placing God above the material world and removed from it. God must be separate from us, or else we would be able to see him here, strolling about as he did in the Book of Genesis. There, after the seven days of creation, God walked in the garden of Eden, enjoying his handi-work in the cool of the evening.

Only the middle element of our diagram, called the transition zone, is new or unusual. A transition zone implies that God and humans meet on common ground. Some-where miracles take place, along with holy visions, angels, enlightenment, and hearing the voice of God. All of these extraordinary phenomena bridge two worlds: They are real and yet they are not part of a predictable cause-and-effect. To put it another way, if we stubbornly cling to material reality as the only way to know anything, skepticism about God is totally justified. Miracles and angels defy reason, and even though holy visions may be catalogued time after time, the ratio-nal mind remains defiant, defending its sure grip on the material plane.

"You really think God exists? Well, let's break it down. You're a doctor, I'm a doctor. Either God is causing these diseases we see every day, or else he can't do anything to stop them. Which one is the God you want me to accept?"

This voice is from a skeptical colleague I used to make rounds with in the hospital, a confirmed atheist.

"I don't want you to accept either one," I would protest.

But he would press the point. "Reality is reality. We don't have to argue over whether an enzyme or hormone is real, do we? God can't survive any kind of objective test. But we all know that. Some of us just choose not to keep on fooling ourselves."

On one level he was right. Materialist arguments against God remain powerful because they are based on facts, but they fall apart once you dive deeper than the material world. Dame Julian of Norwich lived in England in the fourteenth century. Dame Julian asked God directly why he had created the world. The answer came back to her in ecstatic whispers:

> *You want to know your lord's meaning in what I have done? Know it well, love was his meaning. Who reveals it to you? Love. What did he reveal to you? Love. Why does he reveal it to you? For love.*

For Dame Julian God was something to eat, drink, breathe, and see everywhere, as though she were an infatuated lover. Yet since the divine was her lover, she was elevated to cosmic heights, where the whole universe was "a little thing, the size of a hazelnut, lying in the palm of my hand."

When saints go almost mad with rapture,

we find their expressions both baffling and yet very understandable. Although we have all gotten used to the absence of the sacred, we appreciate that journeys into the transition zone, the layer closer to God, continue to happen.

The experience of God feels like flying. It feels as if I'm walking above the ground with such equilibrium that nothing can sway me from my path. It's like being the eye of the storm. I see without judgment or opinion. I just watch as everything passes in and out of my awareness like clouds.[1]

This uplifting experience, which is common to saints and mystics, is the record of a quantum journey. There are no known physical mechanisms that trigger it, yet feeling close to God occurs in every age, among all peoples. We're all capable of going beyond our material bonds, yet we often fail to value this ability. Although we hear in church or temple or mosque that God is love, he doesn't seem to exert much passionate attraction anymore.

I don't believe saints and mystics are really so different from other human beings. If we look at our reality sandwich, the transition zone turns out to be subjective: This is where God's presence is felt or seen. Anything subjective must involve the brain, since it takes millions of neurons firing together before you can have any experience.

Now our search has narrowed down in a way that looks very promising: God's presence, his light, becomes real if we can translate it into a response of the brain, which I will call the "God response." We can get even more specific. Holy visions and revelations aren't random. They fall into seven definite events taking place inside the brain. These responses are much more basic than your beliefs, but they give rise to beliefs. They bridge from our world to an invisible domain where matter dissolves and spirit emerges:

1. **Fight-or-flight response:** the response that enables us to survive in the face of danger. This response is linked to a God who wants to protect us. He is like a parent who looks out for the safety of a small child. We turn to this God because we need to survive.
2. **Reactive response:** this is the brain's creation of a personal identity. Beyond mere survival, everyone pursues the needs of "I, me, mine." We do this

instinctively, and from this response a new God emerges, one who has power and might, laws and rules. We turn to this God because we need to achieve, accomplish, and compete.

3. **Restful awareness response:** the brain can be active or at rest, and this is its response when it wants peace. Rest and activity alternate in every part of the brain. The divine equivalent is a God who brings peace, who enables us to find a calm center in the midst of outward chaos. We turn to this God because we need to feel that the outer world isn't going to swallow us up in its endless turmoil.

4. **Intuitive response:** the brain looks for information both inside and out. Outer knowledge is objective, but inner knowledge is intuitive. No one checks with an expert outside themselves before saying "I am happy" or "I am in love." We rely on our ability to know ourselves from the inside out. The God that matches this response is understanding and forgiving. We need him to validate that our inner world is good.

5. **Creative response:** the human brain can invent new things and discover

new facts. This creative ability apparently comes from nowhere—the unknown simply gives birth to a new thought. We call this inspiration, and its mirror is a Creator who made the whole world from nothing. We turn to him out of our wonder at the beauty and formal complexity of Nature.

6. **Visionary response:** the brain can directly contact "the light," a form of pure awareness that feels joyful and blessed. This contact can be bewildering, because it has no roots in the material world. It comes as a vision, and the God that matches it is exalted—he delivers healing and miracles. We need such a God to explain why magic can exist side by side with ordinary mundane reality.

7. **Sacred response:** the brain was born from a single fertilized cell that had no brain functions in it, only a speck of life. Even though a hundred billion neurons developed from that speck, it remains intact in all its innocence and simplicity. The brain senses this as its source and origin. To match it, there is a God of pure being, one who doesn't think but just is. We need him

because without a source, our existence has no foundation at all.

These seven responses, all very real and
useful to us in our long journey as a species,
form the unshakable basis of religion. If you
compare any two minds—Moses or Buddha,
Jesus or Freud, Saint Francis or Chairman
Mao—each projects a different view of
reality with a matching God. No one can
shoehorn God into a single box. We must
have a range of vision as vast as human
experience itself. Atheists need their God,
who is absent and nonexistent, while at the
other extreme mystics need their God, one
of pure love and light. Only the brain can
deliver this vast range of deities.

You might immediately object that the
human *mind* creates these versions of God,
not just the *brain*. I absolutely agree—in the
long run the mind is much more primary
than the brain in creating all perception.
But for now the brain is our only concrete
way of entering the mind. In cartoons a
lightbulb shows up over somebody's head
when he has a bright idea; this isn't so in
real life. The mind without the brain is as
invisible and unprovable as God.

Also, you might argue that just because
God is seen in a certain way by us, that

doesn't mean he *is* that way. I don't believe this is black or white. God's reality doesn't stand apart from our perceptions but is woven into them. A mother can see her newborn child as wonderful and worthy, and through her perception that baby grows up to become a wonderful, worthy person. This is one of the mysteries of love. A subtle give-and-take is going on at the deepest level between parent and child. In the same way God seems to grow directly out of our deepest inner values. There is a similar give-and-take below the level of mere belief. Peel away all the layers of an onion, and at the center you will find emptiness; peel away all the layers of a human being, and at the center you will find the seed of God.

I believe that God has to be known by looking in the mirror.

If you see yourself in fear, barely holding on with survival at stake, yours is a God of fight or flight.

If you see yourself as capable of power and accomplishment, yours is a God of the reactive response.

If you see yourself as centered and calm, yours is a God of the restful awareness response.

If you see yourself as growing and evolv-

ing, yours is a God of the intuitive response.

If you see yourself as someone who makes personal dreams come true, yours is a God of the creative response.

If you see yourself as capable of working miracles, yours is a God of the visionary response.

If you see yourself as one with God, yours is a God of the sacred response.

Although everyone's brain can create countless thoughts—just to take a number, at ten thoughts a minute, a single brain would conjure up more than 14,000 thoughts a day, 5 million a year, and 350 million in a lifetime. To preserve our sanity, the gross majority of these thoughts are repetitions of past thoughts, mere echoes. The brain is economical in how it produces a thought. Instead of having millions of ways, it has only a limited number. Physicists like to say that the universe is really just "quantum soup" bombarding our senses with billions of bits of data every minute. This swirling chaos must also be organized into a manageable number. So the brain, with its seven basic responses, provides more than sanity and meaning: it provides a whole world. Presiding over this self-created world is a God who embraces everything, but who also must fit into the brain's way of working.

In one way or another, when a person says the word *God*, he is pointing to a specific response from this list:

> *Any God who protects us like a father or mother stems from fight or flight.*
> *Any God who makes laws and rules over society stems from the reactive response.*
> *Any God who brings inner peace stems from the restful awareness response.*
> *Any God who encourages human beings to reach their full potential stems from the intuitive response.*
> *Any God who inspires us to explore and discover stems from the creative response.*
> *Any God who makes miracles stems from the visionary response.*
> *Any God who brings us back into unity with him stems from the sacred response.*

As far as I know, the brain cannot register a deity outside the seven responses. Why not? Because God is woven into reality, and the brain knows reality in these limited ways. It may sound as though we're reducing the Almighty Father, the Primeval Goddess, and the Mystery of Mysteries to a firestorm of electrical activity in the cerebral cortex—but we aren't doing that. We are trying to find the basic facts that will make God possible, real, and useful.

Many people will be sympathetic to this because they long for a God who fits into their lives. No one can make God enter the everyday world, however. The real question is whether he might be here already and going unnoticed. I keep coming back to the transition zone in our "reality sandwich." Unless you are willing to take your vision there, the presence of God is too ghostly to be relied upon. Is the brain prepared for such a journey? Absolutely.

A friend of mine once knew John Lennon very well and continued over the years to grieve his passing. She is a gifted singer, and one night recently she had a dream in which he came to her and showed her an image from the past when they were together. Waking up, she decided to write a new, very intimate song based on her dream, yet in the cold light of day she began to have doubts. I came to London for a visit, and she told me about her indecision.

"After all, it's only a dream, isn't it?" she said. "Maybe I'm foolish to make too much of it."

At that moment her three-year-old ran into the room and plopped himself onto a chair in the corner. He happened to land on the remote control for the television, which came on suddenly. On the screen, amazingly, we saw a nostalgia program showing John Lennon and my friend smiling at the camera, caught in the exact moment she had witnessed in her dream. She burst into tears and got her answer: She would write the song for him.

I believe that this interaction took place in the transition zone. A message arrived from a deeper place than we usually go. To say that it came from spirit or God is totally justified, but the brain also played its part, for this incident began with everyday brain processes—thoughts, emotions, dreams, doubts—that finally crystallized into inspiration. We see a perfect example here of our fifth response, the creative response.

Can we truly satisfy the demands of objectivity when it comes to God? A physicist would recognize our reality sandwich with no difficulty. The material world has long since dissolved for the great quantum thinkers.[2] After Einstein made time and space into fluid things that merge into each other, the traditional universe couldn't hold up. In the reality sandwich of physics there are also three levels:

Material reality, the world of objects and events

Quantum reality, a transition zone where energy turns into matter

Virtual reality, the place beyond time and space, the origin of the universe

Here we run into a semantic problem, because the phrase *virtual reality* is no longer used the way a physicist would understand it. These words now commonly mean computer-simulated reality or even, very loosely, any video game. So I will modify *virtual reality* and call it *the virtual domain*, and to follow suit, *quantum reality* will have to become *the quantum domain*.

It isn't just coincidence that these three layers parallel the religious worldview. The two models have to parallel each other, because they are both delineated by the brain. Science and religion are not really opposites but just very different ways of trying to decode the universe. Both visions contain the material world, which is a given. There has to be an unseen source of creation, because the cosmos can be traced back only so far before time and space dissolve. And there has to be a place where these two opposites meet.

I said before that I don't think mystics are set apart from ordinary people. They are just better quantum navigators. They journey into the transition zone closer to God, and while we might visit there for a few moments of joy, at most a few days, saints and mystics have found the secret of remaining there far longer. Instead of wondering about the mystery of life, a saint lives it. Yet even without adequate words to convey that experience, we find certain similarities from culture to culture:

- The body's heaviness becomes as if weightless.
- A sense of floating or looking down from above is felt.
- Breathing becomes lighter, rarefied, more even.
- Physical pain or discomfort are much lessened.
- A sense of energy streams through the body.
- Color and sound are heightened; increased sensitivity to all senses.

A common phrase for this sensation, which one hears over and over, is "going into the light." It's a phenomenon not limited to saints. Some or all of these bodily changes occur to common people. Existence breaks through its drab routine with a surge of bliss and purity. Some mystics describe these moments as timeless. Afterward a psychological afterglow often persists, a peaceful certainty that one has "come home." In this transition zone that almost reaches God's domain, experience is both inner and outer.

But what if we could steady our flash of ecstasy and learn to explore this strange new territory? Then we would discover the same thing revealed to Dame Julian six hundred years ago: "He is our clothing that wraps us and winds us about, embraces us and all-encloses us, for love. . . . Remain in this, and you shall know more of the same . . . without end." In other words, the sacred isn't a feeling, it is a place. The problem is that when you try to journey there, material reality keeps pulling you back again. The wondrous moment passes. To remain in the transition zone is extremely difficult.

Let me bring these abstract terms down to earth. Some of the following experiences have occurred to all of us:

In the midst of danger, you feel suddenly cared for and protected.

You deeply fear a crisis in your personal life, but when it comes, you experience a sudden calmness.

A stranger makes you feel a sudden rush of love.

An infant or young child looks into your eyes, and for a second you believe that an old soul is looking at you.

In the presence of death, you feel the passing of wings.

Looking at the sky, you have a sense of infinite space.

A stunning glimpse of beauty makes you forget for a second who you are.

Whenever you have any such experiences, your brain has responded in an unusual way; it has responded to God.

If we only knew it, God's most cherished secrets are hidden inside the human skull— ecstasy, eternal love, grace, and mystery. This doesn't seem possible at first glance. If you take a scalpel to the brain, you will cut into soft gray tissue that doesn't respond to the touch. There are lakes of slow-running water in this quivering terrain and open caves where light never penetrates. You wouldn't suspect that a soul is hiding here somewhere, that spirit can find its home in an organ almost as liquid as red blood cells and as mushy as an unripe banana.

The landscape of the brain is deceptive, however. Every burst of light that has blinded every saint in history took place here in the darkness. Every image of God was designed in tissue that appears to be a mass of congested nerves. So to find a window to God, you have to realize that your brain is layered into regions that are ruled by different impulses. The new kingdoms are full of higher thought, poetry, and love, like the New Testament. The old kingdoms are more primordial, like parts of the Old Testament. They are ruled by raw emotion, instinct, power, and survival.

In the old kingdoms each of us is a hunter. The ancestral plains of Africa are buried deep in your cranium, remembered with all their terror and hunger. Your genes remember leopards that leapt out of trees, and in a traffic snarl the old brain wants to hunt that leopard, fighting it to the death. Many doubters have said that God was invented so that these ferocious instincts can be kept in check. Otherwise our violence would turn on us and kill us. But I don't believe this. The oldest hunter lurking in our brains is after bigger prey, God himself. And the motive isn't to fight or die but to find our speck of joy and truth that nothing in the world can erase. The one thing we cannot survive is chaos.

We evolved to find God. This is what

the lightning storm of the brain's endless activity is all about. God for us is not a choice but a necessity. Almost a hundred years ago the great psychologist and philosopher William James declared that human nature contains a "will to believe" in some higher power. Personally James didn't know if God existed or whether there was a world beyond this one. He was almost certain that no proof of God could be found, but he felt it would deprive human beings of something profound if belief was stripped away from us. We need the hunt.

God, it turns out, isn't a person; God is a process. Your brain is hardwired to find God. *Until you do, you will not know who you are.* There is a catch, however. Our brains don't lead us automatically to spirit. Seeking has always been necessary. Some people feel that God is within reach, or at least within stalking range, while others feel he is totally absent. (It is curious that 72 percent of respondents in a recent poll said that they believe in heaven while only 56 percent believe in hell. This is more than naive optimism; the tendency of life is to point us in the right direction.)

A seeker always hopes to see the one, true, final God who will settle all doubts, but instead we hunt for clues. Unable to take in the totality of God, we get hints from the brain, which is constantly exercising an amazing ability to insert a glimpse of spirit in the most mundane situations. To return to a few of those simple examples I gave:

In the midst of danger, you feel suddenly cared for and protected. Spirit is being revealed through fight or flight.

You deeply fear a crisis in your personal life, but when it comes, you experience a sudden calmness. Spirit is being revealed through restful awareness.

A stranger makes you feel a sudden rush of love. Spirit is being revealed through the visionary response.

An infant or young child looks into your eyes, and for a second you believe that an old soul is looking at you. Spirit is being revealed through intuition.

Looking at the sky, you have a sense of infinite space. Spirit is being revealed through unity.

It is typical of modern life to believe that nature is set up to be random and chaotic. This is far from true. Life looks meaningless when you have worn out old responses, old realities, and an old version of God. To bring God back, we have to follow new, even strange responses wherever they lead us. As one spiritual teacher wisely put it, "The material world is infinite, but it is a boring infinity. The really interesting infinity lies beyond."

GETTING WHAT YOU WANT
The Seven Levels of Fulfillment

God is another name for infinite intelligence. To achieve anything in life, a piece of this intelligence must be contacted and used. In other words, *God is always there for you.* The seven responses of the human brain are avenues to attain some aspect of God. Each level of fulfillment proves God's reality *at that level.*

> *Level 1 (Fight-or-Flight Response)*
> You fulfill your life through family, community, a sense of belonging, and material comforts.
> *Level 2 (Reactive Response)*
> You fulfill your life through success, power, influence, status, and other ego satisfactions.
> *Level 3 (Restful Awareness Response)*
> You fulfill your life through peace,

centeredness, self-acceptance, and
inner silence.

Level 4 (Intuitive Response)
You fulfill your life through insight,
empathy, tolerance, and forgiveness.

Level 5 (Creative Response)
You fulfill your life through inspiration, expanded creativity in art or science, and unlimited discovery.

Level 6 (Visionary Response)
You fulfill your life through reverence,
compassion, devoted service, and universal love.

Level 7 (Sacred Response)
You fulfill your life through wholeness
and unity with the divine.

It is very important to absorb this notion
that spirit involves a constant process. It
isn't a feeling, nor is it a thing you can hold
and measure. In the unfolding of spirit
many mysteries begin to make sense. For
instance, consider this famous sentence
from the Vedas: "Those who know It speak
of It not, those who speak of It know It
not." The mystery here is tied up in the
word *It*. If *It* means some kind of revelation,
then you may struggle all your life to join
the elite who have had *It* revealed to them.

Enlightenment turns into something like a secret handshake. But if *It* means a real place that one can journey to, there is no need for frustration. You just find that place, without pointless words. "Don't talk about it, go!" seems like sensible advice.

A striking example that there is a reach-able place beyond material reality is prayer. Beginning more than twenty years ago, researchers devised experiments to try to verify whether prayer had any efficacy. Seri-ously ill patients in hospitals were divided into groups, some being prayed for while others were not. In all cases best medical care was still given, yet it became evident that the prayed-for group seemed to re-cover better. This result was all the more astonishing when it was discovered that the person doing the praying didn't have to know the patient personally, or even know their names. But only in 1998 did a Duke University team verify to all skeptics that prayer indeed has such power.[3] The researchers took into account all manner of variables, including heart rate, blood pres-sure, and clinical outcomes; 150 patients who had undergone invasive cardiac proce-dures were studied, but none of them knew that they were being prayed for. Seven reli-gious groups around the world were asked to pray. These included Buddhists in Nepal, Carmelite nuns in Baltimore, and Virtual Jerusalem, an organization that grants E-mail requests for prayers to be written down and inserted into the Wailing Wall. Researchers found that surgical patients' recovery could be from 50 to 100 percent better if someone prayed for them.

Even before these "highly intriguing" results, as researchers called them, the phenomenon of prayer had already gained sudden new popularity, yet the essential point is often missed. Prayer is a journey in consciousness—it takes you to a place different from ordinary thought. In this place the patient is not a stranger, nor is she removed in space. You and she are joined in a place where the boundaries of the body no longer count. Your intention to make her well has an effect across the space-time boundary. In other words, prayer is a quantum event carried out in the brain.

Of all the clues God left for us to find, the greatest is the light, the Shekhinah. From that clue we can unfold a true picture of the deity. This is a bold claim, but it is corroborated by the fact that science—our most credible modern religion—also traces creation back to light.[4] In this century Einstein and the other pioneers of quantum physics broke through the barrier of material reality to a new world, and in their awe most had a mystical experience. They sensed that when light gave up its mysteries, God's light would be known.

Our vision can't help but be organized around light. The same brain responses that enable you to see a tree as a tree, instead of as a ghostly swarm of buzzing atoms, also enable you to experience God. They reach far beyond organized religion. But we can take any passage from world scripture and decode it through the brain. It is the mechanism that makes the scripture real to us. Our brains respond on the same seven levels that apply to our experience:

1. A level of danger, threat, and survival.
2. A level of striving, competition, and power.
3. A level of peace, calm, and reflection.
4. A level of insight, understanding, and forgiveness.
5. A level of aspiration, creativity, and discovery.
6. A level of reverence, compassion, and love.
7. A level of unbounded unity.

Every Bible story teaches something at one or more of these levels (as do all world scriptures), and in every instance the teaching is attributed to God. Your brain and the deity are thus fused in order for the world to make sense. To repeat, the one thing you cannot survive is chaos.

If you believe in a punishing, vengeful God—clearly related to fight or flight— you won't see the reality of the Buddha's teaching of Nirvana. If you believe in the God of love envisioned by Jesus—rooted in the visionary response—you will not see the reality of the Greek myth wherein Saturn, primal father of the gods, ate all his children. Every version of God is part mask, part reality. The infinite can only reveal a portion of itself at any one time. Indeed, we would have all grown up, in the West at least, calling God "It" except for the linguistic anomaly that Hebrew has no neuter pronoun. In Sanskrit, the ancient Indians had no such problem and referred to the infinite deity as both It and That.

The most startling conclusion of our new model is that God is as we are. The whole universe is as we are, because without the human mind, there would be only quantum soup, billions of random sensory impressions. Yet thanks to the mind/brain, we recognize that encoded into the swirling cosmos are the most valued things in existence: form, meaning, beauty, truth, love. These are the realities the brain is reaching for when it reaches for God. He is as real as they are, but just as elusive.

The Seven Levels of Miracles

A miracle is a display of power from beyond the five senses. Although all miracles take place in the transition zone, they differ from level to level. In general, miracles become more "supernatural" after the fourth or fifth brain response, but any miracle involves direct contact with spirit.

Level 1 (Fight-or-Flight Response)
Miracles involve surviving great danger, impossible rescues, a sense of divine protection.
Example: A mother who runs into a burning house to rescue her child, or lifts a car with a child trapped underneath

Level 2 (Reactive Response)
Miracles involve incredible achievements and success, control over the body or mind.

Example: Extreme feats of martial arts, child prodigies with inexplicable gifts in music or mathematics, the rise of a Napoleon from humble beginnings to immense power (men of destiny)

Level 3 (Restful Awareness Response)
Miracles involve synchronicity, yogic powers, premonitions, feeling the presence of God or angels.
Example: Yogis who can change body temperature or heart rate at will, being visited by someone from far away who has just died, visitation by a guardian angel

Level 4 (Intuitive Response)
Miracles involve telepathy, ESP, knowledge of past or future lifetimes, prophetic powers.
Example: Reading someone else's thoughts or aura, psychic predictions, astral projection to other locations

Level 5 (Creative Response)
Miracles involve divine inspiration, artistic genius, spontaneous fulfill-ment of desires (wishes come true).
Example: The ceiling of the Sistine Chapel, having a thought that sud-

denly manifests, Einstein's insights
into time and relativity

Level 6 (Visionary Response)
Miracles involve healing, physical
transformations, holy apparitions,
highest degree of supernatural feats.
Example: Walking on water, healing
incurable diseases through touch,
direct revelation from the Virgin
Mary

Level 7 (Sacred Response)
Miracles involve inner evidence of
enlightenment.
Example: Lives of the great prophets
and teachers—Buddha, Jesus,
Lao-Tze

I am not imagining that every skeptic and
atheist reading this book has suddenly
jumped to his feet proclaiming that God is
real. This will have to go by stages. But at
least now we have something to hold on to,
and it is something extremely useful. We
can explain those mysterious journeys that
mystics have taken into God's reality. Such
journeys have always deeply moved me, and
I remember exactly where my fascination
began. The first such voyager I ever heard

of was called the Colonel—his story is one of the seeds of this book. As I retell it, I can feel my mind experiencing his reality, which passed through so many phases from danger to compassion, from peace to unity. He will serve as a promise of the unfolding truth that is possible in any of our lives:

I was ten and my father, a doctor in the Indian army, had moved his family to Assam. No part of the country is as green and idyllic. Assam is an Eden, if Eden were covered with tea plantations as far as the eye can see. I could literally hear a song in my heart as I walked to the high-perched school on the hill. It must have been the magic of the place that made me notice an old beggar who used to sit by the road. He was always there under his tree, dressed in tatters, rarely moving or saying a word. The village women believed absolutely that this unkempt figure was a saint. They would sit beside him for hours, praying for a healing (or a new baby), and my grandmother assured me that our neighbor lady had been cured of arthritis by walking past him and silently asking for his blessing.

Strangely, everyone called this old beggar "the Colonel." One day I couldn't control my curiosity and asked why, and my best friend from school, Oppo, found out for me. Oppo's mother had once been healed by the Colonel, and Oppo's father, who was a newspaper reporter in town, had a remarkable tale to tell me:

At the end of World War II, a large force of British troops, the doomed "forgotten army," had been pinned down or captured by the invading Japanese in Burma. Because of the unending monsoon rains, the fighting had been tough and miserable; the treatment received by the prisoners of war was atrocious. Indians served in the British army, and one of them was a Bengali doctor named Sengupta.

Sengupta was on the verge of starving in a POW camp when the Japanese decided to retreat from their position. He didn't know if the British army had somehow advanced close by, but it didn't matter. Instead of marching the POWs to a new prison, their captors lined them up and shot each one in the head at close range with a pistol. This included Sengupta, who was in some way grateful to die and end his torment. He heard the gun blast at his temple, and with a jolt of searing pain he fell over. Only this wasn't the end. By some miracle he regained consciousness several hours later—he judged the passage of time because night had fallen and the prison camp was dead quiet.

It took some moments before Sengupta, who felt that he was suffocating, realized with horror that he had come to under a heavy pile of corpses. In the rush to abandon camp, no one had checked to see if he was really dead, and his limp body had been thrown onto the pile with the others. It seemed like an eternity before Sengupta gathered enough strength to crawl out into the open air; he staggered to the river and washed himself, trembling with fear and revulsion. It was obvious that he was alone and that no Allies were coming to rescue him.

By morning he had made the decision to walk to safety. Deep in a war zone with no sense of Burmese geography, he could only think to return to India—and that is what he did. Surviving on fruit, insects, and rain water, he traveled by night and hid in the jungle by day. The terrain consisted of hill after hill, and the ground was deep in mud. Although he passed occasional villages and peasant farms, he didn't dare trust anyone enough to ask for refuge. He could hear unknown wild animals in the dark at a time when tigers were still found in Burma, and he stumbled over snakes that terrified him.

Sengupta's trek took months before he stepped across the border into Bengal, and eventually the emaciated hero walked into Calcutta, heading for British army head-quarters. He made his report and recounted his achievement, but the British, far from believing him, immediately had him arrested. He was put in irons as a probable Japanese spy or collaborator. Broken emo-tionally as well as physically, he lay in his dark cell and contemplated the fate that had taken him from one prison to another.

Somewhere during this period of dis-grace, under daily interrogation and a later court-martial, Sengupta went through a supreme transformation. It wasn't some-thing he ever spoke about, but the change was startling—in place of bitterness he gained complete peace, he healed his wounds both inner and outer (fitting for someone who would turn into a healer of others) and he stopped struggling, waiting calmly for the inevitable sentence of the court. Amazingly the inevitable never came. In a sudden change of heart the British chose to believe that his story was true, prompted by the immediate end of hostili-ties when the Americans dropped the atomic bomb on Japan.

Within a week Sengupta was dragged out of prison, awarded a medal for valor, and paraded through the streets of Calcutta as a hero. He seemed as strangely oblivious of the cheers as he had been of the suffering. Leaving medicine behind, he became a wandering monk. When he finally grew old and found his resting place under the tree in Assam, he didn't tell anyone his story. It was the locals who dubbed him the Colonel, perhaps tipped off by Oppo's father, the newspaper reporter.

Naturally my first, burning question at the age of ten was how a man could be shot in the head with a pistol at point-blank range and survive. Oppo's father shrugged. When they were captured, most of the British soldiers were armed with ammunition made in India. The Japanese executed them with their own pistols, and no doubt one of the bullets had been defective, filled with powder but no shot. Anyway, that was the best rational guess. So much for the miracle.

Today I ask another question that means more to me: How does such extreme torment, which provides every reason to abandon faith, turn into absolute faith instead? No one could doubt that the Colonel had arrived at some kind of saintliness from his ordeal. He made the mystic journey; he hunted God to the finish. I now realize what a profound miracle the human brain actually is. It has the capacity to see spiritual reality under any circumstance. In Sengupta's case, consider what he might have been over-whelmed by: the terror of death, the possibility of being here one day and gone the next, the fear that good will never prevail over evil, and the fragile freedom that could be extinguished by cruel authority.

It is clear, despite the turmoil that makes belief in God harder than ever, that every level of revelation still exists. *Redemption* is just another word for calling on your innate ability to see with the eye of the soul. Two voices are heard in our heads every day, the one believing in the dark and the other in the light. Only one reality can be *really* real. Our new model, the "reality sandwich," solves this riddle. Sengupta took a journey into the transition zone where transformation occurs. Here, where the material world transforms from dense matter into invisible energy; the mind gets transformed as well.

Sengupta's soul journey passed through fight or flight, restful awareness, intuition, and vision, eventually finding the courage to live entirely in the visionary response for the rest of his life. He ensconced himself in a new way, clothed in love and serenity. The brain discovered that it could escape the prison of its old reactions, rising to a new, higher level that it perceived as God.

*   *   *

So now we have the outline for the entire spiritual journey in our hands: the unfolding of God is a process made possible by the brain's ability to unfold its own potential. Inherent in each of us is wonder, love, transformation, and miracles, not just because we crave these things but because they are our birthright. Our neurons have evolved to make these higher aspirations real. From the womb of the brain springs a new and useful God. Or to be precise, seven variations of God[5] which leave a trail of clues for us to follow every day.

If asked why we should strive to know God, my answer would be selfish: I want to be a creator. This is the ultimate promise of spirituality, that you can become the author of your own existence, the maker of personal destiny. Your brain is already performing this service for you unconsciously. In the quantum domain your brain chooses the response that is appropriate at any given moment. The universe is an overwhelming chaos. It must be interpreted to make sense; it must be decoded. The brain therefore can't take reality as it is given; one of the seven responses has to be selected, and the quantum realm is where this decision is made.

To know God, you must consciously participate in making this journey—that is the purpose of free will. On the surface of life we make much more trivial choices but pretend that they carry enormous weight. In reality, you are constantly acting out seven fundamental choices about the kind of world you recognize:

> *The choice of fear if you want to struggle and barely survive.*
> *The choice of power if you want to compete and achieve.*
> *The choice of inner reflection if you want peace.*
> *The choice to know yourself if you want insight.*
> *The choice to create if you want to discover the workings of nature.*
> *The choice to love if you want to heal others and yourself.*
> *The choice to be if you want to appreciate the infinite scope of God's creation.*

I am not arranging these from bad to good, better to best. You are capable of all these choices; they are hardwired into you. But for many people, only the first few responses have been activated. Some part of their brains is dormant, and therefore their view of spirit is extremely limited. It is no wonder that finding God is called *awakening*. A fully awakened brain is the secret to knowing God. In the end, however, the seventh stage is the goal, the one where pure being allows us to revel in the infinite creation of God. Here the mystic Jews searching for the Shekhinah[6] meet the Buddhists in their search for satori, and when they arrive, the ancient Vedic seers will be waiting in the presence of Shiva, along with Christ and his Father. This is the place which is both the beginning and end of a process that is God. In this process things like spirit, soul, power, and love unfold in a completely new way. Here certainty can replace doubt, and as the inspired French writer Simone Weil once wrote about the spiritual quest, "Only certainty will do. Anything less than certainty is unworthy of God."

Two

MYSTERY
OF MYSTERIES

*This is the work of the soul
that most pleases God.*
—THE CLOUD OF UNKNOWING

The mystery of God wouldn't exist if the world wasn't also a mystery. Some scientists believe we are closer than ever to a "Theory of Everything," or TOE, as the physicists dub it. TOE will explain the beginning of the universe and the end of time, the first and last breaths of cosmic existence. From quarks to quasars, all will be revealed, as the old melodramas used to promise. Is there a place for God in this "everything," or does the Creator get booted out of his own creation? His fate may be important, but when it is wrapped up with ours, it becomes all-important.

Consider again the reality sandwich that has served as our model. As we saw before, it comes in three layers:

Material reality
———— QUANTUM DOMAIN ————
Virtual domain

Anyone could be forgiven for thinking that God is nowhere to be found here, in fact that all the wonders of the sacred world will become mundane on the day that the TOE explains it all away.

For centuries humans looked in the mirror of Nature and saw heroes, wizards, dragons, and holy grails reflected back. The sacred was real, a source of supreme power, and nothing could exist, from a river to a thunderclap, without a god to cause it. Today the mirror has clouded. We have outgrown the need for a thunder god or a hero born on Olympus. What do we see instead? A society that strip-mines old myths to build a city like Las Vegas. If you want to meet myth here, you check into a hotel-casino called Excalibur. The only god is Fortune, the only dragons to conquer are the slot machines, and most of the time they win.

If it is true, as the poetic sentiment goes, that "One touch of Nature makes the whole world kin," then one touch of myth makes the whole world sacred. In a mythless world, something is missing, but do we know what it is? There are many clues to that answer, scattered around in the sacred sites of the world. No one can stand before the Great Pyramid of Cheops (or Khufu, to give him his proper Egyptian name) without feeling the presence of a power that is absent even in the hugest skyscraper. The pharaoh once entombed in the depths of this massive structure was a mortal, but he aspired to be immortal, and he fed that aspiration by erecting the largest single mass of stone ever piled in one place, even to this day. He also backed up his ambition with God. Khufu was venerated as a descendant of the gods and was therefore a god-man himself. Is this a demonstration that the ego of a king knows no bounds? Certainly. But there is more here.

Khufu's link to the gods linked his people at the same time. From time immemorial humans have worried over the same questions: Do I have a soul? What happens after I die? Is there an afterlife, and will I meet God when I get there? The Great Pyramid was an answer erected in stone. You can almost hear the stones crying out, "Now tell me I'm not immortal!"

For a harsh contrast, go back to Las Vegas. What do we see there? Wealth and ambition to rival the pharaohs, but are the people who cram into these pleasure domes any more secure about the great questions? Or does a world without spiritual power force us to seek distraction because underneath, we do not know the answers at all?

The family of man is bound up in the sacred. We cannot allow it to die without strangling our blood ties to a deeper reality: that we all come from one place, that we are on a journey toward a greater good, that our every act is being weighed from a cosmic perspective. Ordinary reality is trivial compared to this heritage. The Theory of Everything will be useless, if not destructive, unless we can use it to keep the sacred alive.

Fortunately, the most solid, reliable things in existence—a seashell, a tree branch, a pothole in the middle of the road—partake of God's mystery. If you believe in a rock, you are automatically believing in God. Let me explain.

Ordinary reality is only the top layer of our sandwich. The material world is full of familiar objects that we can see, feel, touch, taste, and smell. As big objects become very small, shrinking to the size of atoms, our senses fail us. Theoretically the shrinkage has to stop somewhere, because no atom is smaller than hydrogen, the first material particle to be born out of the Big Bang. But in fact an amazing transformation happens beyond the atom—everything solid disappears. Atoms are composed of vibrating energy packets that have no solidity at all, no mass or size, nothing for the senses to see or touch. The Latin word for a packet or package is *quantum*, the word chosen to describe one unit of energy inside the atom, and, as it turned out, a new level of reality.

At the quantum level nothing of the material world is left intact. It is strange enough to hold up your hand and realize that it is actually, at a deeper level, invisible vibrations taking place in a void. Even at the atomic level all objects are revealed as 99.9999 percent empty space. On its own scale, the distance between a whirling electron and the nucleus it revolves around is wider than the distance between the earth and the sun. But you could never capture that electron anyway, since it too breaks down into energy vibrations that wink in and out of existence millions of times per second. Therefore the whole universe is a quantum mirage, winking in and out of existence millions of times per second. At the quantum level the whole cosmos is like a blinking light. There are no stars or galaxies, only vibrating energy fields that our senses are too dull and slow to pick up given the incredible speed at which light and electricity move.

In the animal kingdom some nervous systems are much faster than ours and others much slower. A snail's neurons pick up signals from the outside world so slowly, for example, that events any faster than three seconds would not be perceived. In other words, if a snail was looking at an apple, and I quickly reached in and snatched it away, the snail would not be able to detect my hand. It would "see" the apple disappear before its very eyes. In the same way, quantum flashes are millions of times too rapid for us to register, so our brains play a trick on us by "seeing" solid objects that are continuous in time and space, the same way that a movie seems continuous. A movie consists of twenty-four still pictures flashing by per second, with twenty-four gaps of blackness as each frame is taken away and a new one put in its place. But since our brains cannot perceive forty-eight stop-motion events in one second, the illusion of the movie is created.

Now speed this up by many powers of ten and you get the trick of the movie we call real life. You and I exist as flashing photons with a black void in between each flash—the quantum light show comprises our whole body, our every thought and wish, and every event we take part in. In other words, we are being created, over and over again, all the time. Genesis is now and always has been. Who is behind this never-ending creation? Whose power of mind or vision is capable of taking the universe away and putting it back again in a fraction of a second?

The power of creation—whatever it turns out to be—lies even beyond energy, a force with the ability to turn gaseous clouds of dust into stars and eventually into DNA. In the terminology of physics, we refer to this pre-quantum level as *virtual*. When you go beyond all energy, there is nothing, a void. Visible light becomes virtual light; real space becomes virtual space; real time becomes virtual time. In the process, all properties vanish. Light no longer shines, space covers no distance, time is eternal. This is the womb of creation, infinitely dynamic and alive. Words like *empty*, *dark*, and *cold* do not apply to it. The virtual domain is so inconceivable that only religious language seems to touch it at all. Today in India a devout believer may greet the dawn with an ancient Vedic hymn:

> *In the beginning,*
> *There was neither existence nor nonexis-*
> *tence,*

All this world was unmanifest energy . . .
The One breathed, without breath, by Its
*   own power*
Nothing else was there. . . .
RIG-VEDA

In modern terms, this verse tells us that God can only be found in a virtual state, where all energy is stored before creation. Physics has struggled hard with this state that comes before time and space, and so has popular imagination. It may surprise many to learn that the familiar image of God as a patriarch in a white robe seated on his throne has little authority, even in Judaic scripture. The image appears only once, in the Book of Daniel, whereas we are told many times in the books of Moses that God is without human form.

The best working theory about creation reads as follows: Before the Big Bang space was unbounded, expanded like an accordion into infinite pleats or dimensions, while time existed in seed form, an eternal presence without events and therefore needing no past, present, or future. This state was utterly void in one sense and utterly full in another. It contained nothing we could possibly perceive, yet the potential for everything resided here. As the Vedic seers declared, neither existence nor nonexistence could be found, since those terms apply only to things that have a beginning, middle, and end. Physicists often refer to this state as a *singularity:* space, time, and the entire material universe were once contained in a point. A singularity is conceived as the smallest dot you can imagine, and therefore not a dot at all.

Now if you can imagine that the cosmos exploded into being in a dazzling flash of light from this one point, you must then go a step further. *Because the pre-creation state has no time, it is still here.* The Big Bang has never happened in the virtual domain, and yet paradoxically all Big Bangs have happened—no matter how many times the universe expands across billions of light-years, only to collapse back onto itself and withdraw back into the void, nothing will change at the virtual level. This is as close as physics has come to the religious notion of a God who is omnipresent, omniscient, and omnipotent. *Omni* means all, and the virtual state, since it has no boundaries of any kind, is properly called the All.

It isn't surprising that we find it so difficult to speak about the All. In India seers often referred to it simply as That, or *tat* in Sanskrit. At the moment of enlightenment, a person is able to go past the five senses to perceive the only truth that can be uttered: "I am That, You are That, and all this is That." The meaning isn't a riddle; it simply states that behind the veil of creation, the pre-creation state still exists, enclosing everything.

A physicist friend once stated the same truth in newer words: "You must realize, Deepak, that time is just a cosmic convenience that keeps everything from happening all at once. This convenience is needed at the material level, but not at deeper levels. Therefore if you could see yourself in your virtual state, all the chaos and swirling galaxies would make perfect sense. They form one pattern unfolding in perfect symmetry. Viewed from this perspective, the end point of all creation is now. The whole cosmos has conspired to create you and me sitting here this very second."

Nothing is more fascinating than to watch science blurring its edges into spirit. There are no easier words for the transition zone than "quantum" and no easier words for God than "virtual." To track down a miracle, one must go into these domains. Miracles indicate that reality doesn't begin and end at the material level. "How do I find God?" a young disciple once asked a famous guru in India.[1] "I can't see any evidence that He is anywhere around us, and millions of people live very well without him."

"Everything without God happens in space and time. This is the world you are used to," his guru replied. "Space and time are like a net that has trapped you, but nets always have holes. Find such a hole and jump through it. Then God will be obvious." Every religious tradition contains such loopholes, escape routes into a world beyond ours. In the Gospel of Thomas, Jesus says that his role in life is to point the disciples away from the rule of the five senses, which are totally confined to space-time:[2]

> I shall give you what no eye has seen and what no ear has heard and what no hand has touched and what has never occurred to the human mind.

This promise was certainly carried out whenever Jesus performed any one of his thirty or so miracles, but it is fascinating to observe that often they were performed with considerable reluctance, as if they were somehow beside the point. The real point was to see that our senses aren't trust-worthy at all. The incurable leper only appears that way, the few loaves and fishes are only an illusion, the storm on the Sea of Galilee can be calmed by a mere act of will. After healing the leper with his touch, Jesus sounds particularly impatient with anyone overawed by what he has done.

> Then Jesus dismissed him with this stern warning: "Be sure you say nothing to anybody. Go and show yourself to the priest, and make the offering laid down by Moses for your cleansing; that will certify the cure."

Naturally the miraculously healed man couldn't help himself and told everyone he ran into. Word spread, until Jesus couldn't stay in the town because of the uproar. Teeming crowds wanted their own miracle; he fled to the countryside, where they continued to pursue him. Would we also be so overawed as to miss the larger point? I think so. In India today there is a well-known woman saint who reputedly cured a leper by touching his sores. I remember reading too about a guru who used to let anyone into his house on feast days, holding the laws of hospitality to be sacred. He was not rich, and his followers were distressed that hundreds of guests would appear at his door to be fed. The guru only smiled and made a strange request. "Keep feeding everyone from those buckets of rice and lentils," he said, "but first cover them with a cloth." The buckets were covered so that no one could see into them, and as many times as the ladles were dipped in, there was always more food to go around. In this way the guru performed the same miracle as Jesus.

It is easy to be awed by such stories, but is it helpful when we seek to know facts? From our awe a wealth of superstition, fable, and often false hope has developed. Yet in the blurring of the quantum and the miraculous, a single reality is beginning to emerge. Stephen Hawking indicated in his *A Brief History of Time* that if the laws of nature were deeply explored, we would one day know the mind of God.[3] Here he echoed a famous remark by Einstein: "I want to know how God thinks, everything else is a detail." Because he was a rare visionary, I hope that Einstein would accept as a start the following map of how God thinks:

Virtual domain = the field of spirit
Quantum domain = the field of mind
Material reality = the field of physical existence

If you feel secure with these terms, you can clear up mystery after mystery—literally all the paradoxes of religion start to unravel, and God's ways make sense for the first time. Let me give an example from the field of healing:

Some decades ago an Italian army officer was taken on a stretcher to the shrine of Lourdes. He was suffering from bone cancer in its most advanced metastasized stage. One hip joint was so ravaged that it had all but dissolved, and his leg was kept attached only by a splint. The officer had no desperate expectations of a cure, but he took the holy waters, along with thousands of other pilgrims who flock to this site. Over the next few months a careful X-ray record was kept as his cancer was miraculously healed. This did not just entail the malignancy disappearing: His entire hip joint regrew. Medical science has no explanation for such a thing, and the Italian military officer became one of the authenticated healings attributed to the Virgin Mary at Lourdes. (I believe around seventy of these have been verified since such claims have been examined by a panel of doctors adhering to the strictest standards of proof.)

If we refer to our model, this healing involves a unique event: All three levels of reality were in communication. The soldier's body and his cancer were on the material level. His prayers were on the quantum level. God's intervention came from the virtual level. In one sense this seems to make a miracle seem very cold-blooded and clinical. But in another sense it makes everything a miracle. And why shouldn't that be so? The fact is that stars, mountains, monarch butterflies, and a single skin cell all depend on the same open lines of communication. The flow of reality is miraculous because invisible emptiness gets transformed into the brilliant orange of a butterfly's wing or the massive solidity of a mountain without any effort at all.

This unseen power is sacred and mythic but present all the time. Science is guilty of trying to explain it away instead of explaining it. A real Theory of Everything would instruct us in the art of living on all three levels of reality with equal power and security. Saints strive to get to that point; it is the true meaning of enlightenment.

This is all to say that God's mystery is the same as the mystery of the world. The promise made by Jesus, to show what no human mind has ever conceived, has been fulfilled during our lifetime. Indeed, Niels

Bohr, the great Danish physicist, stated that quantum physics is not only stranger than we think, it is stranger than we *can* think. We are brought face-to-face with one of the mystic's primary beliefs: Whatever can be thought of has already been created by God and is real somewhere, if not in this world, then in another.

Religious trappings offend many rigorous scientists, but do we have to have any? I remember as a young doctor reading about a patient suffering from terminal cancer who was cured literally by an injection of saline, ordinary salt water. He had entered the hospital, his body completely disfigured by swollen malignant lymph nodes. This was in the fifties when medicine was riding a crest of optimism about finding a cure for cancer very quickly. Patients were routinely killed or nearly killed with doses of mustard gas, the same poison used on soldiers in the trenches in World War I but also the first crude chemotherapy.

This man was desperate to be given the latest wonder treatment, known as Krebiozen. His doctor despaired of wasting the drug on someone who would probably be dead before the week was out. But out of pity he arranged for a single dose of Krebiozen and injected it on a Friday. He left over the weekend, fully expecting never to see his charge again, but on his return Monday morning, the patient was jubilant. Every trace of cancer had vanished; his lymph nodes had returned to normal, and he felt completely well. Stunned, his doctor released him as cured, knowing full well that a single dose of Krebiozen could not possibly have made a difference over a few days.

But the story becomes, if anything, much stranger. After some time had passed, the patient read in the newspaper that testing on Krebiozen had proved ineffective. Within a matter of days his cancer returned, and once again he entered the hospital in a terminal state. His doctor had nothing to give him, so he resorted to the most drastic of placebos. He told the man that he would be injected with "new, improved" Krebiozen, while in reality giving him nothing but saline solution.

Again the man was healed in a matter of days. For the second time, he left without evidence of cancer in his body. The story doesn't have a happy ending, because when he later discovered that all hope for Krebiozen was abandoned, he contracted lymph cancer for the third time, and this time he died rapidly.

But the essence of the story is that spirit

acts by flowing from the virtual to the quantum to the material level. This is what all miracles have in common, whether they occur with religious trappings or not. The crucial importance of religion is not to be discarded, however. Faith in God is a way of opening the lines of communication beyond the material. So is prayer or hope. The mind cannot do it simply by thinking. If there is ever going to be a science of miracles, it begins with intangibles that are rooted in spirit.

We are only partway toward solving the mystery. Once again I gaze upon the Great Pyramid of Cheops; only this time I don't see an awesome pile of sandstone but an idea—several ideas, actually. The first is sheer spiritual audacity. This pyramid was once entirely sheathed in a layer of white limestone, because its builders wanted to out-dazzle the sun. That was the whole point, in fact. Without equality to the sun god, these audacious ancients would just have been glorified worker ants. This is a reminder that human beings aspire to be more than human.

The other idea behind the pyramid is wonder. Sacred sites tell us that we are wondrous creatures who should be doing wondrous works. And you can still see that here, for it would be more than four thousand years before another structure encompassed such a volume of space, and that happened on a flat sandbar on the east coast of Florida.

The Vertical Assembly Building at the Kennedy Space Center is tall enough to hold a Saturn V moon rocket upright and has proportions boggling the mind. Standing as it does on a featureless landscape, you think you are close to it when you still have a mile to go. But it isn't just the scale of the thing that awes us. This building is also an idea, the idea that we will find our origins and our cosmic family. The Greek gods were once our family, along with the Indian gods and Jehovah of the Book of Genesis. All were cosmic beings, and we traced our origins back to the beginning of the cosmos.

Now the giant rockets blast off; one will soon go to gather interstellar dust, on the off chance that it will contain even one microorganism. If a single bacterium comes back from deep space, we will have found our own cosmic seed. It's not a whole family, but it's a beginning. As the old myths wear out, new ones spring up in our souls. Prometheus brought us fire, and now these rockets are the fire we send back to the gods. We are returning the gift and also reaching out. We crave to know that we are sacred once again. Are we? The answer isn't in the galactic dust but in ourselves. The deepest levels of the quantum domain are the common ground where our hands reach out to touch God. When that happens, there is a double wonder: What we touch is divine, but it is also ourselves.

Before we proceed any further, I want to offer three lists that summarize where we are. These don't need to be memorized or studied; everything contained in them will be discussed in clear, simple language as we move ahead. But this seems like a good place to pause and reflect. Without using religious terminology, we have discovered a great many facts about God. They are strange facts perhaps, not easily translated into ordinary life. There is no doubt, though, that from these seeds a complete vision of God will blossom.

VIRTUAL DOMAIN = SPIRIT

No energy
No time
Unbounded—every point in space is
    every other point
Wholeness exists at every point

Infinite silence
Infinite dynamism
Infinitely correlated
Infinite organizing power
Infinite creative potential
Eternal
Unmeasurable
Immortal, beyond birth and death
Acausal

QUANTUM DOMAIN = MIND

Creation manifests.
Energy exists.
Time begins.
Space expands from its source.
Events are uncertain.
Waves and particles alternate with one
    another.
Only probabilities can be measured.
Cause and effect are fluid.
Birth and death occur at the speed of
    light.
Information is embedded in energy.

MATERIAL REALITY = VISIBLE UNIVERSE

Events are definite.
Objects have firm boundaries.
Matter dominates over energy.

Three-dimensional
Knowable by the five senses
Time flows in a straight line.
Changeable
Subject to decay
Organisms are born and die.
Predictable
Cause and effect are fixed.

Three

SEVEN STAGES OF GOD

*If you don't make yourself equal to God,
you can't perceive God.*
—ANONYMOUS CHRISTIAN HERETIC,
THIRD CENTURY

Each person is entitled to some version of God that seems real, yet many versions contradict one another. On a long trip to India a few years ago, we had stopped the car to look at a family of Himalayan monkeys playing by the side of the road. Thirty seconds after we got out, a whole band of monkeys, maybe a hundred strong, descended upon us. While everyone was snapping photos and throwing bits of fruit and bread, I noticed not far away an old village woman all by herself, kneeling before a makeshift shrine under a tree. She was praying to Hanuman, a god in the shape of a monkey. I realized then that this pack hung around to grab food from the altar and any handouts they could charm from tourists like us.

What is the difference, I thought, between these chattering, clever animals, who knew all the tricks to catch our attention, and a god? Hanuman, who could fly and was known as "son of the wind," once journeyed to these same Himalayas. When Prince Rama's brother lay dying from a grievous wound received in battle, the flying monkey-king was sent to bring back the one special herb that would save his life. Hanuman looked everywhere but couldn't find the herb, so in frustration he ripped up the whole mountain where the plant grew and sped it back to lay it at Rama's feet.

The old woman kneeling at the rickety shrine certainly knew this story from childhood, but why would she worship a monkey, even a mythic flying one, and even a king? Her face was as devout as anyone praying to the queen of heaven or the son of God. Was her prayer going astray because of whom she prayed to? Was it going anywhere at all?

We are now ready to answer the simplest but most profound question: Who is God? He cannot just be impersonal—a principle or a level of reality or a field. We went into the quantum and virtual domains to establish a basis for the sacred, yet that was only the beginning. In all religions God is described as infinite and unbounded, which creates a huge problem. An infinite God is nowhere and everywhere at the same time. He transcends nature, and therefore you cannot find him. As we said at the outset, one must assume that God leaves no fingerprints in the material world.

This gives us no choice but to find a substitute for infinity that retains something of God, enough so that we feel his presence. The Book of Genesis declares that God created Adam in his own image, but we have been returning the favor almost since the beginning, fashioning God in our image over and over again. In India these images include almost every creature, event, or phenomenon. Lightning can be worshiped as coming from the god Indra, a rupee coin as a symbol of Lakshmi, goddess of prosperity. The taxicabs of Delhi and Bombay may be protected by plastic figures of Ganesh, a cheerfully smiling elephant with a potbelly, dangling from the rearview mirror. In all these cases, however, there is an understanding that only one thing is really being worshiped—the self. The same "I" that gives a person a sense of identity extending beyond the physical body, expanding to embrace nature, the universe, and ultimately pure spirit.

In the West it would be exotic to worship a monkey god but scandalous to worship the self. The anecdote is told of an English anthropologist researching into the beliefs of Hinduism. One day he goes creeping through the forest and spies an old man dancing in a grove of trees. In ecstasy the old man embraces their trunks and says, "Lord, how I love you." Then he falls to the ground and chants, "Blessed are you, my Lord." Jumping to his feet, he raises his arms to the sky and cries, "I am overjoyed to hear your voice and see your face."

Unable to stand the spectacle any longer, the anthropologist jumps out of the bushes. "I must tell you, my good man, that you are quite crazy," he says.

"Why is that?" the old man asks in confusion.

"Because here you are all alone in the woods, and you think that you're talking to God," says the anthropologist.

"What do you mean, alone?" the old man replies.

To anyone who worships God as the self, it is obvious that none of us are alone. The "self" isn't personal ego but a pervasive presence that cannot be escaped. The East seems to have no difficulties here, but as you go west, uneasiness mounts. In the third century of the Christian era, an unknown heretic wrote, "If you don't make yourself equal to God, you can't perceive God." This belief did not succeed as dogma (the heresy here is of course that human and divine are not equal in Christianity), but at other levels it is undeniable.

The God of any religion is only a fragment of God. This has to be true, because a being who is unbounded has no image, no role to play, no location either inside or outside the cosmos, whereas religions offer many images—father, mother, lawgiver, judge, ruler of the universe. There are seven versions of God, which can be associated with organized faiths. Each one is a fragment, but so complete as to create a unique world:

Stage one: God the Protector
Stage two: God the Almighty
Stage three: God of Peace
Stage four: God the Redeemer
Stage five: God the Creator
Stage six: God of Miracles
Stage seven: God of Pure Being—"I Am"

Each stage meets a particular human need, which is only natural. In the face of nature's overwhelming forces, humans needed a God who would protect them from harm. When they felt that they had broken the law or committed wrongdoing, people turned to a God who would judge them on the one hand and redeem their sins on the other. In this way, purely from self-interest, the project of creating God in our own image proceeded—and continues to proceed.

Several of these stages, such as Redeemer and Creator, sound familiar from the Bible, and now that Buddhism has become more popular in the West, the final stage, where God is experienced as eternal silence and pure being, is not as foreign as it once would have been. But we are not comparing religions here; no stage is absolute in its claim to truth. Each one implies a different relationship, however. If you see yourself as one of God's children, then his relationship to you will be as a protector or a maker of rules; this relationship shifts if you see yourself as a creator—then you start to share some of God's functions. You stand on more equal ground, until finally, at the stage of "I am," the same pure being is common to both God and humans. In the progress from stage one to stage seven, the wide gap between God and his worshipers becomes narrower and eventually closes. Therefore we can say that we keep creating

God in our image for a reason that is more than vanity; we want to bring him home to us, to achieve intimacy. Yet whether you see God as an almighty judge who punishes or as a benign source of inner peace, he isn't exclusively that.

To an atheist, all forms of deity are a false projection, pure and simple. We attribute human traits to God such as mercy and love, set these traits upon an altar, and then proceed to pray to them. Every image of God, then, including the most abstract ones, is completely empty (by abstract I mean the God of Islam and orthodox Judaism, neither of which is allowed to be portrayed with a human face). According to the atheist, religion is the ultimate illusion since we are only worshiping ourselves secondhand.

There are two ways to respond to this accusation. The first is the argument that an infinite God should be worshiped in all ways; the second is the argument that God has to be approached in stages, for otherwise one could never close the huge gap between him and us. I think the second argument is the more telling one. Unless we can see ourselves in the mirror, we will never see God there. Consider the list again, and you will see how God shifts in response to very human situations:

God is a protector to those who see themselves in danger.

God is almighty to those who want power (or lack any way of getting power).

God brings peace to those who have discovered their own inner world.

God redeems those who are conscious of committing a sin.

God is the creator when we wonder where the world came from.

God is behind miracles when the laws of nature are suddenly revoked without warning.

God is existence itself—"I Am"—to those who feel ecstasy and a sense of pure being.

In our search for the one and only one God, we pursue the impossible. The issue isn't how many Gods exist, but how completely our own needs can be spiritually fulfilled. When someone asks, "Is there really a God?" the most legitimate answer is, "Who's asking?" The perceiver is intimately linked to his perceptions. The fact that we single out traits like mercy and love, judgment and redemption, shows that we are forced to give God human attributes, but that is absolutely proper if those traits came from God in the first place. In other words, a circle connects the human and the divine. From the virtual level, which is our source, the qualities of spirit flow until they reach us in the material world. We experience this flow as our own inner impulses, and this is also appropriate, because for every stage of God there exists a specific biological response. The brain is an instrument of the mind, but it is a very convincing one. All that we really know about the brain is that it creates our perception, our thinking, and our motor activity. But these are powerful things. On the material plane, the brain is our only way of registering reality, and spirit must be filtered through biology.

No one uses the entire brain at once. We select from a range of built-in mechanisms. There are seven of these, as we saw, that directly relate to spiritual experience:

1. Fight-or-flight response
2. Reactive response
3. Restful awareness response
4. Intuitive response
5. Creative response
6. Visionary response
7. Sacred response

In the opening chapter I gave a thumbnail description of each, but even in abbreviated form you may have begun to see how much of your own spiritual life is based on habitual or even unconscious reflex:

Fight or flight is a primitive, atavistic response to protect yourself, inherited from animals. It energizes the body to meet outside danger and threat. This is the reflex that sends a mother into a burning house to save her child.

The *reactive response* makes us defend our ego and its needs. When we compete and seek to rise above others, we automatically look out for "me" as opposed to "the other." This is the reflex that fuels the stock market, political parties, and religious conflict.

Restful awareness is the first step away from outside forces. This response brings inner calm in the face of chaos or threats. We turn to it in prayer and meditation.

The *intuitive response* calls upon the inner world for more than peace and calm. We ask inside for answers and solutions. This state is associated with synchronicity, flashes of insight, and religious awakening.

The *creative response* breaks free from old patterns. It gives up the known to explore the unknown. Creativity is synonymous with the flow of inspiration.

The *visionary response* embraces a universal "me" in place of the isolated ego. It looks beyond all boundaries and is not fixed by the laws of nature that limit earlier stages. Miracles become possible for the first time. This response guides prophets, seers, and healers.

The *sacred response* is completely free of all limitations. It is experienced as pure bliss, pure intelligence, pure being. At this stage, God is universal and so is the person. This response marks the fully enlightened of every age.

Each of these is a natural response of the human nervous system, and we were all born with the ability to experience the entire range. In the face of danger, a burst of adrenaline creates the overwhelming urge to flee or to stay and fight. When this response is triggered, all kinds of changes take place in the physiology, including increased heart rate, ragged breathing, elevated blood pressure, etc. But if we sit down to meditate, this isn't the state of the nervous system—far from it. The same indicators that were elevated in fight or flight are now decreased, and the subjective feeling is that of peace and calm.

These are well-documented facts medically, but I wish to take a step further, and it is a startling step. I contend that the brain responds uniquely in every phase of spiritual life. Scientific research is incomplete at the higher stages of inner growth, but we know that where the spirit leads, the body follows. Faith healers do exist who transcend medical explanation. Only a few miles from where I was in the Himalayas, yogis sit in trances for days at a time; others can be buried for a week in an almost airless box or bring their breathing and heart rates down to nearly zero. Saints in every religion have been observed to live on little or no food (many of them declaring that they survive solely on the light of God). Visions of God have been so credible that their wisdom moved and guided the lives of millions; extraordinary acts of selflessness and compassion prove that the mind is not ruled by self-interest alone.

We select a deity based on our interpretation of reality, and that interpretation is rooted in biology. The ancient Vedic seers put it quite bluntly: "The world is as we are." To someone living in a world of threat, the need for fight or flight is absolute. This pertains to a Neanderthal facing a saber-tooth tiger, a soldier in the trenches in World War I, or a driver frustrated with road rage on the L.A. freeways. We can match each biological response, in fact, with a specific self-image:

RESPONSE	IDENTITY IS BASED ON . . .
Fight-or-flight response	*Physical body/physical environment*
Reactive response	*Ego and personality*
Restful awareness response	*Silent witness*
Intuitive response	*The knower within*
Creative response	*Co-creator with God*
Visionary response	*Enlightenment*
Sacred response	*The source of all*

Looking at the right-hand column, you have a clear outline of the stages of human growth. The fact that we are born with the potential to go from simple survival to God-consciousness is the remarkable trait that sets our nervous systems apart from all other creatures. It is undeniable that complete inner growth is a tremendous challenge. If you are trapped in traffic, blood boiling with frustration, higher thoughts are blocked out. At that moment, under the influence of adrenaline, you identify with being confined and unable to do anything.

In a different situation, when you are competing for a promotion at work, you see things from the ego's point of view. Now your anxiety isn't over survival (which is the root of the fight-or-flight response in animals) but getting ahead. Once again higher responses are blocked; you would be ruining your chances if you stopped competing and felt only love for the other candidates for the job.

Change the response once more, and this viewpoint will also fade away. When you see a news report about dying children in Africa or a needless war somewhere far away, you may find yourself wanting to find a creative solution to the problem or you may just reflect internally on the pointlessness of suffering. These higher responses are subtler and more delicate. We also call them more spiritual, but in any situation the brain is responding from the highest level it can. The deeper mystery, which we will explore in this part of the book, centers on our ability to rise from an animal instinct to sainthood. Is this possible for everyone, or is the potential there only for the tiniest fraction of humanity? We will only find out by examining what each stage means and how a person rises up the ladder of inner growth.

Despite the enormous flexibility of the nervous system, we fall into habits and repeated patterns because of our reliance on old imprints. This is never more true than with our beliefs. I was once walking down a side street in the old section of Cairo when a man jumped out of the shadows and began ranting at some passersby. Not knowing Arabic, I had no idea what he was preaching, but it was obvious from the vexation and rage in his face that his sermon had to do with fear of God. In every religion there is the same streak of fear whenever a person is certain that the world is dominated by threat, danger, and sin. Yet every religion also contains the strain of love whenever the world is perceived as abundant, loving, and nourishing. It is all projection. I am not finding fault here. We have the right to worship love, mercy, compassion, truth, and justice on the transcendent level, just as we have the right to fear judgment and divine rebuke. If you accept that the world is as we are, it is only logical to accept that God is as we are.

- *God the protector* fits a world of bare survival, full of physical threats and danger.
- *God the almighty* fits a world of power struggles and ambition, where fierce competition rules.

- A *God of peace* fits a world of inner solitude where reflection and contemplation are possible.
- *God the redeemer* fits a world where personal growth is encouraged and insights prove fruitful.
- *God the creator* fits a world that is constantly renewing itself, where innovation and discovery are valued.
- A *God of miracles* fits a world that contains prophets and seers, where spiritual vision is nurtured.
- A *God of pure being*—"*I Am*"—fits a world that transcends all boundaries, a world of infinite possibilities.

The wonder is that the human nervous system can operate on so many planes. We don't just navigate these dimensions, we explore them, meld them together, and create new worlds around ourselves. If you do not understand that you are multidimensional, then the whole notion of God runs off the rails.

I remember as a boy that my mother once prayed for a sign or message from God—I believe she had had a dream that affected her deeply. One day the kitchen door was left open, and a large cobra crawled in. When my mother encountered it, she didn't scream or cry out but fell to her knees in reverence. To her, this snake was Shiva, and her prayers had been answered.

Notice how much your response to this incident depends on interpretation. If you don't believe that Shiva can appear as an animal, it would seem crazy to revere a cobra, not to mention superstitious and primitive. But if all of nature expresses God, then we can choose which symbols express him best. I know one thing: I cannot share anyone else's consciousness. As much as I love my mother, her response is private and unique. What was a glorious symbol of God to her may frighten and repulse others. (I can remember many days sitting in school under the tutelage of Catholic brothers, wondering why anyone would kneel before the horrifying image of the crucifixion.)

I was testing these key ideas with a group when a woman objected. "I don't understand this word *projection*. Are you saying that we just make God up?" she asked.

"Yes and no," I replied. "A projection is different from a hallucination, which has no reality at all. A projection originates inside you, the observer, and therefore it defines your perception of reality—it is your take on infinity."

"Which would make God just a comment about me?" she asked.

"God cannot be just about you, but the portion of him that you perceive must be about you, because you are using your own brain and senses and memory. Since you are the observer, it is all right to see him through an image that is meaningful to you."

I thought of St. Paul's most telling line about the role of the observer: "Now we see as through a glass, darkly." The passage is easier to understand if we set aside the King James poetry in favor of modern English:

> When I was a child, I spoke and saw things like a child. When I grew up, I had finished with childish things. Right now, we all see puzzling reflections, as in a clouded mirror, but then (when we meet God), we shall see face to face. My knowledge now is partial; then it will be whole, the way God knows me already.

The standard interpretation is that when we are confined to a physical body, our perception is dim. Only on the day of judgment, when we meet God directly, will our perception be pure enough to see who he is and who we are. But that isn't the only way to interpret the passage. Paul could be making the point that the observer who is attempting to see who God is winds up seeing his own reflection. Since there is no way around this limitation, we have to make the best use of it that we can. Like a child growing up, we have to evolve toward a more complete vision, until the day arrives when we can see the whole as God does. Our self-reflections tell our own story along the way, usually in symbolic form as dreams do—hence the clouded mirror.

Reality itself may be only a symbol for the workings of God's mind, and in that case the "primitive" belief—found throughout the ancient and pagan world—that God exists in every blade of grass, every creature, and even the earth and sky, may contain the highest truth. Arriving at that truth is the purpose of spiritual life, and each stage of God takes us on a journey whose end point is total clarity, a sense of peace that nothing can disturb.

STAGE ONE:
GOD THE PROTECTOR
(Fight-or-Flight Response)

Neurologists have long divided the brain into old and new. The new brain is an organ to be proud of. When you have a reasoned thought, it is this area of gray matter, primarily the cerebral cortex, that comes into play. Shakespeare was referring to the new brain (and using it) when he had Hamlet utter, "What a piece of work is a man, how noble in reason, how infinite in faculties." But Hamlet was also wrapped up in a murder case that called for vengeance, and as he dug deeper into the sins of his family, he dug deeper into his own mind. The old brain wanted its due; this is the part of us that claws for survival and is willing to kill, if need be, to protect us.

The old brain is reflected in a God who seems not to possess much in the way of higher functions. He is primordial and largely unforgiving. He knows who his enemies are; he doesn't come from the school of forgive and forget. If we list his attributes, which many would trace back to the Old Testament, the God of stage one is

Vengeful
Capricious
Quick to anger
Jealous
Judgmental—meting out reward and
    punishment
Unfathomable
Sometimes merciful

This description doesn't only fit Jehovah, who was also loving and benevolent. Among the Indian gods and on Mount Olympus one encounters the same willful, dangerous behavior. For God is very dangerous in stage one; he uses nature to punish even his most favored children through storms, floods, earthquakes, and disease. The test of the faithful is to see the good side of such a deity, and overwhelmingly the faithful have. Primitive man experienced untold threats from the environment; survival was in question every day. Yet we know that these threats were not destined to prevail. Overarching was a divine presence that protected human beings, and despite his frightening temper, God the protector was as necessary to life as a father is inside a family.

The old brain is stubborn, and so is the old God. No matter how civilized a person's behavior is, if you dig deep enough (Freud compared this to unearthing all the layers of an archaeological site) you'll find primitive responses. We know enough about this region, located at the bottom and back of the skull and rooted in the limbic system, to see that it acts much like our stereotype of Jehovah. The old brain isn't logical. It fires off impulses that destroy logic in favor of strong emotions, instant reflexes, and a suspicious sense that danger is always around the corner. The favorite response of the old brain is to lash out in its own defense, which is why the fight-or-flight response serves as its main trigger.

"I don't care what you're telling us, there's something evil about this thing. It has a mind of its own. No one's going to stop it." The young father had been trying to hide his tears, but now his voice was shaking.

"I know it can feel that way," I replied sadly. "But cancer is just a disease." I looked at him and stopped trying to explain the radiation treatments for his child. The father was beside himself, talking from pure fear and anger. "One day she has a head-ache, nothing to worry about. Now it has turned into this—whatever it is."

"Astrocytoma—it's a kind of brain tumor. Your daughter's has advanced to Stage Four, which means it can't be operated on and is growing very fast."

This conversation took place more than a decade ago. The parents were still in their early thirties, young blue-collar people who had no experience of this kind of catastrophe. Less than twenty-four hours had passed since they brought their twelve-year-old girl in. She had been having dizzy spells with recur-ring pain behind her eyes. After running a battery of tests, the presence of a malignancy showed up. Because cancer grows rapidly in children, the prognosis was likely to be fatal.

"We aren't giving up," I said. "Medical decisions have to be made, and you both need to help." The parents looked numbed. "We're all praying for Christina," I said. "Sometimes it's just up to God."

The father's face went dark again. "God? He could have prevented this whole damn thing. If he's going to let a senseless tragedy happen, why should we pretend he will make it go away?" I didn't respond, and the parents stood up to leave. "You just tell them to start with those treatments. We'll make it through," the father said. He gathered his wife and they returned to their child's bedside.

Hope failed in this moment of crisis, which means, if we are being totally honest, that God failed—the God of stage one, who should have protected his children. In crisis we are all thrown back on a deep sense of physical danger, and not just in the case of a cancer diagnosis. The loss of a job can feel like a matter of life and death. People wrangling over a bitter divorce at times act as if their former spouse has become a mortal enemy. The fact that the old brain exerts its influence age after age accounts for the durability of God's role as protector. Our primitive reactions to danger exist for a reason that is not going to be easily outgrown; the very structure of the brain guarantees this. The brain triggers the endocrine system, which injects adrenaline into the bloodstream to force the body—whatever the higher brain may think—to do its bidding.

Put yourself in the position of an innocent defendant in a lawsuit. A stranger has brought charges against you, forcing you to appear before a judge. Despite your duty to act in accordance with the rule of law, certain primitive feelings will prove inescapable, and they are very Old Testament in nature:

- You will want to get back at your accuser. Jehovah is *vengeful.*
- You will try to find anything that works to prove your case. Jehovah is *capricious.*
- You will boil over whenever you think of the injustice being done to you. Jehovah is *quick to anger.*
- You will want the court to pay attention to you as much as possible, seeing only your side of things. Jehovah is *jealous.*
- You will want your accuser punished after you are found innocent. Jehovah

is judgmental—he *metes out reward and punishment.*

- You will lie awake at night wondering how this could have happened to you. Jehovah is *unfathomable.*
- You will be sustained by faith that the court ultimately won't punish you unjustly. Jehovah is *sometimes merciful.*

(It's worth repeating that Jehovah is just an illustrative example—one could have substituted Zeus or Indra.)

Because his role is to protect, the God of stage one fails when the weak fall prey to illness, tragedy, or violence. He succeeds whenever we escape danger and survive crisis. In the mood of triumph his devotees feel chosen. They exult over their enemies and once again feel safe (for a while) because heaven is on their side.

Reason teaches us that aggression begets retaliation—we know this undeniably, given the tragic history of war. But there is a wall between the logic of the new brain, which is based upon reflection, observation, and the ability to see beyond bare survival, and the logic of the old brain. The old brain fights first—or runs away—and asks questions later.

Who am I? . . .
A survivor.

At each stage the basic question, "Who is God?" immediately raises other questions. The first of these is "Who am I?" In stage one identity is based upon the physical body and the environment. Survival is the foremost consideration here. If we look at biblical history, we find that the ancient Hebrews could survive in a harsh world much more easily than in a purposeless one. The hardships of their lives were many—it took persistent, unending toil to raise crops from the land; enemies abounded; and being in the middle of a much larger nomadic culture, the Hebrews were caught up in one migration after another. How could this life of bare subsistence be reconciled with any sort of benign God?

One solution was to make him a capricious and unpredictable parent. This role is played out with great dramatic conviction in the Book of Genesis, which spends far more time over the fall of Adam and Eve than on their creation.

The first man and woman are the ultimate bad children. The sin they commit is to disobey God's dictum not to eat of the tree of knowledge. If we examine this act in symbolic terms, we see a father who is jealous of his adult prerogatives: he knows best, he holds the power, his word is law. To maintain this position, it is necessary that the children remain children, yet they yearn to grow up and have the same knowledge possessed by the father. Usually that is permissible, but God is the only father who was never a child himself. This makes him all the more unsympathetic, for his anger against Adam and Eve is irrational in its harshness. Here is his condemnation of Eve:

> I will increase your labor and your
>   groaning,
> and in labor shall you bear children.
> You shall be eager for your husband,
> and he shall be your master.

Eve has such a reputation as temptress that we forget one thing—she is not overtly sexual until God makes her so. Being "eager for your husband" is part of the curse, as is the pain of giving birth. The rest of family life will have to bear the sentence pronounced upon God's son:

> With labor shall you win your food
>   from the earth
> all the days of your life.

It will grow thorns and thistles for you,
none but wild plants for you to eat.
You shall gain your bread by the sweat
  of your brow,
until you return to the ground;
for from it you were taken.
Dust you are, to dust shall you return.

This entire scene, which ends with Adam and
Eve driven in shame from paradise, also
divides a family, shattering the intimacy of
the preceding days, when God would walk in
Eden and enjoy himself with his children.
But if paradise quickly turned into a faded
dream—we are not far from the time when
Cain kills his brother Abel—the lesson sank
deep: humans are guilty. They alone made
the world harsh and difficult; on their heads
falls the blame for the agony of childbirth and
the backbreaking toil of eking out a living.

  The Genesis story came about two thousand years before Christ and was written in
final form by temple scribes, perhaps a thousand years after it originated. Women had
been subjugated to men long before that,
and the rigors of farming and childbearing
are as old as humankind. So to arrive at the
God of stage one, it was necessary to argue
back from what already existed.

  When they asked, "Who am I?" the earliest writers of scripture knew that they were mortals subject to disease and famine. They had seen a huge percentage of babies die at birth, and many times their mothers perished as well. These conditions had to have a reason; therefore the family relationship with God got worked out in terms of sin, disobedience, and ignorance. Even so, God remained on the scene—he watches over Adam and Eve, despite the curse put upon them, and after a while he finds enough virtue in their descendant Noah to save him from the sentence of death placed upon every other offspring from the original seed family.

Another irony is at work here, however. The only character in the episode of Eve and the apple who seems to tell the truth is the serpent. He whispers in Eve's ear that God has forbidden them to eat of the tree of good and evil because it will give them knowledge and make them equal to the father. Here are his exact words after Eve informs him that if they eat of the forbidden fruit, they will die:

> Of course you will not die. God knows that as soon as you eat it, your eyes will be opened and you will be like gods, knowing both good and evil.

The serpent is holding out a world of awareness, independence, and decision making. All these things follow when you have knowledge. In other words, the serpent is advising God's children to grow up, and of course this is a temptation they cannot resist. Who could? (The famed authority on myth, Joseph Campbell, points out that at this time the wandering Hebrew tribes had moved into a territory where the prevailing religion was based on a wise, benign goddess of agriculture whose totem animal was the snake. In a complete reversal, the priests of Israel made the female the villain of the piece and her ally a wicked serpent.)

Why would God want to oppose such a natural development in his children—why didn't he want them to have knowledge? He acts like the worst of abusive fathers, using fear and terror to keep his offspring in an infantile state. They never know when he will punish them next—worse than that, he gives no hope that the original curse will ever be removed. Good and bad actions are weighed, reward and punishment are handed out from the judge's bench, yet mankind cannot escape the burden of guilt, no matter how much virtue your life demonstrates.

Rather than viewing the God of stage one harshly, we need to realize how realistic he is. Life has been incredibly hard for many people, and deep psychological wounds are inflicted in family life. We all carry around memories of how difficult it was to grow up, and at any given moment, we feel the tug of old, childish fears. The survivalist and the guilty child lurk just beneath the surface. The God of stage one salves these wounds and gives us a reason to believe that we will survive. At the same time he fuels our needs. As long as we need a protector, we will cling to the role of children.

> *How do I fit in?* . . .
> I cope.

In stage one there is no indication that humans have a favored place in the cosmos—on the contrary. Natural forces are blind, and their power is beyond our control. Recently I saw a news report about a small town in Arkansas flattened by a tornado that struck in the middle of the night. Those who had survived were awakened by a deafening roar in the darkness and had the presence of mind to run into their basements. As they surveyed the wreckage of their lives, the dazed survivors mumbled the same response: *I'm alive only by the grace of God.* They did not consider (nor express out loud) that the same God might have sent the storm. In crisis people seek ways to cope, and in stage one, God is a coping mechanism. This holds true wherever survival is in peril. In the worst ghetto areas ravaged by drugs and street crime, one finds the most intense faith. Horrible situations stretch our coping skills beyond their limits—the random death of children gunned down in school would be an example—and to escape complete despair, people will project beyond hopelessness, finding solace in a God who wants to protect them.

> *What is the nature of good and evil?* . . .
> Good is safety, comfort, food,
> shelter, and family.
> Evil is physical threat and abandonment.

An absolute standard of good and evil is something many people crave, particularly at a time when values seem to be crumbling. In stage one, good and evil seem to be very clear. Good derives from being safe; evil derives from being in danger. A good life has physical rewards—food, clothing, shelter, and a loving family—while if you lead a bad life you are left alone and abandoned, prey to physical danger. But is the picture really so clear?

Once again the family drama must be taken into account. Social workers are well aware that abused children have a strange desire to defend their parents. Even after years of beatings and emotional cruelty, it can be nearly impossible to get them to testify to the abuse. Their need for a protector is too strong—one could say that love and cruelty are so interwoven that the psyche can't separate them. If you try to remove the child from the abusive environment, he is deeply afraid that you are snatching away his source of love. This confusion doesn't end with adulthood. The old brain has an overriding need for security, which is why so many abused wives defend their husbands and return to them. Good and evil become hopelessly confused.

The God of stage one is just as ambiguous. Twenty years ago I read a poignant fable about a town that was perfect. Everyone in it was healthy and happy, and the sun always shone on their doorsteps. The only mystery in the town was that every day a few people walked away, silently and giving no explanation. No one could figure out why this was happening, yet the phenomenon didn't end. We finally discover that a single child has been trapped by his parents in the basement, where he is tortured, out of sight. Those who walk away know this secret, and for them perfection has come to an end. The vast majority don't know, or if they do, turn their heads the other way.

Fables can be read in many ways, but this one says something about our stage one God. Even if he is worshiped as a benign parent, one who never inflicted guilt upon us, his goodness is tainted by suffering. A father who provides with great love and generosity would be considered a good father, but not if he tortures one child. Anyone who considers himself a child of God has to consider this problem. Much of the time, as in the fable, it is papered over. The need for security is too great, and in addition there is only so much we can cope with at any one time.

How do I find God? . . .
Through fear and loving devotion.

If the God of stage one is double-edged, providing with one hand and punishing with the other, then he cannot be known only one way. Fear and love both come into play. For every biblical injunction to "love the Lord thy God with all thy heart, all thy strength, and all thy soul," there is a counterbalance. The injunction to "fear the

Lord" is expressly stated in all faiths, even the faiths supposedly based on love. (Jesus speaks quite openly about the evildoers who will be "cast out with wailing and gnashing of teeth.")

What this means in a deeper sense is that ambivalence is discouraged. Peace of a sort rules in a family where the children are told simply to love their parents but also feel secret anger, hatred, and jealousy toward them. The "official" emotion is only positive. An outsider may call this a false peace, but to the insider it works. But has negativity really gone away? It takes a great deal of growing up before one can live with ambivalence and its constant blending of dark and light, love and hate—this is the road not taken in stage one.

A friend of mine told me a touching story of the day he grew up, as he saw it. He was a protected, even coddled child whose parents were very private. He never saw them disagree; they were careful to draw the boundary between what the adults in the family discussed between themselves and what they told the children. This is psychologically healthy, and my friend remembers an almost idyllic childhood, free of anxiety and conflict.

Then one day when he was about ten, he

woke up late one night to hear loud noises from downstairs. He felt a chill of fear, certain that some crime was taking place. After a moment he realized that his parents were having a loud argument. In great consternation he jumped up and ran downstairs. When he entered the kitchen he saw the two of them confronting each other.

"Don't you lay a hand on her, or I'll kill you!" he shouted, rushing at his father. His parents were bewildered and did everything they could to calm the boy down—there had been no violence, only an angry disagreement—but even though he eventually grasped the situation, something deep had changed. He no longer could believe in a perfect world.

The mixture of love and anger, peace and violence, that we all have to live with had dawned on him. In place of certainty there was now ambiguity—people he once trusted completely had showed that they possessed a darker side. By implication the same holds true for each of us and, by extension, for God.

Everyone must face this conflict, but we resolve it in different ways. Some children try to preserve innocence by denying that its opposite exists; they turn into idealists and wishful thinkers. They show a strong streak of denial when anything "negative" takes place and will remain anxious until the situation turns "positive" again. Other children take sides, assigning all the anxiety-provoking traits to a bad parent while labeling the other as always good. Both of these tactics fall under the category of coping mechanisms; therefore it comes as no surprise to find how much they invade religious belief in stage one, which is all about coping.

The good parent–bad parent solution takes the form of a cosmic battle between God and Satan. There is abundant proof in the Old Testament that Jehovah is willful and cruel enough to assume the role of bad parent by himself. Even a man of titanic righteousness like Moses is deprived in the end of being able to enter the promised land. No amount of fear and love, however you mix them, is enough to satisfy this God. His capriciousness knows no bounds. However, if this portrayal is unacceptable, there must be an "adversary" (the literal meaning of Satan's name) to take the blame away from God. Satan appears in the Old Testament as tempter, deceiver, stealer of souls, and the fallen angel Lucifer, who through pride tried to usurp God's authority and had to be cast down to hell. You could say that he is the light gone bad. But never once is he described as an aspect of God. The division between the two makes for a much simpler story, as it does for a child who has decided that one parent must be the good one and the other bad.

The other coping strategy, which involves denying the negative and seeking always to be positive, is just as common in religion. A lot of harm has to be overlooked to make God totally benign, yet people manage to do so. In the family drama, if there is more than one child, interpretations become fixed. One child will be absolutely sure that no abuse or conflict was ever present, while another will be just as certain that it was pervasive. The power of interpretation is linked to consciousness; things can't exist if you are not conscious of them, no matter how real they may be to others. In religious terms, some believers are content to love God and fear him at the same time. This duality in no way involves any condemnation of the deity. He is still "perfect" (meaning that he is always right) because those he punishes must be wrong.

In this case faith depends on a value system that is preordained. If some ill befalls me, I must have committed a sin, even if I didn't have any awareness of it. My task is to look deep enough until I find the flaw inside myself, and then I will see the perfect judgment God has rendered. To someone outside the system, however, it appears that an abused child is figuring out, through convoluted logic, how to make himself wrong so that the cruel parent remains right. In stage one, God has to be right. If he isn't, the world becomes too dangerous to live in.

What's my life challenge? . . .
To survive, protect, and maintain.

Every stage of God implies a life challenge, which can be expressed in terms of highest aspiration. God exists to inspire us, and we express this through the aspirations we set for ourselves. An aspiration is the limit of the possible. In stage one, the limit is set by physical circumstances. If you are surrounded by threats, to survive is a high aspiration. This would be true in a shipwreck, a war, a famine, or an abusive family. However, each stage of God must give scope to the whole range of human abilities; even in the worst situations a person aspires to do more than cope.

You might think that the next step would be escape. In stage one, however, escape is blocked by the reality principle. A child can't escape his family, just as famine victims often can't escape drought. So the mind turns instead to imitating God, and since God is a protector, we try to protect the most valuable things in life. Protectors take many forms. Some are policemen protecting the law, firemen protecting safety, social workers protecting the helpless. In other words, stage one is the most social of all the seven worlds we will examine. Here one learns to be responsible and caring.

The reward for learning to protect others is that in return they give you their love and respect. Notice how furious the police become if they are taunted by the very people they are sworn to defend (this occurs in riots, political demonstrations, and racially divided neighborhoods). The protector craves respect. He is also inflexible about rules and laws. Being a guardian, he sees danger everywhere; therefore he is motivated to keep people in line "for their own good." This is essentially a parental feeling, and you will find that police officers can be fatherly, in both the good and bad sense. They may be quick to forgive offenses where the perpetrator acts humbled and chastised, but they are also prone to dispensing rough justice when a bad guy shows no remorse. Outright defiance is the worst response to a protector, who then feels completely justified in holding you to the letter of the law, just as Jehovah felt justified in punishing infractions of his law. Divine authority could be very cruel even to the chosen people, but those outside the law (meaning anyone with a different religion) deserve no mercy.

What is my greatest strength? . . .
Courage.

What is my biggest hurdle? . . .
Fear of loss, abandonment.

It isn't hard to figure out what you have to do to survive in a harsh world—you have to show courage in the face of adversity. The Old Testament is a world of heroes like Samson and David who fight battles and defeat enemies. Their victory is proof that God favors them. But as we saw, no amount of effort will totally appease this God. The courage to fight must eventually turn into the courage to oppose him.

If we take it back to the family, a vicious circle is involved. If you are afraid of your father because of his violent and unpredictable temper, the prospect of facing him

head-on will arouse even more fear. Thus
the incentive to keep quiet gets strength-
ened. Unfortunately, keeping quiet only
makes the fear worse, since it has no
release. The only way out is to overcome
the hurdle, which is true at every stage of
God. As in the family, the devotee of a fearful God will not move on to a higher stage
until he says, "I am tired of being afraid.
You are not my God if I have to hide from
your anger."

In social terms we see this played out in
rebellion against authority. A policeman
who decides to testify against his fellow officers on charges of corruption walks a fine
line. From one perspective he is a traitor,
from another he has found a conscience.
Which one is true? It all depends on where
you are heading. Some people have to preserve the system, and since corruption is
inevitable, they must decide how much bad
can be stomached in the name of the common good. Fathers and mothers make such
decisions every day over the bad behavior of
their children, just as the police do over
behavior under the law. But others look at
the same system and decide that doing good
isn't consistent with breaking the rules you
are assigned to enforce. Parents can't teach
truth-telling while at the same time being

liars; policemen can't accept bribes and at the same time arrest crooks.

There is no clear line here. As organized religions demonstrate, it is possible to live a long time with an angry, jealous, unfair God, even though he is supposed to be the highest judge. Neither side of the line is better than the other; ultimately one must learn to live with ambivalence.

The important issue is psychological. How much fear are you willing to live with? When this hurdle is cleared, when personal integrity is more important than being accepted within the system, a new stage begins. Thus the exhilaration felt by many war protesters. To them, demonstrations against authority mark a new birth of morality that is guided by principle rather than outside force. Now translate this to an inner war, with one voice urging rebellion and the other threatening you with punishment for breaking the law, and you have the core drama of stage one.

What is my greatest temptation? . . .
Tyranny.

You would think from the story of Adam and Eve that God's children were tempted to sin, but to me this is just the official version. The guardian wants you to obey; therefore he must make disobedience a wrongful act. The real temptation lies on God's side, just as it does with any protector who acts in his name. God's temptation is to become a tyrant. Tyranny is protection that has gone too far. It exists in families where the parents cannot balance rules with freedom. It exists in systems of law where mercy has been forgotten.

The desire to rule is so seductive that we don't need to delve very far into this particular temptation. It is more interesting to ask how it is ever escaped. The tyrant more often than not has to be deposed, overthrown by force. In some societies, as in some families, this happens through violence. The children rebel against authority by killing it; this takes place symbolically— through reckless teenage behavior with drinking and driving, for example. But short of violence there is a subtler mechanism for escaping any temptation, which is to see through the need for it. In Mafia films the gangsters inevitably run a protection racket. Under the pretext of keeping harm away from a storekeeper, they sell him insurance in the form of their protection. But this scheme works only through a lie, since the violence being held at bay comes from the gangsters themselves—they are the threat and the insurance. In spiritual terms, God's protection is valued only by denying that he is also the source of the threat. In the end, nothing is outside the deity, so asking him to protect you from storms, famine, disease, and misfortune is the same as asking the perpetrator.

I was reading a psychiatric case study in which a father was very worried about his three-year-old daughter. The little girl couldn't sleep well and suffered from bouts of severe anxiety. The father sat up with her every night, reading fairy tales to her and trying to offer reassurance.

"I read to her about Little Red Riding Hood and the big bad wolf," he told the therapist, "and when she gets scared, I tell her that there's nothing to worry about. I'm here to protect her."

"So you can't understand why she still seems so frightened?" the therapist remarked.

"Not at all," said the father. "Do I need to be even more reassuring?"

"No, you need to ask yourself why you choose frightening stories when she is so frightened to begin with."

The answer in this case is that the father was blinded by his need to be reassuring, a need rooted in his past—he had had an absent father who wasn't around to calm his child's fears. This is a telling anecdote, because it poses the central question in stage one: *Why did God have to make such a frightening world?* Was it just out of the temptation to tyrannize us? The answer doesn't lie with God but in our interpretation of him. To get out of stage one, you must arrive at a new interpretation of all the issues raised so far—Who is God? What kind of world did he create? Who am I? How do I fit in? In stage two the basic problem of survival has been overcome. There is much less need for fear, and for the first time we see the emerging influence of the new brain. Even so, just as the reptilian brain is buried inside the skull, not abolished by the cerebrum or canceled out by higher thought, the God of stage one is a permanent legacy that everyone confronts before inner growth can be achieved.

STAGE TWO:
GOD THE ALMIGHTY
(Reactive Response)

If stage one is about survival, stage two is about power. There is no doubt that God has all the power, which he jealously guards. At the beginning of the scientific era, when the secrets of electricity were being discovered and the elements charted, many worried that it was sacrilege to look too closely at how God worked. Power was not only his but rightfully so. Our place was to obey—a view that makes perfect sense if you consider heaven the goal of life. Who would endanger his soul just to know how lightning works?

Freud points out, however, that power is irresistible. It is one of the primary goods in life, along with money and the love of women (Freud's worldview was inescapably masculine). If Hamlet's dilemma is rooted in stage one, the hero of stage two is Macbeth, who finds it convenient to murder the king, his symbolic father, but then must wrestle with the demons of ambition. In the first act of *Macbeth*, when he meets the three witches on the heath, they predict that more and more power will come to him, until in the end he is king. But this is more than a prediction. Power is Macbeth's curse. It inflames his guilt, it forces him to abandon love; he lives in the shadows of night, sleepless and afraid of being plotted against; and in the end power drives him mad. The kind of God implied by the drive

to power is dangerous, but he is more civilized than the God of stage one. In describing this new God we would say that he is

Sovereign
Omnipotent
Just
The answerer of prayers
Impartial
Rational
Organized into rules

Compared to the God of stage one, this
version is much more social. He is worshiped by those who have formed a stable
society, one that needs laws and gover-
nance. The Almighty is not so willful as his
predecessor; he still metes out punishment,
but you can understand why—the wrongdoer disobeyed a law, something he knows
in advance not to do. Justice is no longer so
rough; the kings and judges who take their
power from God do so with a sense of being
righteous. They deserve their power—or so
they tell themselves. As with Macbeth, the
wielders of power get caught up in urges
that are all but irresistible.

The drama of power is based on the reactive response, a biological need to fulfill ego
demands. This response has not been stud-

ied well; we can surmise that it is associated with the midbrain, which lies between the oldest animal structures of the old brain and the rationality of the cerebral cortex. This is a shadowy region, and for decades no one really believed that ego—meaning your sense of identity and personality—was innate. Then studies in infant development by Jerome Kagan and others began to demonstrate that babies do not simply learn to have a personal identity. Almost from the moment of birth some newborns are outgoing, demanding in their needs, bold, and curious about the outside world, while others are introverted, quiet, undemanding, and shy about exploring their environment. These traits persist and expand through childhood and in fact remain for life. This implies that the ego response is built into us.

The ruling dictum of the reactive response is "More for me." Taken too far, this leads to corruption, since eventually an insatiable appetite must run into the desires of others. But in biological terms the drive for more is essential. A newborn infant exhibits a total lack of discipline and control. Child psychiatrists believe that all boundaries are fluid in the beginning. The baby is enclosed in a womblike world where the walls, crib, blanket, and even

mother's arms are still part of an undifferentiated, amorphous entity. To take this
blob of sensation and find out where "I"
begins is the first task of growing up.

The birth of ego is primitive at first.
When an infant touches a hot stove and
draws away in shock, he remembers the
pain not only as discomfort but as something "I" don't want. This sense of ego is so
primary that we forget what it was like not
to have it. Was there a time when I saw my
mother smiling down at me and felt that
her emotions were mine? Apparently not—
without being able to think or reflect, the
seed of ego came into the world with us.
Need, desire, pain, and pleasure were felt as
"mine" and remained that way, only growing in intensity.

Nor do we find any altruistic gods in
world mythology. The first commandment
given to Moses is "You shall place no other
God before me." Jehovah survives all com-
petitors in the Old Testament—we don't
even witness much of a contest. But in other
systems, such as the Greek and the Hindu,
the war for power is constant, and one gets
the sense that Zeus and Shiva have to keep
their eyes open if they want to remain at the
top of the pantheon. The Judaic God is a
surprising victor in his emergence from a

small, conquered nation that had ten of its twelve tribes wiped off the face of the earth by powerful foes, yet the subjugated Hebrews were able to look beyond their situation. They projected a stable, unshakable God who could not be touched by any shift of power on earth—the first God Almighty to survive all challengers.

Jehovah succeeded because he exemplified a world that was fast evolving—the world of competition and ambition. Raw power is violent, while the power achieved through ambition is subtle. At the level of survival, you get the food you need by stealing it from others; sex is connected with rape or the stealing of women from another tribe. The God of stage two doesn't condone rape and pillage, however; he has structured a hierarchical world, one in which you can appeal to the king or the judge to settle who owns the crops and whose wife is legitimate. The struggle to bring in laws to replace sheer might divides stage one and stage two, although there is always the threat of reversion. Power addicts you to getting what you want, exposes you to the temptation to trample other people's needs according to the rule that might makes right. To prevent this we have a new God, an omnipotent judge who threatens even the most powerful king with retribution if he goes too far.

Who am I? . . .
Ego, personality.

Every parent is aware of the phase in a toddler's life associated with the "terrible twos," when power dawns. The two-year-old who throws tantrums, coaxes, wheedles, and manipulates any situation to get his way is testing his ego boundaries. Earlier time was spent mastering basic skills of bodily coordination, but now the time is ripe for discovering just how far I, me, mine will get you. Exasperated as they might get, good parents do not stifle this sudden fascination with power. They realize that balance grows out of excess; without the testing of limits, the ego would either be cowed into submission or lost in grandiose fantasies.

From its first days, the ego finds that making things go your way isn't automatic. Parents say no, and more important, have their own lives, which means that a child cannot usurp every moment of their attention. These are shocking discoveries, but as a young child adapts to them, he prepares for the bigger shock ahead—that there are other children who want to grab the love and attention that used to be yours by right. This contest of competing egos creates the drama of stage two.

If you know yourself to be competitive and ambitious, it goes without saying that at some level you have given your allegiance to the God of this stage. Society rewards these traits so much that we tend to over-look their roots. Imagine that you and your older brother are both trying out for the same position on a Little League baseball team. When the time comes for the coach to make his decision, your feelings are those of a devotee before God the Almighty:

- You have to abide by the coach's decision. The Almighty is *sovereign.*
- Even if you want to fight back, the adults have all the power. The Almighty is *omnipotent.*
- You have to believe that playing your best will make the decision fall in your favor. The Almighty is *just.*
- You can't help but hope that the coach knows how desperately you want to be on the team. The Almighty *answers prayers.*
- The coach is assumed to know what he is doing and capable of judging who is better than someone else. The Almighty is *impartial and rational.*

- You have to study the rules of baseball and abide by them. It does no good simply to beat your brother up to win a spot on the team. The Almighty *lays down rules and laws.*

This psychology is not mere projection; the same kind of thinking conforms to the way society works. Thus the ego forms a bridge from the family, where your needs and whims are indulged, to the setting of school, where rules override your whims and many other children are taken into account.

The ego is always tempted to return to the infant paradise in which food and love came automatically, without competition. This fantasy comes to the surface in adults who believe that they deserve everything they have earned, no matter by what means. When John D. Rockefeller was asked where his immense wealth came from, he gave the famous reply "God gave it to me." It is essential in stage two to feel this connection, for otherwise one would be competing with the Almighty. In Genesis, after God has created the first man and woman on the sixth day, he says,

Be fruitful and multiply, fill the earth and subdue it, rule over the fish of the sea, the birds of heaven, and every living thing that moves upon the earth.

When power was handed out, several features were notable. First, it was handed to both man and woman. This original couple precedes Adam and Eve; it remains a mystery why the writers of the books of Moses felt called upon to create human beings a second time, in a more sexist version. Second, there is no suggestion of aggression or violence. God gives humans plants to eat, with no suggestion that they are to kill anything for food. Finally, God looked at his work "and he saw that it was good," implying that he felt no competitiveness with mankind over who was to rule. In future ages, keeping the peace would often depend on surrounding a monarch with the aura of God-given rule. (Macbeth owes his worst troubles not to the fact that he committed murder but that he seized the crown unlawfully, against the divine right of kings.)

The fantasy of getting everything for me doesn't often come true, however; this isn't the time for the meek to inherit the earth. Stage two is dominated by a God who justifies strength and competition, with no thought that being a loser is possible.

How do I fit in? . . .
I win.

The theme of stage two can be summarized as "Winning is next to godliness." The Almighty approves of accomplishment. The Protestant work ethic sealed his approval into dogma. It is a very simple dogma, free of theological complications. Those who work the hardest will get the greatest reward. But did this belief actually derive from spiritual insight, or did people find themselves in a world where work needed to be done and added God's stamp of approval afterward? Any answer we give would have to be circular, because the human situation is always being projected onto God, only to come back as spiritual truth.

In stage one the Fall brings about the curse of having to labor until you return to the dust from whence you came. For work to be glorified now in stage two seems contradictory, yet this is exactly how inner growth proceeds. A certain problem is posed that cannot be solved in an earlier stage, and then it gets resolved by finding a new way to approach it. In other words, each stage involves a change of perspective or even a new worldview.

If we take the Bible as our authority,

there is ample evidence to support the
notion that God approves of work, competition, and winning. None of the kings of
Israel is punished for going to war. Joshua
could not have brought down the walls of
Jericho with a blast on a ram's horn if God
hadn't aided him. A warrior God sides with
David when he fights the Philistines against
impossible odds—in fact, most of the Old
Testament victories require miracles or
God's blessing to be achieved.

On the other hand, Jesus is adamantly
opposed to war, and in general to work. He
has no consideration for money, even
promising (or so the disciples understood
him) that one has only to wait for deliverance, and this meant deliverance from
work, among other things. The Sermon on
the Mount is in favor of letting God handle
all earthly needs. One glance proves the
point beyond a doubt:

> Do not store up for yourselves treasure
> on earth, where it grows rusty and
> moth-eaten, and thieves break in to
> steal it. Store up treasure in heaven
> instead. . . .
>
> No servant can be a slave to two mas-
> ters. . . . You cannot serve God and
> Mammon [money].

Behold the lilies of the field. They do not toil, nor do they spin [cloth], yet I tell you, Solomon in all his glory was not attired like one of them.

This sort of talk was disturbing. In the first place, it undercut the power of the rich. Jesus explicitly tells a wealthy man who is worried about the state of his soul that if he doesn't give away his money, he has no more chance of getting to heaven than a camel of passing through the eye of a needle—no chance at all.

Even if you ignore the letter of what is being said—society has found countless ways to serve God and money at the same time—Jesus holds a completely different view of power than anyone around him. He doesn't equate power with achievement, work, planning, saving, or accumulation. If you take away those things, the ego collapses. All are necessary in order to build wealth, wage war, or divide the strong from the weak. These were the very goals Jesus did not want to further; therefore his rejection of power makes perfect sense. He wanted the human wolves to lie down with the lambs.

However, this poses a huge conflict for we who follow the demands of our egos, who want to feel that we can be good and win at the same time. Some sort of work ethic is inevitable in stage two, yet it will always be haunted by the fear that God doesn't really approve of the things society rewards so lavishly.

How do I find God? . . .
Awe and obedience.

Stage two is much less paralyzed by fear of God than stage one, but the next closest emotion to fear—awe—is much present. The most primitive God could strike you dead with a sudden bolt of lightning, leaving the survivors to guess what you did to offend him. This new God punishes by the rules. Most of his rules make sense in broad outline; every society mandates against murder, theft, lying, and coveting property that belongs to someone else. Yet the Almighty doesn't have to make sense. As the medieval church fathers declared, God does not have to justify his ways to man. Eventually this attitude will change, but as long as the deity inspires awe, the way to him is through blind obedience.

Every stage of God contains hidden questions and doubts. In this case the hidden question is: Can God really make good on his threats? The Almighty has to make sure that no one is tempted to find out, which means that he must exhibit his strength. The righteous must receive tangible rewards, the wrongdoers must feel his wrath. Psalm 101 affirms that a deal has been struck between God and the faithful:

I sing of loyalty and justice;
I will raise a psalm to thee, O Lord.

I will follow a wise and blameless course,
  whatever may befall me.
I will go about my house in purity of
  heart. . . .
I will hate disloyalty; I will have none of it.

As part of this loyalty oath, the psalm lists what will not be tolerated: crooked thoughts, backbiters, the proud and pompous, the wicked in general.

I remember receiving a lesson in God's power when I was three. My parents had hired a nurse, or *ayah*, to take care of me because my mother was preoccupied with a new baby. My ayah was from Goa, a heavily Christian part of India with a strong European influence, and her name was Mary da Silva. Every day Mary took me to the park in my pram. After an hour or so, she would take me out and place me on the ground. Then she would draw a circle around me in chalk, telling me in a solemn voice that if I ventured outside the circle, the goddess Kali would eat my heart and spit out the blood. Naturally this promise frightened me to death, and I never dared to go anywhere near the boundary.

We are all like cows who will not cross a road that has a metal cattle guard laid down, for fear that they will catch their hoofs in it. Ranchers pull a simple trick on the animals by painting the shape of a cattle guard on the pavement, the mere sight of which will make the cows pull back. God's laws could be just such a phantom; for fear of hurting ourselves, we pull away from disobedience, even though we have never experienced divine punishment in real life. To this end we take ordinary misfortunes such as illness, bankruptcy, and loss of loved ones, and interpret them as coming from God.

What is the nature of good and evil? . . .
Good is getting what you want.
Evil is any obstacle to getting
what you want.

Obedience isn't an end unto itself. For obeying God's laws, the worshiper expects a reward. In stage two this takes the form of getting what you want. God permits you to fulfill your desires, and he makes you feel righteous in the bargain. In his role as Almighty, the deity now begins to answer prayers. In this value system, the rich can clothe themselves in virtue while the poor are morally suspect and seem shameful. (Lest anyone assume that this is a biblical tradition or just the fruit of the Protestant work ethic, in China mercantile success as a measure of goodness has been going on for centuries. Only the most self-denying sects of Buddhism have escaped the equation of wealth and God's favor.)

As cut-and-dried as it appears, measuring good and evil according to rewards has its pitfalls. As every young child finds out to his dismay in preschool, others want the same things that you do, and sometimes there isn't enough to go around. Social rules prevent you from grabbing, hitting, and running away. Therefore the ego has to figure out how to aggrandize "me" while at the same time being good. Rarely does the solution emerge as pure honesty and cooperation.

As a result, manipulation is born. The goal of manipulation is to get what you want but not look bad in the process. If I want your toy and can charm you into giving it to me, then no one (including my conscience) can accuse me of stealing. This calculus is very important when you fear guilt, even more so if you fear that God is watching and keeping tabs. It seems strange that arch-manipulators are motivated by conscience, yet they are; the ability to tell right from wrong yet not completely heed the difference is what separates a manipulator from a criminal or a bully.

Are these simply the kinds of shortcuts we are all tempted to use in order to get our way? If you turn to the Old Testament, there is no mistaking that God himself is manipulative. After destroying the world in a flood, his covenant with Noah blocks him from using totalitarian force. Thereafter he is subtler—praising those who hew to the law, withdrawing to show anger, sending an endless string of prophets to attack sin through preaching that stirs up guilt. We continue to use the same tactics in society, pressuring conformity to what the majority believe is good while disguising the evils that are done to the band of wrong-thinkers (pacifists, radicals, communists, etc.) who refuse to fall into line.

What is my life challenge? . . .
Maximum achievement.

Stage two isn't just a matter of naked power. It brings a sense of optimism to life.

The world exists to be explored and conquered. If you watch a two-year-old as I, me, mine takes over, the sense of delight is inescapable. Ego gives you strength, although its lessons are often painful.

The Buddhist doctrine of ego death as a road to enlightenment is something most people cannot accept. Ego death is based on a good argument, which goes as follows: the more you center your life on I, me, mine, the more insecure you will become. The ego believes in acquiring more and more. Its appetite for pleasure, power, sex, and money is insatiable. But more and more doesn't make anyone happy. It leads to isolation, since you are getting your share at the cost of someone else's. It forces you to fear loss. Even worse, it makes you identify with externals, and that tendency can only wind up leaving you empty inside. At the deepest level, pleasure can never be the road to God because you get trapped in the cycle of duality (seeking pleasure and avoiding pain) while God is beyond all opposites.

Convincing as the benefits of ego death may sound, few people would willingly sacrifice the needs of I, me, mine. In stage two this is particularly true because God gives his blessing to those who achieve.

I was once consulted by a retired executive who was certain he had a hormone problem. I asked him about his symptoms.

"Where can I begin?" he complained. "I've lost all my energy. Half the time I don't want to get out of bed in the morning. Hours go by while I just sit in a chair, feeling gloomy and wondering if life has any point to it."

On the surface this was a case of depression, probably brought on by the man's recent retirement. Medically it's well documented that sudden retirement can be dangerous. Men with no history of heart attack or cancer can unexpectedly die of these illnesses; one study found that the average life expectancy of retired executives was only thirty-three months on average.

I dutifully ran a battery of tests, but as I suspected, there was nothing wrong with this man's endocrine system. The next time I saw him, I said, "Would you do something simple for me? Just close your eyes and sit in silence for ten minutes. Don't look at your watch, I'll keep time for you."

Although a bit suspicious, he did as I asked. Ten minutes passed, the last five obviously being hard for him, to judge by his fidgety movements. Opening his eyes, he exclaimed, "Why did you make me do that? How pointless could anything be?"

"You were getting pretty restless," I remarked.

"I wanted to jump out of my chair," he said.

"So it doesn't look like our problem is lack of energy." My remark took him aback, and he looked baffled. "I don't think this is a hormone problem, metabolism, or depression," I said. "You've spent years organizing your external life, running a business, directing a large work force, and all that."

"Right, and I miss all that more than I can tell you," he mourned.

"I understand. And now that you have no external focus, what do you find? You've paid almost no attention to organizing your inner life. Your problem isn't lack of energy, it's chaos. Your mind was trained to order everything around you at the cost of discovering what it would be like to have internal order."

This man had devoted his life to the values of stage two, and the challenge he faced now was to expand, not outwardly, but inside. In stage two the ego is so bent on accomplishment that it ignores the threat of emptiness. Power for its own sake has no meaning, and the challenge of acquiring more and more power (along with its symbols in terms of money and status) still leaves a huge vacuum of meaning. This is why absolute loyalty is demanded by God at this stage—to keep the faithful from looking too deeply inside. Let's clarify that this is not an actual demand made by the Almighty; it is another projection. The retired executive in my anecdote had a decision to make, whether to begin to cultivate an inner life or to start up some enterprise that would give him a new external focus. The course of least resistance would be to gear up a second business; the harder road would be to heal the disorder of his inner life. This is the choice that carries everyone from stage two to stage three.

What is my greatest strength? . . .
Accomplishment.

What is my biggest hurdle? . . .
Guilt, victimization.

Anyone who finds satisfaction in being an accomplished, skilled worker will find stage two a very tempting place to rest on the spiritual journey. Often the only ones who break free to a higher stage have had some drastic failure in their lives. This isn't to say that failure is spiritually worthy. It carries its own dangers, primarily that you will see yourself as a victim, which make the chances for spiritual progress worse than ever. But failure does raise questions about some basic beliefs in stage two. If you worked hard, why didn't God reward you? Does he lack the power to bestow good fortune—or has he forgotten you entirely? As long as such doubts don't arise, the God of stage two is the perfect deity for a competitive market economy. He has been cynically referred to as the God of getting and spending. However, there is still the problem of guilt.

"I came from a small town in the Midwest, the only student from my high school to ever make it to the Ivy League. Getting in was the prize I valued the most," a friend of mine recalled.

"A month ago I was leaving work at my law firm, on the way to a new restaurant. I was late, and as it happened, a homeless man had chosen the doorway of our building to spend the night. He was blocking the door, and I had to step over his body to get into the cab. Of course I've seen homeless people before, but this was the first time I literally had to walk over one.

"I couldn't shake that image the whole time I was riding uptown, and then I remembered that the first month I was in college, twenty years ago, I was walking in the part of Boston known as the Combat Zone. It was one string of bars and adult bookstores after another. I was scared and intrigued at the same time, but as I was leaving, a stumblebum on the sidewalk ahead of me went into a seizure. He fell down, and some people ran to call an ambulance, but I just kept on walking. Twenty years later, sitting there in the cab, I could feel the old remorse wash over me. I had been lying to myself, you see. The homeless man in front of my building wasn't the first time I had walked over somebody."

Despite its external rewards, stage two is associated with the birth of guilt. This is a form of judgment that requires no all-seeing authority, except at the beginning. Someone has to lay down the commandments defining absolute right and wrong. Afterward, the law-abiding will enforce their own obedience. If you translate the process back to the family, the origins of guilt can be traced along the same lines. A two-year-old who tries to steal a cookie is reprimanded by his mother and told that what he is doing is wrong. Until that point taking a cookie isn't stealing; it is just following what your ego wants to do.

If the child repeats the same act again, it turns into stealing because he is breaking a commandment, and in most families some sort of punishment will follow. Now the child is caught between two forces—the pleasure of doing what he wants and the pain of being punished. If a conscience is to develop, these two forces have to be fairly equal. In that case, the child sets up his own boundaries. He will take a cookie when it is "right" (permitted by mother) and not take one when it is "wrong" (causes guilt through a bad conscience).

Freud called this the development of the superego, our internal rule maker. *Super* means above, in that the superego watches over the ego from above, holding the threat of punishment ever at the ready. Learning to modify the harshness of the superego can be extremely difficult. Just as some believers never get to the point of accepting that God might be willing to bend the rules every once in a while, neurotics have never learned how to put their conscience in perspective. They feel tremendous guilt over small infractions; they develop rigid emotional boundaries, finding it hard to forgive others; self-love remains out of reach. Stage two brings the comfort of laws clearly set down, but it traps you into putting too much value on rules and boundaries, to the detriment of inner growth.

What is my greatest temptation? . . .
Addiction.

It's no coincidence that a wealthy and privileged society is so prone to rampant addictions.[1] Stage two is based on pleasure, and when pleasure becomes obsessive, the result is addiction. If a source of pleasure is truly fulfilling, there is a natural cycle that begins with desire and ends in satiation. Addiction never closes the circle.

Stage two is also power-based, and power is notoriously selfish. When a doting parent finds it almost impossible to let a coddled child break free, the excuse may be "I love you too much, I don't want you to grow up." Yet the unspoken motive is self-centered: I crave the pleasure it brings me to have you remain a child. The God of stage two is jealous of his power over us because it pleases him. He is addicted to control. And like human addiction, the implication is that God is not satisfied, no matter how much control he exerts.

Psychiatrists meet people every day who complain about the emotional turmoil in their lives and yet are blindly addicted to drama. They cannot survive outside the dance of love-hate; they create tension, foster mistrust, and never leave well enough alone. Other addictions are also based on behavior: the need to have something wrong in your life (or to create it if it doesn't exist), the obsession over things going wrong—this is the "what if" addiction—and finally the compulsion to be perfect at all costs.

This last addiction has taken secular form in people who crave the perfect family, perfect home, and perfect career. They do not even see the irony that such "perfection" is dead; it can be bought only at the price of killing our inborn spontaneity, which by its nature can never be controlled. There is a corresponding spiritual state, however, that aims to please God through a life that has no blemish whatever. In the loyalty oath of Psalm 101, the believer makes promises no one could live up to:

I will set before myself no sordid aim . . .
I will reject all crooked thoughts;
I will have no dealing with evil.

Such absolutism itself amounts to an addiction—and it is here in stage two that fanaticism is born.

The fanatic is caught in a self-contradiction. Whereas an orthodox believer can feel satisfied if he obeys the law down to the last detail, the fanatic must purify his very thoughts. Complete control over the mind is unachievable, but this doesn't prevent him from imposing ever-stricter vigilance on "crooked thoughts." Fanatics are also obsessed by other people's purity, opening an endless quest to police human imperfection.

This fate lies in wait for those who get stuck in stage two: They lose sight of the actual goal of spiritual life—to free humans and allow them to live in innocence and love. This loss cannot be repaired until the devotee stops being so concerned with the law. To do that he must find an inner life, which will never happen as long as he is policing his own desires. Vigilance kills all spontaneity in the end. When a person begins to see that life is more than trying to be perfect, the bad old desires rear their heads again. Only this time they are seen as natural, not evil, and the road is open for stage three. It comes as a source of wonder when turning inward breaks the spell of I, me, mine and ends its cravings.

STAGE THREE:
GOD OF PEACE
(Restful Awareness Response)

No one could accuse the earlier God of stages one or two of being very interested in peace. Whether unleashing floods or inciting warfare, the God we've seen so far relishes struggle. Yet even such powerful ties as fear and awe begin to fray. "You believe that you were created to serve God," an Indian guru once pointed out, "but in the end you may discover that God was created to serve you." The suspicion that this might be true launches stage three, for until now the balance has all been in God's favor. Obedience to him has mattered far more than our own needs.

The balance begins to shift when we find that we can meet our own needs. It takes no God "up there" to bring peace and wisdom, because the cerebral cortex already contains a mechanism for both. When a person stops focusing on outer activity, closes his eyes, and relaxes, brain activity automatically alters. The dominance of alpha-wave rhythms signals a state of rest that is aware at the same time. The brain is not going to sleep, but it is not thinking, either. Instead there is a new kind of alertness, one that needs no thoughts to fill up the silence. Corresponding changes occur in the body at the same time, as blood pressure and heart rate decrease, accompanied by lessened oxygen consumption.

These various changes do not sound overly impressive when put in technical terms, but the subjective effect can be dramatic. Peace replaces the mind's chaotic activity; inner turmoil ceases. The Psalms declare, "Commune with your own heart on your bed, and be still." And even more explicitly, "Be still and know that I am God." This is the God of stage three, who can be described as

Detached
Calm
Offering consolation
Undemanding
Conciliatory
Silent
Meditative

It hardly seems possible that this nonviolent deity emerged from stage two—and he didn't. Stage three transcends the willful, demanding God that once prevailed, just as the new brain transcends the old. Only by discovering that peace lies within does the devotee find a place that divine vengeance and retribution cannot touch. In essence the mind is turning inward to experience itself. This forms the basis of contemplation and meditation in every tradition.

The first solid research on the restful awareness response came with the study of mantra meditation (specifically Transcendental Meditation) in the 1960s and 1970s. Until then the West had paid little scientific attention to meditation. It didn't really occur to anyone that if meditation was genuine, some shift in the nervous system must accompany it. Early experiments at the Menninger Foundation had established, however, that some yogis could lower their heart rate and breathing almost to nil. Physiologically they should have been on the brink of death; instead they reported intense inner peace, bliss, and oneness with God. Nor was this phenomenon simply a curiosity from the East.

In December 1577 a Spanish monk in the town of Avila was kidnapped in the middle of the night. He was carted off to Toledo, to be thrown into a church prison. His captors were not bandits but his own Carmelite order, against whom he had committed the grave offense of taking the wrong side in a fierce theological dispute. As advisor to a house of Carmelite nuns, he had given them permission to elect their own leader instead of leaving it to the bishop.

From our modern perspective this dispute is all but meaningless. But the monk's superiors were seriously displeased. The monk underwent horrendous torture. His unlit cell "was actually a small cupboard, not high enough for him to stand erect. He was taken each day to the rectory, where he was given bread, water, and sardine scraps on the floor. Then he was subjected to the circular discipline: while he knelt on the ground, the monks walked around him, scouring his bare back with their leather whips. At first a daily occurrence, this was later restricted to Fridays, but he was tortured with such zeal that his shoulders remained crippled for the rest of his life."

The tormented monk has come down to us as a saint, John of the Cross, whose most inspired devotional poetry was written at this exact time. While imprisoned in his dark cupboard, Saint John cared so little about his ordeal that the only thing he begged for was a pen and paper so he could record his ecstatic inner experiences. He felt a particular joy at communing with God in a place the world couldn't touch:

On a dark, secret night,
starving for love and deep in flame,
O happy, lucky flight!
unseen I slipped away,
my house at last was calm and safe.

These opening lines from "Dark Night" describe the escape of the soul from the body, which delivers the poet from pain to joy. But for this to happen, the brain has to find a way to detach inner experience from outer. In medicine we run across instances where patients seem remarkably immune to pain. In cases of advanced psychosis, someone who has become catatonic is rigid and unresponsive to stimulation. There is no sign of reacting to pain—just as with a patient whose nerves are dead. Chronic schizophrenics have been known to cut themselves with knives or burn their arms with lit cigarettes while showing no awareness of pain.

We cannot simply lump a great poet and saint, however, with the mentally ill. In the case of St. John of the Cross, there was a pressing need to separate from his tormentors. He had to find an escape route, and perhaps that was the psychological trigger for his ecstasy. In his poetry he flees to his secret lover, Christ, who caresses and soothes him in his arms:

. . . and there
my senses vanished in the air.

I lay, forgot my being,
and on my love I leaned my face.
All ceased. I left my being,
leaving my cares to fade
among the lilies far away.

Saint John describes with precisely chosen words the transition from the material level our bodies are trapped in to the quantum level where physical pain and suffering have no bearing. Lying beneath the spiritual beauty of the experience, its basis is the restful awareness response.

To put yourself in a comparable situation, imagine that you are a marathon runner. Marathons test the body's extremes of endurance and pain; at a certain point long-distance runners enter "the zone," a place that transcends physical discomfort.

- The runner no longer feels pain as part of his experience. The God of peace is *detached.*
- The runner's mind stops fighting and struggling. The God of peace is *calm.*
- The zone makes one feel immune to harm. The God of peace *offers consolation.*

- Winning and losing are no longer a driving force. The God of peace is *undemanding*.
- There is no need to fight; the zone will take care of everything. The God of peace is *conciliatory*.
- The runner's mind quiets down. The God of peace is *silent*.
- In the zone one expands beyond the limits of the body, touching the wholeness and oneness of everything. The God of peace is *meditative*.

I have heard of professional football players who claim that at a certain point in every game, the game takes over, and they feel as if they are going through the motions of a dance. Instead of using every ounce of will to make it downfield to catch a pass, they see themselves running ahead and meeting the ball as if destined. The God of peace isn't found by diving within so much as he rises from within when the time is right.

Who am I? . . .
A silent witness.

The God of stage three is a God of peace because he shows the way out of struggle. There is no peace in the outer world, which is ruled by struggle. People who attempt to control their environment—I am thinking of perfectionists and others caught up in obsessive behavior—have refused the invitation to find an inner solution.

"I wasn't raised with any feelings about religion," one man told me. "It was a nonissue in my childhood and remained that way for years. I laid out some huge goals for myself, which I intended to accomplish on my own—the important job, the wife and kids, retirement by the age of fifty, all of it."

This man came from considerable wealth, and for him a job wasn't important unless it meant CEO. He achieved that aim; by his mid-thirties he headed up an equipment-supply company in Chicago. Everything was moving on track until a fateful game of racquetball.

"I wasn't pushing myself or playing harder than usual, but I must have done something because I heard a loud snap, and all at once I was falling over. The whole thing happened in slow motion. I knew at once that I had torn my Achilles tendon—only the strangest thing was happening." Instead of being in excruciating pain, he felt extremely calm and detached. "The whole thing could have been happening to someone else. I lay there while someone called an ambulance, but my mind was floating somewhere beyond."

The sensation at that moment was of a sweet, even blissful calm. The man—we will call him Thomas—had never experienced such a state, and it persisted even when his ankle did start to swell and ache with pain. During the time Thomas was hospitalized in traction, he noticed that his newfound peace gradually waned. He found himself wondering if he had experienced something spiritual after all, but after some intense scrutiny of scriptures, Thomas couldn't really put his finger on any specific passage that corresponded to what had occurred.

It is common for people to break into stage three with this kind of abruptness. In place of an active, excited mind, they find a silent witness. Interpretations differ widely. Some people jump immediately into religion, equating this peace with God, Christ, or Buddha; others register the whole thing simply as detachment: "I used to be inside the movie," one person explained, "but now I am sitting in the audience watching it."

Medically we know that the brain can choose to cancel out awareness of pain. Until the discovery of endorphins—the brain's own version of morphine—there was no biological explanation for this self-anesthesia. Yet endorphins are not enough to account for Saint John's ecstasy or the inner calm of the man who tore his Achilles tendon. If you examine the body's painkilling mechanisms, it becomes clear that the brain does not give itself a simple injection of opiates when pain is present. There are many situations where pain cannot be overcome at all or only partially, and sometimes it takes a trick to get the brain to react. If you take people suffering from intractable pain, a certain number will get relief if you inject them with saline solution while telling them that it is a powerful narcotic. The whole area of treatment is psychological—it is a matter of changing someone's interpretation. One also recalls the famous "show surgeries" under the Maoist regime, where patients stayed cheerfully awake during appendectomies, chatting and drinking tea. Their only anesthesia was provided with acupuncture, yet when attempts were made to duplicate this feat outside China, results were unreliable at best. The difference in perception was too great between Eastern belief and Western skepticism.

In between the pain and the brain something must intervene that decides how much discomfort is going to be felt, and the amazing thing is that this decision maker can control our body's response totally. The switch for pain is flicked mentally. It is just as normal to feel no pain as to feel a great deal. To someone who has entered stage three, the decision maker is not a mystery. He is the presence of God bringing peace, and the pain being relieved is more than physical; it includes the pain of the soul caught in turmoil. By going inward, the devotee has found a way to stop that pain.

How do I fit in? . . .
I remain centered in myself.

A dangerous God was just right for a dangerous world. The God of peace is no longer dangerous because he has created a world of inner solitude and reflection. When you go inward, what do you reflect on? The inner world seems to be a landscape we all know very well. It is filled with thoughts and memories, desires and wishes. If you focus on these events, which rush by in the stream of consciousness, the inner world isn't a mystery. It may be complex, because our thoughts are so varied and come from so many places, but a mind filled with thought is not an enigma.

Someone who has arrived at stage three is

reflecting on something very different. A therapist would call it the core or center of a person. At the mind's center there aren't any events. You are simply yourself, waiting for thoughts to happen. The whole point of "remaining centered" is that you aren't easily thrown off balance. You remain yourself in the midst of outer chaos. (One is reminded of the football player who is so focused that the game starts to play itself while he begins to move to catch the ball as though preordained.)

In many ways finding your center is the great gift of stage three, and the God of peace exists to assure his worshiper that there is a place of refuge from fear and confusion. "Now I shall lie down in peace, and sleep," says Psalm 4, "for you alone, O Lord, makest me unafraid." The absence of peace in the world is never far from the minds of the writers of scripture. Some of the strife is just part of how life is, but much of it is political. The angels who greet the shepherds with the news of Christ's birth include the promise of peace on earth and goodwill among men, reflecting the fact that a messiah's function was to settle the turbulent history of the chosen people once and for all.

A warrior God didn't solve the problem, nor did laying down countless laws. The

God of peace can't simply dictate an end to strife and struggle. Either human nature has to change or else it must disclose a new aspect that transcends violence. In stage three the new aspect is centeredness. If you find your own inner quiet, the issue of violence is solved, at least for you personally. A friend of mine who has been deeply influenced by Buddhism goes even further: he says that if you can find the motionless point at your core, you are at the center of the whole universe.

"Haven't you noticed driving down the highway that you can pretend not to be moving? You reverse your point of view, so that you remain still while the road and the scenery do all the moving. The same trick can be done when you are out jogging. Everything else is in motion, flowing past you, but you yourself remain hovering in place." Most of us would find it easy to pull off this trick, but he sees a greater significance here. "That still point which never moves is the silent witness. Or at least it's as close as most of us can get. Once you find it, you realize that you don't have to be lost in the endless activity going on around you. Seeing yourself at the center of everything is just as legitimate."

In the East much the same argument has

been made. Buddhism, for example, doesn't believe that personality is real. All the labels we apply to ourselves are just a flock of different birds that happen to roost on the same branch. The fact that I am over fifty, Indian, a physician by training, married with two children, and so forth doesn't describe the real me. These qualities have chosen to roost together and form the illusion of an identity. How did they all find the same branch? Buddhism would say that I pulled them in by attraction and repulsion. In this lifetime I preferred to be male rather than female, Eastern rather than Western, married rather than single—and on and on. Choosing to be this instead of that is totally arbitrary. For each choice, its opposite would be just as valid. However, because of tendencies from my past (in India we would say my past lives, but that isn't necessary) I make my particular choices. I am so bound up in these preferences that I actually think they are me. My ego looks at the house, the car, the family, the career, the possessions, and it says, "I am those things."

But in Buddhism, none of it is true. At any moment the birds resting on the branch can fly away. In fact this will happen when I die. If my soul survives (the Buddha did not commit himself about what happens after death) my choices will dissolve in the wind once I give up this body. So who am I if not all these millions of choices that cling to me like a glued-on overcoat? I am nothing except the still point of awareness at my center. Strip away every experience I have ever had and that remains. To realize this truth is to be free, so Buddhism teaches. Therefore seeing yourself as a motionless point while driving down the freeway becomes a valued experience. You are one step closer to finding out who you really are.

How do I find God? . . .
Meditation, silent contemplation.

The fact that stage three is self-centered cannot be denied. The Old Testament clearly states that the way to peace is through reliance on God as an outside power. He is the focus of attention, always. Verses on this point read, "Great peace have they who love your laws" and "You will keep him in perfect peace whose mind is fixed on you, because he puts his trust in you." Giving up trust in God and looking instead to yourself could be very dangerous. It could also be heresy. After the Fall, sin separated man and God. The deity is "up there" in his heaven, while I am "down here" on earth, a place of tears and struggle. In this scheme I am permitted to pray to God, calling out for his help and comfort, but he decides whether to return the call. It is not for me to try to make the connection permanent. My imperfection—and the laws of God—forbid it.

A few clues indicate that I can risk a different approach, however. In the Bible one finds such verses as "Seek ye the kingdom of heaven within." And the means of going inward, chiefly meditation and silent contemplation, are not that far removed from prayer. If it is true that "in silence shall you possess your soul," then how much can God care how I find silence? The religious arguments become secondary once we realize that a biological response lies behind restful awareness, no matter what faith we clothe it in.

The Eastern origins of meditation are undeniable, and in the Hindu tradition, going inward begins a spiritual quest that will eventually end in enlightenment. Dr. Herbert Benson of Harvard, who played the key role in popularizing meditation without religion, based his "relaxation response" on the principles of Transcendental Meditation, minus its spiritual implications. He removed the mantra, replacing it with any neutral word that could be repeated mentally while slowly breathing in and out (he suggested the word *one*). Others, including myself, have disagreed with this approach and based our approach on the central value of a mantra as a means of unfolding deeper spiritual levels inside the mind. To us, the recited word has to be connected to God.

The spiritual properties of mantras have two bases. Some orthodox Hindus would say that every mantra is a version of God's name, while others would claim—and this is very close to quantum physics—that the vibration of the mantra is the key. The word *vibration* means the frequency of brain activity in the cerebral cortex. The mantra forms a feedback loop as the brain produces the sound, listens to it, and then responds with a deeper level of attention. Mysticism isn't involved. A person could use any of the five senses to enter this feedback loop. In the ancient *Shiva Sutras*, more than a hundred ways of transcending are described, among them looking into the blue of the sky and then looking beyond it, seeing the beauty of a woman and then finding what is behind that beauty. The whole intent is to go past the senses in order to find their source. (The cliché that Buddhists stare at their navels is a distortion of the practice of concentrating the mind on a single point; the navel is imagined as just such a point. In some traditions it also serves as a focus of energy that is supposed to have spiritual significance.)

In all cases the source is a finer state of brain activity. The theory is that mental activity contains its own mechanism for becoming more and more refined until complete silence is experienced. Silence is considered important because it is the mind's source; as the mantra grows fainter and fainter, it eventually fades away altogether. At that point one's awareness crosses the quantum boundary. For the first time in our stages of inner growth, the material plane has been left behind; we are now in the region where spiritual activity commands its own laws.

The argument persists that nothing of this kind is happening, that a brain learning to calm down may be comforting, but it isn't spiritual. This objection can be settled by noting that there really is no fundamental disagreement going on. The cerebral cortex produces thought by using energy in the form of photons; their interaction takes place on the quantum level, which means that every thought could be traced back to its source at a deeper level. There are no "spiritual" thoughts that stand apart on their own. But ordinary thinking doesn't cross the quantum frontier, even though it could (as Benson's nonspiritual technique shows). We are kept on the material level because we pay attention to what the thought means. Our attention is pulled outward rather than inward.

A mantra, as well as Benson's neutral word *one*, has little or no meaning to distract us. Therefore it is an easier vehicle for going inward than prayer or verbal contemplation (in which one takes an aspect of God to think about and dwell on).

There is no doubt that people resist the whole notion of God being an inner phenomenon. The vast majority of the world's faithful are firmly committed to stages one and two, believing in a God "up there," or at any rate outside ourselves. And the problem is complicated by the fact that going inward isn't a revelation; it is just a beginning. The quiet mind offers no sudden flashes of divine insight. Yet its importance is stated eloquently in the medieval document known as "The Cloud of Unknowing," written anonymously in the fourteenth century. The author tells us that God, the angels, and all the saints take greatest delight when a person begins to do inner work. However, none of this is apparent at first:

For when you first begin, you find just a darkness and, as it were, a cloud of unknowing. . . . This darkness and this cloud, no matter what you do, stands between you and your God.

The blockage takes two forms: one cannot see God with the mind's reason and understanding, nor can he be felt in "the sweetness of your affection." In other words, God has no presence emotionally or intellectually. The cloud of unknowing is all we have to go on. The only solution, the writer informs us, is perseverance. The inner work must continue. Then a subtle argument is made. The writer informs us that any thought in the mind separates us from God, because thought sheds light on its object. The focus of attention is like "the eye of an archer fixed on the spot he is shooting at." Even though the cloud of unknowing baffles us, it is actually closer to God than even a thought about God and his marvelous creation. We are advised to go into a "cloud of forgetting" about anything other than the silence of the inner world.

For centuries this document has seemed

utterly mystical, but it makes perfect sense once we realize that the restful awareness response, which contains no thoughts, is being advocated. The writer has delved deeply enough to find the God of stage three, who is beyond material considerations. The step he took was a brave one under the weight of priests, cathedrals, shrines, holy relics, church laws, and all the other material trappings of medieval religion, but it would be a brave step today as well, because we are still addicted to the outward life. People want a God they can see and touch and talk to.

Consider how radical the argument really is, as revealed in the next section of the book:

> *In this work it profits little or nothing to think upon the kindness or worthiness of God, or upon our Lady, or upon the saints and angels in heaven, or upon heavenly joy. . . . It is far better to think upon the naked being of God.*

This "naked being" is awareness without content, pure spirit, which naturally does not unfold itself in a few hours or days. As with any stage, this is one you enter, then explore. To someone who loves religion, it can be a bleak place at first, one marked by

loss of all the rituals and comforts of organized faith. The value of stage three lies
more in promise than in fulfillment,
because it is a lonely road. The promise is
given by our anonymous writer, who
emphasizes over and over that delight and
love will eventually arise out of silence.
The inner work is done for only one purpose—to feel the love of God—and there is
no other way to achieve it.

> *What is the nature of good and evil?* . . .
> Good is clarity, inner calm, and
> contact with the self.
> Evil is inner turmoil and chaos.

The reader may have gotten this far and
wondered how many people ever evolve to
stage three. Looking around the world, one
sees tremendous suffering and struggle. Even
in a prosperous society the prevailing belief
system usually promotes the value of work
and achievement. "You never get something
for nothing" and "God helps those who help
themselves," as the sayings go.

Every stage of inner growth is hard-won.
There is no outside force that picks you up
by the nape of the neck and drops you ahead
on the journey. It is also true that outward
circumstances do not determine anyone's

belief system. I remember the widespread shock when Aleksandr Solzhenitsyn first arrived in America in the early 1970s when the Cold War was at its coldest. He was expected to praise the superiority of the West with all its individual freedoms, compared to the soulless repression he had left behind in Russia. Even though he had suffered terribly in the Gulag prison camps for eight years after writing a letter against Stalin, Solzhenitsyn shocked everyone when he denounced the spiritual emptiness of American consumerism, and subsequently he could only survive by retreating into the solitude of the New England woods, as ignored as Thoreau was when he did the same thing a hundred and fifty years earlier.

This clash of values confronts everyone on the threshold of stage three. Good and evil are no longer measured by what happens outside oneself; the compass is turned inward. Good is measured by remaining centered in the self, which brings clarity and calm. Evil is measured by disturbance to that clarity; it brings confusion, chaos, and inability to see the truth.

The inner life can never be a common experience. Fifty years ago the sociologist David Riesman noted that the vast majority are "outer directed" and the small

minority "inner directed." Outer direction comes from what others think of you.
If you are outer directed you crave
approval and shrink from disapproval; you
bend to the needs of conformity and easily absorb the prevailing opinions as your
own. Inner direction is rooted in a stable
self that can't be shaken; an inner-directed
person is free of the need for approval;
this detachment makes it much easier for
him to question prevailing opinions. Being
inner directed doesn't make you religious,
but the religion of the inner directed is
stage three.

What is my life challenge? . . .
To be engaged and detached at the same
time.

Now we are in a better position to understand why Jesus wanted his disciples to be
"in the world but not of it." He wanted
them to be both detached and engaged—
detached in the sense that no one could
grab their souls, engaged in the sense that
they remained motivated to lead a worthy
life. This is the balancing act of stage three,
and many people find it hard to manage.
    The writer of "The Cloud of Unknow-
ing" says that going within is not the real

dilemma, nor is rejection of society and its values. Here is how our writer describes spiritual work:

See that you are in no way within your-self. And (to speak briefly) I do not want you to be outside yourself, or above, or behind, or on one side, or on the other.

This leaves only nowhere, and that is where the writer says we should be. God can't be contained in the mind; he is nothing compared to our myriad thoughts and ambitions. But there is a tremendous secret to this nothing and nowhere:

Who is it that calls it nothing? Surely it is our outer man and not our inner. Our inner man calls it All; for it teaches him to understand all things bodily or spiritual, without any special knowledge of one thing in itself.

This is a remarkable description of how silence works. We aren't talking about the silence of an empty mind—in fact, those who achieve inner silence are also thinking in the ordinary way. But the thought takes place against a background of nonthought. Our writer equates it with knowing something that doesn't have to be studied. The mind is full of a kind of knowing that could speak to us about everything, yet it has no words; therefore we seek this knowingness in the background. At first nothing much seems to exist there; this is the phase of darkness and "the cloud of unknowing." But the hunt is on, and if you keep to your plan, rejecting outward answers over and over, never giving up on your belief that the hidden goal is real, eventually your seeking bears fruit.

During this whole time, your work inside is private, but outer existence has to go on. Thus the balancing act Jesus referred to as being in the world but not of it. Or as we are stating it, being detached and engaged at the same time.

What is my greatest strength? . . .
Autonomy.

What is my biggest hurdle? . . .
Fatalism.

Having explained how the inner and outer life are meant to be balanced, the question arises, can it actually be done? In stage three a person finds that he is autonomous. By breaking free of social pressures, he can be himself. Yet there is the risk of fatalism, a feeling that being free is just a form of isolation with no hope of influencing others. How can another person, someone not at this stage, understand what it means? The whole thing sounds like a paradox, and once again the writer of "The Cloud of Unknowing" hits it right on the head.

He points out that worldly people (and our own egos) aspire to be everywhere, while God is nowhere; they want to amount to something, yet God is nothing. The spiritually dedicated are thus consigned to the margins of society—the most extreme examples being monks and nuns. Renunciation is almost a requirement, because an inner God does not conform.

Although every culture values its saints, the danger of turning inward, as far as society is concerned, is obvious. In 1918, long before anyone in England could foresee the importance of Gandhi to the fate of the British empire, the noted scholar Gilbert Murray made a prophetic statement: "Persons in power should be very careful of how they deal with a man who cares nothing for sensual pleasure, nothing for riches, nothing for comfort or praise or promotion, but is simply determined to do what he believes to be right. He is a dangerous and uncomfortable enemy, because his body, which you can always conquer, gives you so little purchase upon his soul."

Purchase means something you can grab on to, and that is what's missing in stage three. Gandhi, because he had renounced the outer trappings, couldn't be grabbed anywhere in the usual places. Those in power couldn't threaten him with losing his job, house, family, or even with imprisonment and death (they tried all of these means anyway). I am not implying that stage three is as far as Gandhi got in his spiritual journey, but he illustrates the point: detachment renders the use of power impotent. The God of peace doesn't validate how good you are by giving you money or status. You validate yourself from within, and this equates with God's blessing. At this stage of inner growth, the power of going inward is veiled; there is darkness and a cloud of unknowing. Yet somehow the pull toward spirit is real. For all the outer sacrifices, something seems to have been gained. What that something is becomes clear later; at this moment there is a period of adjustment as the person accommodates to a new world so different from that of every day.

What is my greatest temptation? . . .
Introversion.

I've taken great pains to show that stage three is not about becoming an introvert. That is the great temptation, especially for those who misinterpret the words *going inward* and *inner silence*. Words have a hard time at the quantum level. We are not talking about silence in the sense of no thought; we aren't talking about the inside of a person as opposed to the outside. But the ego has a fondness for co-opting anything spiritual and turning it to other purposes. Someone who by nature wants to shrink from the world can use as his excuse that spirituality should be inward. Someone who feels pessimistic in general can find comfort in rejecting the whole material world.

Introversion is not a spiritual state, however. Behind it lie all kinds of negative assumptions about the value of external life. The introvert is hiding his light under a bushel basket, the very thing Jesus warns against. I know one man who describes himself as an internal defector. His basic attitude is disgust with the world. He thinks all politics are corrupt, all business greedy, all ambition futile, all personal attachments a trap. Needless to say, it can be very drain-

ing to be around this man, but he sees himself as a good, indeed almost model Buddhist. His path of renunciation—as he sees
it—really amounts to rejection. The two
are so close that it takes diligence not to
mistake them.

The telling difference is that rejection
involves a great deal of ego. "I" make a decision that "they" (other people, the world in
general) are unsuitable. The ego has many
reasons for such rejection, and many sound
plausible. To be involved in the world is a
muddy, sometimes dispiriting business. On
the other hand, the goal of spirituality is
inclusive. God enfolds the whole creation,
not just the nice parts. If you start out by
rejecting this or that, how will you end up
accepting it? Introversion rejects everything
except those few acceptable bits of experience that make it through the gates set up by
the ego.

True renunciation is quite different. It
consists of realizing that there is reality
behind the mask of the material world. The
"nothing and nowhere" of God are real,
and in the face of that one's attention is
pulled away from outer rewards. Thus the
richest man in the world could be a renun-
ciate, if he has the proper insights, while a
greedy, selfish monk, no matter how clois-

tered he may be, could fall very short of renunciation. In the same way, someone can be extremely active and extroverted; this doesn't harm the inner search. The whole issue in stage three has to do with allegiance. Do you give your allegiance finally to the inner world or the outer? Many challenges come our way on this long journey, and no matter what answer you give verbally, it will be in the fire of experience that real answers come.

STAGE FOUR:
GOD THE REDEEMER

(Intuitive Response)

The brain knows how to be active and it knows how to be calm. Why isn't that the end of it? Where could the mind go once it has found peace within itself? The higher stages of spirituality seem mysterious when framed this way, because there is nowhere to go beyond silence. We have to look at what silence can grow into, which is wisdom.

Psychologists are well aware that wisdom is a real phenomenon. If you pose a battery of problems to subjects who span a range of ages, the older ones will predictably give wiser answers than the younger. The posed problem could be anything: deciding on whether you've been cheated in a business deal, or how to settle an international incident that could lead to war. A wiser answer might be to wait and see before acting on impulse, to ask for advice from several sources, or not to take any assumptions for granted. It doesn't matter really what the problem is. Wisdom is a perspective applied to any situation.

Just as stage three sees the birth of a peaceful God, stage four sees the birth of a wise God. He is willing not to act on his vengeful impulses; he no longer holds old sins against us; his outlook has gotten beyond right- and wrongdoing. In the role of God the Redeemer, he begins to take back all the judgments that weighed down life; therefore his wisdom creates a sense of being loved and nurtured. In this way the loneliness of the inner world begins to soften. The qualities of God the Redeemer are all positive:

Understanding
Tolerant
Forgiving
Nonjudgmental
Inclusive
Accepting

You will notice that none of these qualities is the result of thinking—if we found
them in a person, we would call them qualities of character. The psychological version of wisdom is inadequate here. To a
psychologist, wisdom is correlated with age
and experience, but something much
deeper is involved. Spiritual masters speak
of a mysterious faculty known as "second
attention." First attention is concerned
with the task at hand, with the data being
brought in by the five senses. It expresses
itself as thoughts and feelings. Second
attention is different. It looks beyond the
task at hand, somehow viewing life from a
deeper perspective. From this source wisdom is derived, and the God of stage four
appears only when second attention has
been cultivated.

I know an ambitious writer who received
a windfall from a book that had surprised
everyone by becoming a best-seller. Elated
with the influx of hundreds of thousands of
dollars, he decided to venture it all in a risky
oil leasing company. His friends pointed out
that the vast majority of such opportunities
bleed the investors dry before any oil is discovered. The writer was undeterred, and
with no experience whatever, he plunged
into his investment, going so far as to visit

the proposed oil wells, which were dotted throughout Kansas.

I met him again at a publishing event six months later. He sounded mournful; all his money had gone down the drain. "Every-one is being very kind about it," he said with embarrassment. "My friends resist their I-told-you-so impulses. But losing the money isn't really the hardest part, and it isn't the humiliation, either. What I have to live with is different. You see, from the very outset, I knew that this investment would fail. I hadn't the slightest doubt that I was making a terrible decision, and I walked through each day like a schizophrenic, totally confident on one level and totally doomed on the other."

This is a dramatic example of the fact that we all inhabit more than one level of reality at the same time. First attention organizes the surface of life; second attention organizes the deeper levels. Intuition and wisdom both grow out of second attention and therefore cannot be compared to ordinary thinking. Yet this man didn't pay heed to his intuition; he went ahead with his doomed project, ignoring the unconscious part of himself that knew in advance what would happen. The God of stage four enters one's life only after you make friends with the subconscious.

Therapists have an exercise for this, which consists of imagining yourself in a dark cave. You have entered to find the perfect mentor, who is waiting for you at the end of a tunnel. You begin to walk toward him, feeling calm and expectant—the cave is warm and safe. As you get near the end of the tunnel a room opens up, and you see your mentor with his back to you. He slowly turns around—this is the point at which you are supposed to realize who, out of everyone you have ever met, will be facing you. Whoever it turns out to be, whether your grandfather, a former teacher, or even a person you don't know, like Einstein or the Dalai Lama, you would expect certain qualities in your mentor:

- A mentor should know who you are and what your aspirations are. God the Redeemer is *understanding*.
- A mentor should accept you faults and all. God the Redeemer is *tolerant*.
- When you bring up things that you have never told anyone because they make you feel guilty and ashamed, a mentor should absolve that guilt. God the Redeemer is *forgiving*.
- Wise as he is, a mentor should not interfere in your decisions or brand

them wrong. God the Redeemer is *nonjudgmental.*
- A mentor should be able to understand a whole range of human nature. God the Redeemer is *inclusive.*
- You should feel safe with your mentor and bonded with him in intimacy. God the Redeemer is *accepting.*

No gender is implied in the role of mentor (the original Mentor, who appeared as tutor and guide to the son of Ulysses, took a male shape but was actually Athena, goddess of wisdom). For the first time, in fact, we can say that the God of stage four has a bias toward the female. Intuition and the unconscious have generally been seen as feminine in contrast to the masculine power of reason. The same division is expressed biologically as right-brain versus left-brain dominance. The fact that the right brain oversees music, art, imagination, spatial perception, and perhaps intuition doesn't mean that the God of stage four lives there, although the implication is strong. Myths around the world include heroes who speak directly to gods, and some anthropologists have speculated that just as the right brain can bypass the left to receive nonverbal, nonrational insights, so ancient humans could bypass the claims of rationality and perceive gods, fairies, gnomes, angels, and other beings whose material existence is much doubted by the left brain.

Today we are more inhibited. Very few people can say that they have talked with the Virgin Mary, while the rest of us have internalized divine voices as intuition. A gut feeling is as close to the oracle of Delphi as many people are going to get. That we can bypass reason to gain insight is certainly true. Intuition involves no cogitation or working through. Like lightning, it flashes across the mind, carrying with it a sense of rightness that defies explanation.

I think the two hemispheres of the brain are likely to be the source of first and second attention, because "dominant" doesn't mean domineering. We can all intuit and reason at the same time. Doctors have all met patients who know in advance whether or not they have cancer, or whether a surgery will turn out well. In my early practice there was a woman who was fearful of her husband's life when he was on the verge of entering the hospital. As it happens, his surgery was minor and in no way threatened his life.

"I know all that," she insisted, "but it's really his surgeon that worries me. I just don't have a good feeling about him." Everyone, including her husband and me, tried to reassure her. Doctor X was a prominent and skilled surgeon, yet the wife remained fretful.

As it happens, there was a freakish occurrence. In the middle of his procedure her husband had a rare reaction to the anesthesia. He died on the table, unable to be revived. I was in shock; the wife was beyond consolation. She had known what would happen, and yet at the rational level, she had no basis for halting the surgery. This clash of first and second attention forms the central drama of stage four. The big question is how we can learn to trust second attention, since the unconscious has a reputation for being unreliable, if not dark and menacing. Once you start identifying with the knower—that part of yourself that is intuitive, wise, and perfectly at home in the quantum world—then God assumes a new shape. He turns from all-powerful to all-knowing.

Who am I? . . .
The knower within.

You will never trust your intuition until you identify with it. Self-esteem enters here. At the earlier stages of inner growth, a person is esteemed who belongs to the group and upholds its values. If the knower within tries to object, he is stifled. Intuition actually becomes an enemy, because it has a nasty habit of saying things you aren't supposed to hear. A soldier sacrificing his life on the front lines can't afford to think about the barbarity of war and the rightness of pacifism. If his inner voice says, "What's the point? The enemy is just me in another man's skin," self-esteem gets torn to shreds.

A person who has arrived at stage four long ago gave up group values. The enticements of war, competition, the stock market, fame, and wealth have faded. Being stranded in isolation is not a good fate, however, and so the knower within comes to the rescue. He provides a new source of self-esteem based upon things that cannot be known any other way. If you are thrilled by the following lines from the great Persian mystic Rumi, you definitely understand how the inner world can be more thrilling than anything outside:

When I die
I will soar with angels,
And when I die to the angels,
What I shall become
You cannot imagine.

In stage four the emptiness of outward life is rendered irrelevant because a new voyage has commenced. The wise are not sitting around contemplating how wise they are; they are flying through space and time, guided on a soul journey that nothing can impede. The hunger to be alone, characteristic of anyone in stage four, comes from sheer suspense. The person cannot wait to find out what comes next in the unfolding of the soul's drama.

The word *redemption* conveys only a pale sense of how all-involving this whole expedition is. There is much more to the knower within than just being free from sin. Someone who still felt burdened with guilt and shame, however, would never embark on the voyage. You don't have to be perfect to try to reach the angels, but you do have to be able to live with yourself and keep your own company for long stretches of time. A sense of sin hinders that ability. As a somewhat cynical friend of mine, a psychiatrist, likes to say, "You will know a lot about human motivation once you realize one thing: ninety-nine percent of humanity spends ninety-nine percent of their time trying to avoid painful truths."

Those who spend their time in other ways can seem mysterious. The knower within has little to do with the five senses; it doesn't care how rationality looks at a situation. The knower just knows. This mystery is the subject of a famous Zen parable: A young monk goes to his master, the abbot of the monastery, saying, "I must know the meaning of life. Will you tell it to me, sir?"

The master, who was famed for his skill in calligraphy, picks up his brush and swiftly writes the word *Attention* on a piece of paper. The disciple waits, but nothing more happens. "Sir, I am determined to sit here until you tell me the meaning of life," he repeats.

He sits down, and after a moment the master picks up his brush and again writes the word *Attention* on the paper.

"I don't understand," the disciple protests. "It is said that you have attained the highest enlightenment. I am very eager to learn. Won't you tell me your secret?" But for the third time the master has nothing to say, only dipping his brush in the black ink and writing the word *Attention*. The young monk's impatience turns to discouragement.

"So you have nothing to teach me?" he says mournfully. "If only I knew where to go. I have been seeking for so long." He gets up and leaves. The old master follows him with a compassionate look as he takes his brush and with a single stroke writes the word *Attention*.

This little story loses its Zen-ness once you grasp that the master is talking about second attention. He can't answer the disciple's earnest questions because there are no answers at the level of first attention. The disciple could also have no idea of the excitement felt by the master, because from the outside there is no sign. We made the same point by observing that God leaves no traces in the material world. In stage four you find yourself fascinated with God, not because you need protection or comfort, but because you are a hunter after his quarry. The chase is all the more challenging when the prey leaves no tracks in the snow.

How do I fit in? . . .
I understand.

In stage three the inner world evidences little activity. Ships don't sail in a dead calm. They rest and wait. The inner world comes alive in stage four, where calmness and peace turn into something much more useful. One begins to understand how reality works, and human nature starts to unfold its secrets. Here are some examples:

There are no victims.
Everything is well ordered; things happen
  as they should.
Random events are guided by a higher
  wisdom.
Chaos is an illusion; there is total order to
  all events.
Nothing happens without a reason.

Let's call this a package of insight, centered on the question of why things turn out the way they do. It's a profound question. We all ask it, but we tend to ask in passing. Our passion is not to figure out the workings of fate. If some things seem preordained while others are accidental, so be it. In stage four, however, fate becomes a pressing issue. The person has experienced enough instances when "an invisible hand" must be at work. The instances may be small, but there is no turning away from them.

Recently I fumbled on the computer and lost a large chunk of very important work. I could hardly sleep that night, and the only remedy was a piece of software that might rescue my lost chapters, if they could be rescued at all. It was agonizing waiting for overnight delivery, which of course wasn't on time. I picked up the phone and had dialed the express company when a neighbor knocked at the door. "I think this must be for you," he said, holding out the package, which he had noticed while walking across our yard. It had arrived at the wrong entrance to the house, an old sealed-off door, and the deliveryman hadn't been able to ring the bell since we don't have one back there.

Besides getting to me just at the moment I was about to create a bit of chaos over the phone, the package was found by someone who had never unexpectedly dropped by before. How did all these ingredients, albeit tiny ones, happen to coincide?

In stage four you will not rest easy until you understand the answer. After paying enough attention (always the key word) you begin to see that events form patterns; you see that they also hold lessons or messages or signs—the outer world somehow is trying to communicate—and then you see that these outer events are actually symbols for inner events. (In my case, the inner event was an angry tension that I wanted to be saved from.) The ripples flow out from the center, getting wider and wider, until you begin to see that the "invisible hand" has a mind behind it, as well as great wisdom in what it does.

The conclusion of this little package of insight is that there are no victims. Wise people often say this, but when they declare that all is wisely and justly ordered, their listeners remain baffled. What about wars, fires, random murders, aircraft disasters, despotism, gangsters, and on and on? All of these imply victims and often cruel victimizers, too. How could the poet Browning have the audacity to claim that God is in his heaven and all's right with the world? He found out from God himself, but it was a God not to be met until stage four.

Here is a good place to ask what the inner knower actually knows. As we commonly define it, knowledge is experience that has been recorded in memory. No one would know that water boils at 100 degrees Centigrade unless there was memory of this. So the wise must have much more experience than the rest of us, or else they were born with more brain capacity. But is that really the case? After a divorce a person may lament that as early as the honeymoon it was obvious that the marriage wouldn't work out. Yet somehow only hindsight shows the importance of that intuition. How much is reliable to begin with?

Only the wise seem to know. Wisdom consists of being comfortable with certainty and uncertainty. In stage four life is spontaneous, yet it has a plan; events come as a surprise, yet they have an inexorable logic. Strangely, wisdom often arrives only after thinking is over. Instead of turning a situation over from every angle, one arrives at a point where simplicity dawns. In the presence of a wise person one can feel an interior calm, alive and breathing its own atmosphere, that needs no outside validation. The ups and downs of existence are all one. The New Testament calls this "the peace that passes understanding," because it goes beyond thinking—no amount of mental churning will get you there.

How do I find God? . . .
Self-acceptance.

The inner world has its storms, but much more terrible are its doubts. "Doubt is the dry rot of faith," as one Indian saint has said. No one can get very far in stage four if there is self-doubt, because the self is all there is to rely on. Outside support has lost its reassurance. In ordinary life, such a loss is dreaded. The outcast, the man without a country, and the traitor are roles no one wants to play. I have sat in a movie theater and heard dozens of people break into sobs when the Elephant Man is being hounded through a train station by a curious mob. His hideous head masked in a canvas bag, he is finally cornered and turns on his pursuers to cry in anguish, "I am not an animal, I am a human being!"

This is our own unconscious speaking its deepest fear. There is an element of freakishness to all outsiders, because we define normality by being accepted. In stage four, however, all moorings are loosed. "I was once almost engaged to this woman," a friend who had spent some years in a monastic setting told me. "It was a long time ago, and I had no kind of experience in this area. One night we were sitting in the dark on the sofa. Her head was nestled on my chest, and I felt so close to her that I said, 'You know, as much as I love you, I think I love humanity just as much.'

"She sat up with a horrified look on her face. 'Don't you realize that's the worst thing you can say to me?' she exclaimed. And I didn't. We broke up soon afterward, and yet I still don't truly understand why she was so disturbed."

Two worldviews had collided at that moment. To the woman, her lover's words were a betrayal, because she looked to him for support; by choosing to love her instead of someone else, he made her more complete; he added to her identity with outside validation. The man felt the opposite—in his eyes, including humanity in his love made her greater. At bottom, he didn't understand the kind of support she needed. He wanted to experience a state where all love is included in one love. Such an aim is hard to achieve, and most people don't even see its value (not for themselves, at least—they might value it in Saint Francis or a bodhisattva). Since infancy we have all gained security from having one mother, one father, our own friends, one spouse, a family of our own; this sense of attachment reflects a lifelong need for support.

In stage four the whole support structure melts away—the person is left to get support internally, from the self. Self-acceptance becomes the way to God. Not that an inner voice coos reassuring words, or that a new spiritual family is sought out. When Jesus says to his followers that they must die, he is referring to a state of inner detachment. It isn't a cold, heartless detachment but a kind of expansion that no longer needs to distinguish between me and you, yours and mine, what I want and what you want. Such dualities make perfect sense to the ego, yet in stage four the goal is to get beyond boundaries. If that involves giving up the old support systems, the person willingly pays the price. The soul journey is guided by an inner passion that demands its own fulfillment.

> *What is the nature of good and evil?* . . .
> Good is clarity, seeing the truth.
> Evil is blindness, denying the truth.

From the outside someone in stage four seems to have opted out. With no social bonds left, there is really no social role, either. The band of misfits that gathers on the fringes of every culture is composed of madmen, seers, sages, psychics, poets, and visionaries. Which is which cannot be distinguished easily, and the fact that all seem to be getting a free ride irks many people. Socrates was condemned to death simply for being wise—the authorities called it "corrupting the city's youth" and following "novel religious beliefs"—and throughout history the same story has played out over and over. The deepest insights are usually not socially acceptable; therefore they are seen as insane, heretical, or criminal.

In stage four good and evil are still contrasted, but with much less harshness than before. Good is clarity of mind, which brings the ability to see the truth. Evil is blindness or ignorance, which makes the truth impossible to see. In both cases we are speaking about self-centered qualities. The person accepts responsibility for defining "the truth" as he or she sees it. But that raises another accusation. What if the truth is simply whatever is convenient? Perhaps stealing a loaf of bread becomes right because "my truth" is that I am hungry. This sort of situational ethics isn't the real issue, however. In stage four the truth is much more elusive and even mystical. It contains a kind of spiritual purity difficult to define. When Jesus taught his followers that "the truth will set you free," he didn't mean a certain set of facts or dogmas but revealed truth. In modern language we might come up with a different translation: seek the knower within, and it will set you free.

In other words, the truth becomes a quest from which no one can deter you. Goodness means remaining true to your quest, evil is being drawn away from it. In the case of Socrates, even a sentence of death left him impervious. When offered an escape route across the sea if he would sneak out of Athens in the company of his friends, he refused. Their idea of evil—dying at the hands of a corrupt court—was not his. His evil would have been to betray himself. No one could comprehend why he wasn't afraid of death. Surrounded by tearful, frustrated pupils, he explained that death was an inevitable outcome. He was like a man who had calmly taken every step toward the edge of a cliff, knowing exactly where he was headed. Now that he had come to the jumping-off point, why should the last step cause any fear? This is really a perfect example of stage four reasoning. The quest has a purpose, and one sees it to the end. By drinking his cup of hemlock, Socrates died a traitor to the state who had upheld a total commitment to himself: this was a gesture of ultimate goodness.

What is my life challenge? . . .
To go beyond duality.

I have saved the topic of sin until we understood the inner world better. Sin is a stubborn issue. Because no one was perfect in childhood, we all carry the imprints of guilt and shame. Even in cultures that do not have a legend of the Fall, with its inheritance of original sin, guilt remains. The question is whether it is inherent. That is, did we do something to deserve feeling guilty, or is human nature created that way?

Sin can be defined as a wrong that leaves an impression. Wrong deeds that you forget have no consequence, along with those that were inadvertent—leaving a pot boiling unattended that catches fire is accidental, not sinful. In the East any act that leaves an impression is called karma; this is a much broader definition than sin and it includes no moral blame. People often speak of bad karma, concentrating on the aspect of wrong; but in its purest form, karma can be right or wrong and still leave an imprint.

The importance of this distinction becomes clear in stage four, because as right and wrong become less severe, the desire arises to be free of both. It would make little sense to have this aim before stage four. A tremendous amount of effort is expended in earlier stages trying to be good. God punishes those who aren't, and what he doesn't accomplish, a guilty conscience will. But the God of stage four, intent on redemption, sees sinners and saints in the same light, and all actions as equal. This valuation is scandalous. Society exists to draw the line between right and wrong, not to erase it. When Jesus associated with lepers and outcasts, when he neglected religious observances and pared the hundreds of Jewish laws down to two (put no other gods before

God and love your neighbor as yourself), the good people around him assumed he was either crazy or criminal.

In actuality, he was extremely responsible. In one phrase—"As you sow, so shall you reap"—Jesus stated the law of karma quite succinctly. He had no intention of getting away with wrongdoing but instead pointed to a higher spiritual rule: your actions today define your future tomorrow. Regardless of whether an act is deemed good or bad, this higher rule can't be side-stepped. Those who think it can have not looked deep enough. By stage four there is enough insight to realize that all past actions have a way of coming home to roost. This dynamic turns out to be more important than identifying sin.

What, then, would forgiveness of sin amount to? How do you redeem your soul? Finding the answer is the life challenge of this stage. A redeemed soul sees itself as new and unblemished. To reach this state of innocence would be impossible according to the law of karma, for the cycle of sowing and reaping never ends. (Unlike sin, karma grips us even in the case of accidents and inadvertent mistakes—regardless of circumstances, an action is an action and has consequences.)

The problem is further complicated by the fact that each person performs millions of actions in a lifetime, and these overlap on all levels. Emotions and intentions are both tied in. Is a man virtuous who gives money to the poor out of a selfish desire to save his soul? Is it right to marry a woman who is carrying your baby even if you don't love her? The parsing of good from bad becomes extremely complicated, and the doctrine of karma makes the calculation harder rather than easier, because the mind can always find some tiny detail that was overlooked previously.

It can take a lifetime to solve this riddle, but in theory at least the answer is simple: you redeem your soul by turning to God. A redemptive God is the only being in the cosmos exempt from karma (or sin). Or to be more accurate, God transcends karma because he alone isn't in the cosmos. A person in stage four has no interest in praying for a miraculous delivery from all his past evils; what he wants is a way to get outside the cosmos as well. In other words, he wants the rule of "As you sow, so shall you reap" repealed.

How can that possibly happen? Clearly no one can repeal the law of cause and effect. In the East, using the terminology of karma, they say that evil acts pursue a soul across time and space until the debt is paid. Even death cannot abolish a karmic debt; this only happens by becoming a victim of the same evil you committed or by working off bad imprints through good ones.

At the level of second attention, however, this cycle is irrelevant. One doesn't need to repeal the law of karma at all. Despite all the activity on the surface of life, a speck of awareness inside is not touched. The instant they wake up in the morning, a saint and a sinner are in the same place. They both feel themselves to be alive and aware. This place stands outside reward and punishment. It knows no duality; therefore in stage four your challenge is to find this place, hold on to it, and live there. When you have accomplished this task, duality is gone. You are free from all bondage of good or bad actions. In Christian terms, your soul is redeemed and returned to innocence.

What is my greatest strength? . . .
Insight.

What is my biggest hurdle? . . .
Delusion.

I said earlier that in stage four all the moorings are cut loose. Now we know why.

The inner quest is all about undoing attachments. These do not come free all at once, nor is every attachment equal. It is entirely normal to arrive at profound insights about yourself and still feel as ashamed or guilty as a little child over certain things. The soul is like a ragged army on the march. Some aspects push ahead; others lag behind.

The reason for this is again karmic: not all our past actions leave equal imprints. Some people are haunted for life by incidents from their past that are seemingly small. I know a man who has had to fire hundreds of employees, reorganize businesses that eventually went under, and in various ways decide the fate of many people. His decisions caused grief and complaints every time, no matter how well intentioned they were. He sleeps undisturbed by any of that, while in his heart of hearts he cannot forgive himself for not being at his mother's bedside when she died. The thought of having left so much unsaid makes him guilty every day. He knows at some level that his love for his mother is felt by her, but that doesn't heal the guilty wound.

Because of its intense subjectivity, stage four requires new tactics. No one outside yourself can offer absolution. To get past an obstacle requires your own insight; if you can't get past it, you keep fighting off delusion until you do. In this man's case, his delusion is that he is bad for not being with his mother (he had in fact no choice, since his trip home was delayed beyond his control); the insight is that his genuine love doesn't have to have an outward show. But beyond these particulars, there is only one insight and one delusion in stage four. The insight is that everything is all right; the delusion is that we have made unforgivable mistakes. The reason that everything is all right goes back to redemption; in the eyes of God, all souls are innocent. The same reason tells us that we are deluded to keep holding on to past mistakes. They cannot blemish our souls, and their residual effect, in terms of guilt, shame, and payback, will be washed away in good time.

What is my greatest temptation? . . .
Deception.

This is meant both in terms of self-deception and deceiving others. Every stage of inner growth contains more freedom than the one before. Breaking free from sin is a great accomplishment in stage four, but the price of redemption is constant vigilance. It is hard to keep examining yourself all of the time. A voice inside often urges you to be easier on yourself, take things as they are, act the way everyone else does. To follow this advice would make existence much more pleasant. Socrates could have apologized for offending the morals of Athens; he could have preached the accepted wisdom instead of his own. But to fall into this easy way amounts to deception, because the inner march of wisdom cannot be stopped. (Plato put it eloquently: "Once lit, the flame of truth will never go out.") Unless you are willing to deceive yourself into believing otherwise, a person in stage four really is free of outside values.

How long this temptation lasts varies with each person. In myth one is redeemed instantly by a merciful God when in fact it is a long process with many turnings. "I think my soul is like one of those squirrels in the park," someone once remarked to me. "When you try to feed a squirrel, he won't take the peanut from your hand in one go. He darts toward you, then he loses his nerve and darts away. The slightest gesture scares him off, and only after a few feints will he get up the nerve to reach out for what he wants." The parallel is exact. At some level everyone wants to be rid of guilt. As Rumi says in one aphorism, "Outside all notions of right and wrong there is a field—will you meet me there?" However much you want to, it isn't possible to dash toward this place. Our old imprints are very strong; guilt and shame arise as a reminder that it takes more than an act of will to escape notions of right and wrong. The process has to continue without deception. You can't fool your sense of being imperfect or sinful—choose your terms—in the hope that the slate can be wiped clean once and for all. There is a lot of work to do in the form of meditation, self-reflection, taking responsibility. You have to act on the truth as it occurs to you. Every step forward must be tested, and the temptation to go backward persists until the very end.

Whatever is involved in total self-acceptance has to be met. The triumph of stage four turns out to be a paradox in the end. At the very point when you see that you are all right, that you need never worry about good and evil again, the realization dawns that you never did wrong to begin with. Redemption returns the soul to a sense of innocence that never actually went away. Or to put it more simply, the whole process of being true to yourself brings as its reward a higher level of awareness. At this level, the issues of duality have been left behind, and when that happens, the subjective feeling is one of being redeemed.

STAGE FIVE:
GOD THE CREATOR
(Creative Response)

There is a level of creativity that goes far beyond anything we have discussed so far. It dawns when intuition becomes so powerful it must break out into the environment. This "super-intuition" controls events and makes wishes come true, as though an artist is working not in paint and canvas but in the raw material of life. The following example from my own life began in mundane circumstances that grew more and more amazing:

Some months ago I was in my office looking over a project that needed some cover art, but I knew no professional illustrators. As soon as I had the thought "I wonder whom I can find?" the phone rang. It was my grown daughter, Mallika, calling from India, and when I mentioned my problem, she immediately suggested an Irish artist named Suzanne Malcolm (not her real name). Neither of us had any idea where she lived. I hung up and thought nothing more about it, until that afternoon when a publisher friend called from London. On the off chance, I asked if he knew Suzanne Malcolm, but he didn't. An hour later he found himself at a cocktail party when the person next to him got a call on his cellular phone. He put it to his ear and said, "Suzanne?"

My publisher friend gave in to a sudden impulse. "Could that possibly be Suzanne Malcolm you're talking to?" he asked. Astonishingly, it was. My friend took down her telephone number and also asked her to call me. By this time—we are still on the same day—I had flown to Los Angeles for a scheduled lecture. I was early, however, so I pulled my rental car over to the curb; I had no idea exactly where I was. Checking my messages on the cell phone, I found one from Suzanne Malcolm. This was good news, and I dialed the number she had left me.

"Hello?" a woman's voice answered.

"Suzanne," I said, introducing myself, "I was wondering whether you could fly over from Dublin. I think I have an art assignment for you."

"Well, actually, I'm not in Ireland at the moment. I'm in Los Angeles."

"Really? Where are you staying?" I asked.

"I'm not sure," she replied. "Oh yes, it's 3312 Dominic." I looked outside the car window and felt a shudder pass through me—I was parked directly in front of her house.

How unwittingly we fall into God's reach. This example clearly goes beyond intuition, because no one involved in the story had any. It amounts to more than synchronicity, since this wasn't just a chance encounter that turned out to be significant. What can we call it when a string of events begins with a faint intention, only to be orchestrated across two continents, several time zones, and the random lives of four people?

The answer is creativity. The mind field, being beyond time and space, can manipulate them for its own use. Usually its workings are not exposed to view. We don't observe how the wheels of fate turn—until stage five, that is. Now the time has come when fate no longer has to be hidden from view. This happens when a person gives up all notions of accident, coincidence, and random events, and instead claims responsibility for each and every incident, however trivial. Events no longer happen "out there" but are guided by one's own intentions. Stage five joins the individual to God in a partnership as co-creators. When you are ready to form this alliance, the God you meet has these qualities:

Unlimited creative potential
Control over space and time
Abundant
Open
Generous
Willing to be known
Inspired

This is the most intimate God we have projected so far, because of a quality that is the key to stage five: openness. God the Creator is willing to share his power with his creation. His abundance and generosity follow from his openness. The Creator is much vaster than any previous God, and our minds have to grasp just what it means to have all of time and space at our disposal.

When Adam and Eve ate the forbidden fruit, it immediately created a sense of shame in them. This first moment of self-consciousness caused them to hide from God, and to some extent we have been hiding ever since. In other words, the conviction of sin has deprived us of our own creativity, which could parallel if not equal God's. Getting back to the source has been a constant theme ever since the first stage. In stage five, at long last, there is no trace of original sin, no imperfection to atone for.

To return to my first example, the fact that I found my illustrator doesn't mean that I arrived at stage five. The crucial question is over the role I played. If I see myself outside the process, then I am not a co-creator. Lazarus, after being raised from the dead, was incredibly astonished, but he didn't raise anyone himself, nor did he claim to be his own miracle worker. To be in alliance with God, you must uphold your side of the partnership, which involves some very specific beliefs:

You have to see yourself at the center of the creative process.

You have to accept responsibility for all outcomes.

You have to recognize that all thoughts have consequences, even the most minor.

You have to identify with a larger self than the one living here and now in this limited physical body.

Many people on the spiritual path willingly accept one or more of these beliefs, but the deciding factor is whether you live them out. One prerequisite is years of meditation, contemplation, or prayer; another is doing a great deal of inner work to remove self-doubt and beliefs about one's imperfection. Above all, this is a stage of power, and that implies getting straight about whether you deserve to wield it. People in stage five are usually inward and private, but they all know that their intentions count. Things happen because they want them to, no matter whether the results feel good or bad and irrespective of whether or not they bring any obvious benefit. Behind their screen of privacy, these people are not necessarily grand, rich, or famous. They are overjoyed, however, by knowing that God is sharing his creative genius with them.

Brain research sheds little light on what mechanism is involved here. It is surmised that when people are in a creative state, the cerebral cortex first establishes restful awareness. Creativity exhibits the alpha rhythms of relaxation; subjectively the person feels open and receptive. Unlike other periods of relaxation, this state is on the lookout for something—a stroke of inspiration—and when it occurs a spike of activity is registered by the mind as a moment of "Eureka!" Famous artists and inventors all testify to this experience, and in their work it can have profound implications. A eureka isn't ordinary thinking. Truly creative people tend to introduce a question into their minds and then wait for the solution to arrive—hence the necessity of going into a relaxed mode.

What is the brain doing for those hours or days before the creative solution appears? We have no idea. While incubating a great theoretical breakthrough, Einstein's brain exhibits the same mundane activity as anyone else's.

Yet it is undeniable that the mind is doing something highly unusual, particularly if we extend creativity beyond what an Einstein or Michelangelo does. If creativity means carving your own destiny out of space-time, it would be fruitless to look for evidence on the material level. We are speaking of quantum creativity here. For quite a while I have put aside our quantum model because I wanted to portray God from a more human, personal standpoint. As soon as we start approaching the miraculous, however, the quantum world has to return; there is no other viable way to explain such powers.

"There are no miracles," an Indian master once remarked, "unless you look at all of life as a miracle." He meant something quite specific here. The world seems to be a given, not the product of a miracle, whereas turning water into wine seems absolutely miraculous. The two fuse, however, at the quantum level. If I look outside my window I can see an old gnarled oak standing between myself and the ocean. Is that tree simply there, a given object in the land-scape? Not at all. To a neutrino, which can pass through the entire earth in a few mil-lionths of a second, solid objects are as vaporous as fog. My nervous system must create an oak tree from the fog of quantum data. Everything about that tree is mal-leable. To a proton, which takes billions of years to be born and then decay, the life of an old oak is less than a split second. To a mayfly, with its life span of one day, the oak tree is literally eternal. To a Druid priest, the tree would be sacred, the home of forest deities, and therefore a tremendous source of power. To a logger it is just a day's work.

Take any quality the tree might have, and it changes according to the perceiver. Now consider the environment of the tree. Every quality possessed by the air, the sea, the earth, and the sun are equally under my control. In a catatonic state, I would see nothing that I see now. In a state of reli-gious inspiration, colors, smells, and sounds might be acutely sharp. This is more than a subjective shift. To perceive the world, my brain must convert virtual photons into sensory information.

Having covered this area already, I will just emphasize the most important point: *there is no tree "out there."* No sights, sounds, textures, tastes, or smells exist without a brain to create them. We are so accustomed to accepting the world as a given that we overlook our creative role in it, but one can imagine a sightless world—it is the one that blind cave fish inhabit. Since their environment contains no photons of visible light, eyes aren't needed. This isn't a loss to them; it is just a choice not taken. Likewise, when one person is able to create outcomes in his life while another person merely experiences random events, the difference is a choice not taken.

So many of us limit our choices that we look upon higher creativity as miraculous, but it isn't. In your mind's eye, see a scene from your childhood. Most people can do this easily, putting themselves back at the beach with their families, for example. With a vivid enough imagination, you can even get absorbed in the scene, feeling the sun's heat and brightness, letting the surf surge over your body. There is no essential difference between doing this in your mind and actually going to the beach in person. In both cases the brain is shaping virtual photons into a pattern of experience. When Jesus turned water into wine, he used the same ability, only he obliterated the arbitrary line between imaginary results and real ones.

In stage five a person flirts with crossing that line. This is not yet the phase for complete miracles like levitation or raising the dead. Here one takes the role of apprentice, willing to peer into the master's box of secrets yet not quite a master oneself. In other words, there is still a small separation between the individual mind and its source at the virtual level. Imagining yourself in stage five is much like being the most privileged pupil of Mozart or Leonardo da Vinci. To be accepted as an artist in the master's eyes, the following relationship would have to develop:

- You need to trust that your teacher really is a great master. God the Creator has *unlimited creative potential.*
- You expect the master to be able to work confidently in his chosen medium. God the Creator uses the medium of reality itself: he *controls time and space.*

- You want your master to have a great deal to teach. God the Creator is *abundant* and *generous*.
- The master shouldn't be so lost in himself that he isn't approachable. God the Creator is *open*.
- You don't want the master to hold back his real knowledge. God the Creator is *willing to be known*.
- You want the master to transcend mechanical ability and tap into the source of genius. God the Creator is *inspired*.

At earlier stages of inner growth, it would seem blasphemous, or at the very least impudent, to undertake this kind of relationship. Earlier stages did not desire or permit such intimacy. But by stage five, a person realizes that God is not a being with desires. Since he has no preferences, everything is permitted. The inhibitions that hold us back—and this holds true at every level of growth—exist inside ourselves. Because he is infinite and therefore all-inclusive, God sees all choices with the same eye—his vision includes no judgment. When a person realizes this, God suddenly opens his deepest secrets, not because God changed his mind but because our perspective has.

Who am I? . . .
God's co-creator.

The master-apprentice metaphor stretches only so far. God is never to be met in person, and he doesn't announce what he has to teach. The entire process is internal. As a co-creator, however, you are expected to do more than just live and have random desires, as most people do. A co-creator takes a certain orientation toward his desires. This doesn't mean controlling or manipulating what you wish for. Those are choices made at the ego level. In stage five, the process is about becoming the author of your own life; some have called it writing your destiny script. How is that done?

First of all, one has to see the difference between before and after. Before you become the author of your own life, you feel inadequate and powerless. Unforeseen things happen all the time. Every day presents some kind of obstacle, large or small. Indeed there may be massive confusion about what you want in the first place. If you are operating from a place of conflict and confusion, outside circumstances seem to have the upper hand.

By contrast, after you assume authorship of your own life, outcomes are never in doubt. No matter what happens to you, each event has a place and a meaning. You see that your spiritual journey makes sense, even down to the smallest details. It isn't that your ego wakes up every morning and arranges your day. Events still unfold unpredictably, yet at the moment they occur, you know that you are adequate to meet them. No question arises that doesn't have its own answer somewhere inside it. The adventure is to uncover the creative solutions that most appeal to you. Like an author who can make any world he chooses on the page, you gain authorship based on your own inclinations, with no outside help and no second opinions.

Stage five isn't the last phase, since we haven't crossed the line into miracles. You can tell if you are in stage five by the way you get what you want. If you rely almost entirely on an internal process, then you are, with a minimum of effort, a co-creator of reality.

How do I fit in? . . .
I intend.

If we get down to specifics, the act of creation is reducible to one ingredient: intention. In stage five you don't have to master esoteric techniques; there are no magic tricks to making a thought come true, no secrets of miracle-working. You just intend a thing and it happens. When highly successful people are interviewed, many times they repeat the same formula: "I had a dream and I stuck with it, because I was certain that it would come true." This attitude is a symptom—one might say *the* symptom—of co-creation. Of course, there is a great deal of work to be done to arrive at any great accomplishment, but in stage five the end result is preordained, and therefore the work itself isn't primary. It's just what you need to do to get to the goal. In fact, many famous achievers testify that the astonishing events of their careers seemed to be happening on automatic, or as if to someone else standing outside themselves. Whatever it feels like, intention lies at the heart of the process.

To break this down into specific behavior, the following qualities can be seen in people who have mastered the art of intention:

1. They are not attached to the past or how things should turn out.
2. They adapt quickly to errors and mistakes.

3. They have good antennae and are alert to tiny signals.
4. They have a good connection between mind and body.
5. They have no trouble embracing uncertainty and ambiguity.
6. They remain patient about the outcome to their desires, trusting the universe to bring results.
7. They make karmic connections and are able to see the meaning in chance events.

These qualities also answer the earlier question of what good comes from inner silence. The good is creative. In these seven qualities some huge life lessons are embedded. One could write a book about this list alone, but here is a brief synopsis: Making any idea come to life always involves intention. If you have a flash of genius, that flash remains inside your head until it materializes. So the important issue is how it gets materialized. There are efficient ways and inefficient ways. The most efficient way is shown to us by the mind itself. If I ask you to think of an elephant, the image just appears in your head, and even though millions of neurons had to coordinate this image, using chemical and electromagnetic energy, you remain aloof from that. As far as you are concerned, the intention and the outcome are one; all intervening steps remain invisible.

Now consider a larger intention, such as the intention to go to medical school. Between having this idea initially and fulfilling it are many steps, and these are not internal at all: raising tuition money, passing exams, gaining admission, etc. Yet, just like the image of the elephant, each of these steps depends upon brain operations being invisibly coordinated. You think, move, and act using intention. In stage five this automatic pilot is extended to the outer world. That is, you expect the entire process of becoming a doctor to unfold with the least effort, unhindered by obstacles. The boundary between "in here" and "out there" is softened. All events take place in the mind field first and then exhibit their outward manifestation.

Having realized this fact, your behavior is now free to follow the seven principles outlined in our list. You can be detached from how things are going to work out because you have left it to the cosmos. Past success and failure don't matter since each intention is computed afresh, without regard for old conditioning. You are able to be patient about each step, given that timing is worked out perfectly on another level. Over the months and years of getting to be a doctor, you remain a silent witness as pieces of the process fall into place. Even as you go through action, the "doing" of it remains impersonal. On the ego level you may feel disappointment that event A occurred instead of event B, which you expected, but at a deeper level you know that B happened for a better reason. When that reason reveals itself, you make the karmic connection. Since no one is perfect, you will still make mistakes, but you adapt to these quickly; there is no need for stubbornness since after all you are not in charge of how things work out—your chief responsibility was to have the intention in the first place. (Skeptics might wonder what prevents you from intending the perfect murder or embezzling a million dollars, but the universe tends to support what is best for you, not just what your whims dictate.)

Finally, as any intention unfolds, you aren't just passively riding along like a passenger on a train. Your role is to remain as sensitive and alert as possible. The turning points in life arrive as small signals at first; these only amplify when you choose to follow them. So being vigilant about tiny clues is a major part of spiritual evolution. God always speaks in silence, but sometimes the silence is louder than at other times.

How do I find God? . . .
Inspiration.

I often hear people quote Joseph Campbell's advice to "follow your bliss." But how exactly is this done? I might get bliss from eating chocolate cake, but if I follow that, the results would be uncomfortable after a while; greedy, selfish, abusive, controlling, and addicted people could mistakenly believe that they are following their bliss, too. In stage five bliss becomes better defined as inspiration. Rather than having intentions that originate with your ego, you feel that you are called to do something highly meaningful. Self-gratification is still intense, but it is no longer narrow (in the way that having an orgasm or eating in a great restaurant is). The sense of being outside yourself is often present and, as God takes over, the fruition of your desires feels blissful—whereas the fulfillment of ego desires often surprises us by feeling very flat: ask anyone how they feel six months after winning the lottery.

To be inspired is a high state of attainment. Four decades ago, the psychologist Abraham Maslow first spoke of *peak experiences*, his terminology for a breakthrough into expanded consciousness. A peak experience shares many qualities with inspiration, including feelings of bliss and being outside oneself. Peak experiences have been reported atop Mount Everest, but they also might arrive in the ecstasy of music making, falling in love, or winning an important victory. The conscious mind receives a supercharged burst from the unconscious, and even though this may happen only once in a lifetime, that feeling of empowerment can influence the course of events for many years.

By contrast, ever since Freud uncovered the basis of neurosis, psychology has insisted that human nature is freighted with violence and repression. The unconscious was not a region close to God but a dark, murky terrain. Our worst instincts thus became normalized, overlaid with better instincts such as love and peacefulness, but never to be escaped. Maslow felt differently, that it was not normal to be violent or evil in any way.

Although Maslow theorized that peak experiences gave glimpses of the real norms of the psyche, it was nearly impossible to prove that anyone lived at a peak for any length of time. Out of the whole population, Maslow and like-minded researchers could barely find 5 percent who even temporarily made such a transition. When they did, remarkable things happened. Such individuals felt as a normal experience that they were safe, confident, full of esteem for themselves and others, deeply appreciative of what life brought to them, and constantly in a state of wonder that the world could remain so fresh and alive every day, year in and year out.

This handful of people were labeled "self-actualized" and then more or less forgotten. The norm did not get redefined. This wasn't a failure of insight. To redefine human nature in such positive terms seemed unrealistic. Freud had already laid down as law that human nature contains hidden tendencies that break out like caged monsters to overwhelm us but are always present beneath the surface.

Maslow himself, believing with all his heart that human nature is trustworthy and capable of great inner growth, had to admit that tremendous obstacles stand in our way. Most people are too needy to grow, because as long as our needs are frustrated, we spend most of our time being driven to fulfill them. Need comes in four levels, Maslow said: the first is physical, the need to feed and clothe ourselves; next comes the need for safety, followed by the need to be loved, and finally by the need for self-esteem. A huge amount of inner work is devoted to these basic requirements of life. Maslow taught that needs are stacked up, one above the other, into a hierarchy. Only at the top of the pyramid does a person get the chance to feel self-actualized.

By this measure most of spiritual life is wishful thinking. When someone turns to God in order to feel safe or to be loved, need is the real motivation. In any event, God doesn't intervene to rectify the situation. To be driven by need is just how life works. To bring back the sacred, it must accomplish something that love, security, self-esteem, or good fortune cannot. This is where inspiration comes in, because when we are inspired, we don't act from need at all. Inspiration, as the Bible says, is an act of grace, a blessing.

In stage five this sense of being blessed begins to spread beyond a particular moment. You don't have to be spiritually advanced to feel triumphant when you reach the top of Everest or win the Nobel Prize. Spiritual advancement shows up when the small things carry a share of blessing, too. As Walt Whitman wrote, "A morning glory at my window satisfies me more than the metaphysics of books." (This is a poet who scandalized his readers by declaring that the smell of his armpits was more holy than any church.) Someone in stage five sees grace in all things.

> *What is the nature of good and evil?* . . .
> Good is higher consciousness.
> Evil is lower consciousness.

"For me, a new phase began in a very trivial way," a woman once told me. "I was in a hotel room sitting next to the window. My plans for the day had been ruined by heavy rains that had moved in overnight, and I was a little glum. Down the block I could see a skyscraper looming up, when all at once I thought, 'It would be nice to see a patch of sun on that building.' I've probably never had a more trivial idea in my life.

"All at once, in the midst of a downpour, the clouds parted, and a brilliant shaft of sunlight landed right where I was looking. It paused for a moment, as if to say, 'Okay, do you get it?' and then the gray closed back in. I wasn't shaken; oddly enough I wasn't even surprised, but that tiny incident had a huge impact on me. I began to believe that my thoughts were connected to outer reality."

Once attained, this connection becomes the most valuable thing in a person's existence, and losing it becomes one's worst fear. In stage five the fall from grace becomes a personal threat. Is such a fear groundless? Yes and no. It is inevitable that no one in stage five can make every wish come true, and bad things, in terms of pain and failure, continue to occur. This stokes the fear. Many people who have attained tremendous success find themselves spinning out of control, losing their center and no longer relying on the inner assurance that is needed at every level of awareness. Outward pressures are sometimes to blame, or inner demons may rise to the surface. In any case, stage five is not a magic haven.

On the other hand, these setbacks are only temporary. The ego has forgotten that a learning process is involved. When things don't go right, failure is not the issue, much less evil. Being a co-creator implies complete mastery, and during apprenticeship that hasn't yet been attained. We don't live in a society that gives credibility to what has been discussed here. Despite all the clichés about making your dreams come true, no one is really taught that success depends on your state of consciousness. Gurus and masters are scarce; the legacy of wisdom has been shelved in books. This means that almost anyone who strives spiritually must become his own guide. Even God, who is the real guide, becomes known as an aspect of the self. In this context, falling to a lower state of consciousness is felt as a real and present danger, for you risk losing the only relationship that ultimately matters, that between you and yourself. In reality this can never happen, but the shadow of evil still lurks over stage five.

Maslow argued that the whole problem of evil boils down to needs that persist in unconscious form from our past. Nazi Germany was a country devastated by war and economic turmoil in the 1920s. We know from the biographies of Hitler and Stalin that they were abused as children, denied love. Eventually these frustrated needs took the form of cruelty, paranoia, and oppression. Common unhappiness comes from lower needs being unmet; evil comes from all being unmet.

Stage five amplifies our power so much that misusing it would amount to evil. Leaders who have a hypnotic hold over their followers go beyond ordinary persuasion. They have hit upon a source of power that crosses the boundaries of identity; in some way the leader actually infiltrates the "I" of his listener. Anyone who has entered stage five deeply fears having that kind of influence, for it amounts to letting one's own unconscious desires take over. Clarity is lost in the intoxication of power, without the person realizing that a destructive child is playing with the controls of the mind. The evil that results can be traced back to a lower level of awareness, exactly the thing most feared.

What is my life challenge? . . .
To align with the Creator.

There is more than one way to arrive at any goal, and not all are sacred. Jesus was born into a world of magicians and miracles. He by no means invented all the powers that can accomplish things beyond the five senses. In those episodes where he drives out demons or defeats the sorcerer known as Simon Magus, Jesus draws a line between God's way and other ways. Magic is not seen as holy.

In the late nineteenth century a famous English performer named Daniel Dunglas Home developed the amazing ability to walk on air. He could, for example, exit out through a tall window seventy feet off the ground and come back in through the adjoining one. Home performed this feat widely and did not charge or accept fees. Later in life he converted to Catholicism, but was excommunicated when he revealed that he had accomplished his air walk with the aid of "discarnate spirits" using him as their medium.

I offer this anecdote at face value, without comment about how Home accomplished what he did (no definitive debunking was ever done, although skeptics point out that he usually insisted on performing in dimly lit rooms). For ages the distinction between holy and unholy power has been made. Is it valid? If God is all-encompassing, does he care how any power is attained?

I would say that the question has to be reframed. If we assume that our quantum model holds good, then nothing is unholy. Beyond right and wrong, the Creator may permit us to explore anything he himself has allowed to exist.

Yet it wouldn't be good to attain any level of consciousness that does not bring benefit to yourself, and since you do not know how your soul's journey has been mapped out, deciding what is good or bad for you shouldn't be left to your ego. The ego always wants to accumulate and acquire; it wants to be safe; it hates uncertainty. Yet on the road of evolution there are periods of great uncertainty and even lack of safety. Therefore the challenge is to align with a higher intention for yourself—God's will.

In stage five, although one may be able to make almost any wish come true, the ones that *should* come true matter more. Here we are guided to increase bliss, love, charity to others, and peaceful existence on the planet. An inner sense of rightness must be cultivated; an inner sense of ego must be diminished. Power never arrives in a vacuum. The larger will that rules events always tries to make itself known. If you align with it, the path through this phase is smooth; if you don't, there are many ups and downs, and your ability to manifest your desires can run into as many obstacles as it overcomes.

What is my greatest strength? . . .
Imagination.

What is my biggest hurdle? . . .
Self-importance.

Artists who create with paint or music start with a blank canvas or page; they go inward and an image appears, at first faint but growing. The image carries a feeling with it of wanting to be born. If the inspiration is genuine, this impression never fades. Creator, creation, and the process of creating are fused. I would call this the literal meaning of imagination; it is much more than having a nice idea you would like to carry out.

In stage five the fusing isn't complete. The greatest artists still suffer pangs of doubt and failure of inspiration. So do co-creators. In particular, there is the danger of trying to take over the process, which severs the alliance with God. Self-importance can halt progress for a long time. This is easy to trace in artists: reading a biography of Ernest Hemingway, you cringe as the balance of ego and genius tragically shifts. A writer gifted beyond measure in his thirties, Hemingway describes how his stories wrote themselves, how in magical moments he stood aside from the process and allowed it to happen. In the same mental state, the poet William Blake declared, "My words are mine and yet not mine."

Over the years, this delicacy of awareness departed, and Hemingway descended into a much more ordinary kind of struggle. Immersed in the labor of writing, he churned out massive manuscripts that were products of confused labor. On the spiritual plane the danger of losing the connection looms for anyone still in the grip of self-importance. Eventually Hemingway succumbed to failure and self-destruction. The God of stage five is more forgiving; no one is ever deprived of the evolutionary impulse. Struggles with self-importance can last a long time, but they always end once the person finds a way to give more of the responsibility back to God. In other words, the way to power is to give up power. This is the great lesson the ego is confronted with in this phase.

What is my greatest temptation? . . .
Solipsism.

The power to make your wishes come true is very real, but it is as much feared as desired. This fear is succinctly stated in the saying "Be careful what you wish for—it might come true." And many people do find themselves feeling ambivalent when they get the dreamed-for job or the dreamed-for wife. I say that this is really a false danger, however; the nature of inner growth is that as you gain more power, you deserve to have it. If something comes true that has its disadvantages, the balance of good and bad reflects your own awareness. This we will discuss in stage six, where actual miracles become possible.

What's much more dangerous here is solipsism, believing that only your mind is real, while all objects out there in the world are mirages that depend upon you, the perceiver, and without you they would melt away. Some paranoid schizophrenics suffer from precisely this illusion, and will go to any lengths to stay awake, so great is their fear that nodding off will bring the world to an end.

In stage five the temptation is to stay locked in yourself. I mentioned that when desire becomes most efficient, no outer struggle is needed. It is as if God takes over and things unfold on automatic pilot. But this cannot become an excuse for lethargy. The person still plays his part. Paradoxically, he may go through the same motions as someone who doesn't have any awareness of being a co-creator. The difference takes place inside one's mind. To a co-creator, life has a true flow; things are connected in patterns and rhythms; all details make sense.

When this point of view is alive, all work becomes deeply satisfying. One is no longer obsessed with failure or performance anxiety. More important, the achieved result brings fulfillment. This is lost, however, if you fall into solipsism. The ego, as it takes charge of holding the world together, forgets that creation depends upon grace. Stage five isn't really measured by how much you can achieve. Someone who achieves close intimacy with God may choose to accomplish very little. But no matter what is achieved, there is a constant feeling of being blessed. This becomes the object of all desiring, not the outward show.

STAGE SIX:
GOD OF MIRACLES
(Visionary Response)

God the Creator gave open access to the entire cosmos, including its dark places and secret compartments. To accept his generosity, a person must also be unafraid of his own dark places, and this is rarely the case. Who can see himself purely as a child of light? I once read in an inspirational book the following: *This is a recreational universe. Your ability to play in it is limited only by how much you can appreciate.* On reading these words it occurred to me that the world's greatest saints and masters may be simply enjoying themselves. They have the ability to live in the light while the rest of us cannot.

It is hard to imagine yourself as a citizen of the universe, utterly without hindrance and limitation. The Catholic Church recognizes dozens of saints who could levitate, be in two places at once, emit light from their bodies as they prayed, and perform healings. (As late as the 1950s parishioners in Los Angeles testified to seeing their priest rise from the ground when he lost himself in the passion of his sermon.)

Yet for all their miracles, or because of them, we think of saints as being without fun, loving relationships, sexual impulses. It's impossible to imagine a saint with money and a good car. Without the right appurtenances—white robe, sandals, a halo of virtue—the enlightened need not apply.

In stage six all of these assumptions are tested. Full-blown miracles are now possible. Here we accept God's invitation to transform material existence, and there is ecstatic joy in that. For example, one of the most charming saintly souls in recent times was a nun of the late Victorian era named Sister Marie of Jesus Crucified, who lived among the Carmelites near Bethlehem. She had been born a poor Arab in the region, one Mariam Baouardy, and worked as a housemaid before taking her vows.[2]

Upon entering the convent in 1874 it was

discovered that this novice had the alarming habit of suddenly swooping up to the tops of trees, where she flitted from branch to branch like a bird. Some of the twigs she landed on were not strong enough to hold a bird. This feat embarrassed Mariam, since she had no way of predicting or controlling her ecstasies, and on at least one occasion (eight were observed in total), Mariam timidly asked her companion to turn her back and not look.

In her ecstatic state, the "little one," as Mariam was known, sang constantly in praise of God. The prioress in charge, rather than falling to her knees in awe, ordered Mariam to come back to earth immediately.

> *At the moment she heard the word "obe-dience," the ecstatic came down "with a radiant face" and perfect modesty, stopping at several branches to chant "Love!"* . . .
>
> *"Why do you rise like this?" the Mother Superior interrogated her.*
>
> *"The Lamb [Christ] carries me in his hands," Mariam answered. "If I obey quickly, the tree becomes like this," and she put her hand close to the ground.*

Somewhere in a remote corner of the world, someone whose name is completely unknown to us is taking flight, I am sure. The fact that skeptics deny the existence of miracles matters not at all. The existence of miracles announces the God of stage six, who has the following qualities:

Transformative
Mystical
Enlightened
Beyond all causes
Existing
Healing
Magical
Alchemist

Words can convey only a hint of the Being we are talking about. A God of miracles is buried so deep in the quantum world that even those who have spent years in prayer and meditation may have detected no trace of him. The material world is set up to do without his presence, which makes the God of miracles profoundly mystical even by religious standards. Was Jesus exaggerating when he made his most dramatic claim about the powers God can bestow?

I tell you this: if you have faith no bigger than a mustard seed, you will say to this mountain, "Move from here to there," and it will move; nothing will prove impossible for you.

There is an explanation for this promise. The most mystical of the gospels is the Book of John. Consider its description of creation: "In the beginning was the word, and the word was with God, and the word was God." In other parts of the Bible, a writer who wanted to refer to divine wisdom would call it "the word," but here John says "the word *is* God." Clearly no ordinary word is implied. Something like the following is meant: Before there was time and space, a faint vibration existed outside the cosmos. This vibration had everything contained in it—all universes, all events, all time and space. This primordial vibration was with God. As far as we can fathom, it *is* God. Divine intelligence was compressed in this "word," and when the time came for the universe to be born, the "word" transformed itself into energy and matter.

In stage six, a person returns to the word, in all its primordial power, to discover the source. Behind everything is a vibration— not in the sense of a sound or an energy wave, because those are material, but a "mother vibration" at the virtual level that includes everything. In India the sound of the divine mother took the name *om*, and it is believed that meditating on this sound will unlock all the mother's secrets. Perhaps *om* is the very word John is referring to. No one will know for sure who hasn't arrived at stage six. But we can imagine it because the greatest miracle workers tend to have disciples, and in all ages disciples say much the same thing about a sacred master:

- Being in his presence is enough to change your life. The God of miracles is *transformative*.
- There is a holy aura about the master that the mind cannot fathom. The God of miracles is *mystical*.
- A sacred master exhibits higher states of consciousness. The God of miracles is *enlightened*.
- The master's actions follow a secret reasoning that sometimes makes no sense to his followers. The God of miracles is *beyond all causes*.
- The master purifies other people of their imperfections and may be able to cure illness. The God of miracles is *healing*.
- The master can perform wonders that defy explanation. The God of miracles is *magical*.

- The master may be interested in esoteric science. The God of miracles is an *alchemist*.

These qualities don't tell us, however, about the inner workings of a saint's mind. What brain mechanism, if any, gives visions of God and makes miracles possible? All we really have is scattered clues. Some researchers have speculated that the two hemispheres of the brain become completely balanced in higher states of consciousness. A yogic tradition holds that the breath also becomes balanced; instead of favoring one nostril, a person finds that a soft, faint breath rhythm flows from both. Another speculation holds that the brain becomes more "coherent," meaning that the wave patterns that are usually jumbled and disconnected fall in synch, rather like the synchronized beating of millions of heart cells during normal cardiac rhythm. But such coherence has been rarely spotted and is open to dispute.

So what we are left with is an elusive brain function that I will call the visionary response. It is marked by the ability to change energy states outside the body, causing objects and events to be transformed. As vague as that sounds, to someone in stage six, miracles are as easy as any other mental process. No brain researcher has come within miles of describing the necessary shift that must be achieved to perform a miracle.

Once you admit the existence of the visionary response, it is fascinating to learn how important symbols and images are. Healing, for example, is never the same from one culture to the next. In our culture the human heart is seen as a machine—the old ticker—that wears out over time. We fix it through mechanical repairs, as one might a worn-out clock. So when we find out that widowers have a high incidence of sudden death from heart attacks, the fact that sadness can kill doesn't compute very well. Not many sad machines die.

In certain regions of the Amazon, the body is considered an extension of the jungle. In this environment ants are carriers of bad things—toxins, poisons, rotted food, etc. According to an account by a visiting anthropologist, a villager once came to the local medicine man with a swollen abscess in his jaw due to a rotting tooth. The medicine man tied a string around it, and immediately a troop of large ants emerged from the man's mouth and marched down the string. They carried away the poison, and the villager recovered without having his tooth extracted.

Symbols aside, how did this healing work? One is reminded of the psychic surgeons of the Philippines, who seem to penetrate a patient's body with their hands and pull out all manner of bloody tissue, none of it anything that would be seen inside a body at autopsy. In many cases patients report that they can actually feel the surgeon's fingers, and dramatic recoveries have been reported.

In quantum terms we can offer an explanation for what medicine men are accomplishing on the outskirts of the miraculous. The medicine man is not using hypnosis, but at the same time he isn't operating on the physical plane, either. As we know from our quantum model, any object can be reduced to packets of energy. Up to now, however, our consciousness could not change these invisible patterns of photons except in a very limited way. We can imagine a healthy body, for example, but that image doesn't keep us from getting sick. The medicine man turns a mental image into physical reality—in fact, this is what all miracle workers do. At the quantum level they "see" a new result, and in that vision the new result emerges.

A power struggle ensues, and the medicine man must be more powerful than his

patient in order to make any kind of permanent change in his condition. What he is
trying to alter are the energy patterns that
have become distorted, thus causing the
disease. A rotten tooth, a tumor, or a
detached retina are all a cluster of photons,
a warped image made of light.

The key question is not whether a medicine man is real or fake but how powerful
his consciousness is, for he alone makes the
patient enter into altered reality with him,
along with any nearby observers. I have to
emphasize "nearby" because this is a field
effect, and just as a magnet can attract iron
only at a certain distance, the miracle
worker has a limited range of ability. It is
even said that having too many people in
the room can defeat the phenomenon. The
lump of consciousness that they form is too
large to handle, like a lump of iron too large
for a magnet to pull.

When the Virgin Mary appeared near
Fatima, Portugal, in 1917, a huge crowd
estimated at seventy thousand gathered for
the apparition, which had been promised to
three local peasant children. Those closest
to the children reported that the sun
whirled in the sky and dove toward the
earth in a rainbow radiance, but others farther away saw only a bright light, and at a

greater distance nothing at all was witnessed. The children themselves fell to their knees and talked with Mary herself.

When the wonder is over, the observer leaves the miracle worker's sphere of influence. The field effect no longer works, so everyone recaptures his normal state of awareness. The transition can be bumpy—some people faint or feel dizzy. The miraculous world fades, giving rise to a sense of vagueness over what actually happened. At the level of ordinary life, the events remain baffling, hence the widespread skepticism over holy apparitions, psychic surgeons, and jungle medicine men. But the visionary response describes another level of consciousness where energy patterns are shifting with every thought. The fact that these shifts change the outer world is amazing to us but natural to the person in stage six.

Who am I? . . .
Enlightened awareness.

We have come a long way with the question "Who am I?" Starting with the physical body in stage one and steadily moving to less physical planes, now we arrive at nothing but awareness. "I" am not even the mind, only the light. My identity floats in a quantum fog as photons wink in and out of existence. Observing these shifting patterns, I feel no attachment to any of them. They come and go; I am not even troubled by having no permanent home. It is enough to be bathed in the light.

Of the million ways you could define enlightenment, identifying with the light is a good one. Miracle workers do more than access energy patterns. As the Vedas say, "This isn't knowledge you learn; it's knowledge you turn into." Jesus spoke in parables but could easily have been literal when he declared to his disciples, "You are the light of the world."

At any given moment, it is impossible to compute how many human beings have turned into miracle workers. According to mystical Judaism, thirty-six pure souls, known as the Lamed Vov, hold the world together, keeping God from destroying the sinners who offend him. Some sects in India reduce this number to seven enlightened masters at any one time. However, we are also told in the Old Testament that God would spare Sodom and Gomorrah if fifty righteous men could be found, only to whittle the number down to one (Lot, whose wife was turned into a pillar of salt—but the cities were destroyed anyway). By implication, if you aspire to join any of these groups, your chances are slim. Is it plausible to hold out for enlightenment?

The vast majority of people have said no by their actions if not their words. It should be pointed out that miracle-working is accessible before sainthood. When you see any image in your brain, you are shifting reality. A mental image is faint and quickly fades away, but no matter. The critical operation behind a miracle is one that you can perform. The difference between you and a miracle worker is that you do not create a strong enough force field to make your mental image project itself onto the outer world.

Even so, if you come into the force field of a greater soul, your reality can shift quickly. I heard an interesting account about a Western-trained doctor who had traveled into the depths of the Colombian rain forest. While climbing the slippery rock face beside a waterfall, he lost his footing and took a severe fall. His back was injured to the extent that he couldn't walk. The expedition was a hundred miles from the nearest town, and there were no phones or electricity.

For several days he rested in a small village, hoping that he might get free enough of pain to make it out on his own, but his condition worsened as the injured tissue became more inflamed. In desperation he finally agreed to allow a tribal shaman to work on him. The shaman came in and began to enter a trance, taking hallucinogenic herbs and chanting for several hours. In the middle of the ritual, the injured doctor found himself dozing and drifting off. When he awoke the shaman was gone, and so was his back pain. To his astonishment, he could stand up and walk as if nothing untoward had occurred.

"I have no idea how this happened," he recounted, "but I wonder about one thing. I had reached the point of total desperation before I permitted them to call this medicine man in. I didn't believe in him, but at least I was willing not to disbelieve."

I think that this man closed the gulf between himself and the healer in a significant way. He permitted the shaman to go into the light without resistance. Some faith healers will often precede the laying on of hands by asking, "Do you believe that God can cure you?" From the larger perspective, no one has the power to keep God out totally. We can only open or close our acceptance of the light. It helps to create a process that will gently create more willingness to be open. No matter what documentation is offered for miracles, many people will say, "But have you seen one yourself?" I have come as close as I need to, just recently, in fact. I have a cousin, a veteran of combat in Kashmir, who was struck with a virulent case of hepatitis C a few years ago. We are a family of doctors, and he received every sort of treatment, including interferon, but to no avail. His platelet counts dropped alarmingly and his viral count from the hepatitis soared.

A few months ago he turned to an energy healer in India, who passed his hands over my cousin's liver to extract the disease entity. In a short time, his platelet counts were back to normal, his viral count had subsided, and there were no symptoms of any disease. To me this is a miracle. It seems to be a teachable one as well. You can take most people in our society and school them successfully in the art of "healing touch," which requires a practitioner to run her hands over the body a few inches over the skin to feel where there are energy hot spots (detected as a patch of warm air over that region). The practitioner then moves this excess energy to dispel it, and in many cases some healing is achieved, usually in the form of more rapid recovery than from conventional treatments.

Are there really warm patches over the diseased portions of our bodies? If so, why should that make any difference in a patient's recovery? The answer depends on the fact that the basis of healing isn't material but quantum. Things are real in the quantum world if you *make* them real, and that is done by manipulating light. With care and patience, anyone can be taught to do that; healing touch is only one mode. If we formed a school for teaching nurses how to get streams of jungle ants to emerge from a sick person's mouth, some pupils would be decidedly talented at it. Likewise, any miracle may be within reach, if only we begin to alter our conception of who we are and how our minds work.

How do I fit in? . . .
I love.

When he realizes that he is bathed in light, the feeling that comes over a miracle worker is one of intense love. This is because he is absorbing the qualities of spirit that the light contains. When Jesus said "I am the light," he meant "I'm totally in God's force field." In India people from every walk of life are eager to put themselves in a saint's force field, which is called *darshan*, a Sanskrit word that means to be in someone's sight. A few years ago I went for darshan at the home of a woman saint outside Bombay known to her followers simply as Mother.

Her home was tiny, a brick bungalow in a small village. I was escorted upstairs to an even tinier sitting room where she was waiting on a sofa by the window. Her attendant, an older woman, waved me silently to a chair. Mother herself, dressed in a gold sari and with large, expressive eyes, appeared to be around thirty. We all sat quietly. The warm drizzle outside turned to tropical rain; no other sound made itself felt. Time passed, and I began to notice a wonderful sweetness in the room, which made my mind very peaceful. My eyes closed, but I was aware that Mother was looking at me. After half an hour, her attendant quietly asked if I had any questions to ask.

"Feel free," she said. "After all, you are talking to God. Whatever you ask she will take care of."

I didn't find this startling. In India when a person reaches a state of consciousness that is completely intimate with God, he or she is respectfully referred to in this way. But I had no questions. I could feel without a doubt that this young woman was creating an atmosphere of her own that was very tender and loving. It offered such reassurance that one could believe, at that moment, in a "mother energy" inherent in the universe.

In stage six all gods and goddesses are aspects of oneself expressed as fine energy states. I am not declaring myself a devotee when I say that Mother could make these energies felt. The only real surprise is that she could do this for a stranger, since we all feel the mother energy as children around our own mothers. In India it is well known that darshan isn't the same with every saint. Some saints have a presence that is almost trancelike; others create a flavor like honey or the fragrance of flowers. The "darshan junkies" who spend hours in the presence of holy people can recite which *shakti*, or power, is felt around one saint or the next. And it is believed that these flavors of God can be absorbed by visitors like water by a sponge.

The most touching moment with Mother came as I was leaving. Her attendant showed me to the door and sent me away with a remark in broken English. "Now you have no more troubles," she said cheerfully. "God is going to pay your bills!"

No one could claim that stage six alone

reveals God's love. But the analogy to mag-
netism works well here. A compass needle
exposed to the earth's weak magnetic field
trembles toward north; it does this unerringly, but if you shake the compass the
needle wavers. Hold it close to a huge elec-
tromagnet, however, and the needle will
lock into place without wavering.

Likewise, we are all in the force field of
love, but in early stages of spiritual growth,
its power is weak. We waver and can easily
be thrown off in other directions. Conflicted emotions are at play, but more
important, our perception of love is
blocked. Only after years of cleaning out the
inner blockages of repression, doubt, negative emotions, and old conditioning does a
person realize that God's force is immensely
powerful. When this occurs, nothing can
pull the mind away from love. Love as a personal emotion is transmuted into a cosmic
energy. Rumi puts it beautifully:

Oh God
I have discovered love!
How marvelous, how good, how beautiful
    it is! . . .
I offer my salutation
To the spirit of passion that aroused and
    excited this whole universe
And all it contains.

Rumi believes that every atom in creation dances in a passion for God, such is a stage six awareness. It takes a quantum leap in consciousness to love God all the time, yet when the leap is finally made, there is really no God to love, not as a separate object. The fusion of the worshiper and what he worships is nearly complete. But that is enough to animate everything in creation. "This is the love," Rumi declares, "that brings our body to life."

How do I find God? . . .
Grace.

In stage six it is no longer necessary to seek God, just as we do not have to seek gravity. God is inescapable and constant. Sometimes he is felt with ecstasy, but just as often there can be pain, anguish, and confusion. This mixture of feelings reminds us that two entities are coming into conjunction. One is spirit, the other is body. The body can perceive spirit only through the nervous system. As the intensity of God increases, the nervous system is overwhelmed by it. There is no choice but to adapt, yet adaptation can cause sensations of intense burning, tremors, blackouts, and fainting, along with fear and semipsychotic states. It is still quite common to come across medical "explanations" of saintly visions as epileptic seizures, for example, and the blinding light of holy visions as a by-product of severe migraines. How do we know that this isn't true?

One obvious rebuttal is that migraines and epilepsy aren't inspiring. They do not bring wisdom and insight, whereas saints appear to be pure examples of grace at work. One thinks of the Polish mystic Father Maximilian Kolbe, a saintly figure who died under the Nazis at Auschwitz.[3] Although emaciated and a longtime sufferer from tuberculosis, Kolbe gave away most of his meager rations to other prisoners. When utterly parched with thirst, he was offered a contraband cup of tea by a doctor also imprisoned in the camp, but refused to take it because the other inmates had nothing to drink. Without complaint, Father Maximilian endured incessant beatings and torture. In the end, he was present when another prisoner was condemned to die of starvation in an underground vault. Kolbe volunteered to take the man's place. When the crypt was opened some days later, everyone had perished but he, and he was killed with a lethal injection.

In his own eyes Kolbe was not a martyr. A few fellow prisoners, and even some Nazis, gave firsthand accounts of the state of grace he occupied. A Jewish survivor testified under oath that Father Maximilian emanated light when he prayed at night. (This account is seconded by several others in the years before the priest was arrested.) In demeanor he was simple and humble. When asked how he could endure with such gentleness the treatment he was receiving at the hands of the Nazis, he said only that evil must be met with love.

Few saint stories are more moving than this one, which leaves us feeling that grace might be superhuman. In one sense it is, in that God's presence overcomes the most intense conditions of pain and suffering. In another sense, though, grace offers constant support in everyday life. There is no way to tell, as we work through each stage of inner growth, whether we are actually doing anything through our own will. An Indian master was once asked, "When we strive to reach higher states of consciousness, are we really doing anything or is it just happening to us?"

"It could be seen either way," he replied. "You are doing your part, but the real motivation comes from outside you. If you wanted to be strictly accurate, it is all happening to you."

If God is like a force field in stage six, grace is his magnetic pull. Grace adapts itself to each person. We make our choices, some of which are good for us, some bad, and then grace shapes the results. To express this another way, each of us does things that have unexpected consequences. Our foresight is limited; therefore our actions are always subject to blindness about what will happen next.

The word *karma* includes both the action and the unpredictable results. Five people can make a fortune, yet for each one the money creates different consequences, which can range from misery to contentment. The same holds true for any action. Why isn't karma mechanical? Why doesn't action A always lead to result B? The law of karma is often compared to simple cause and effect, using the analogy of billiard balls being hit with a cue stick. The angles and bounces in a billiard game are very complex, but a skilled player can compute his shot in advance with extreme accuracy, thereby predicting the path of a ball even after it has left his control.

If karma were mechanical, the same would hold for our actions. We would plan them out, let them go, and be sure of a certain result. Theoretically nothing prevents this. In actuality we are stymied by the sheer complexity of what needs to be calculated. Everyone performs millions of actions every day—strictly speaking, every thought is a karma, along with every breath, every bite of food, etc.—so the billiard game in this case has a nearly infinite number of balls. But something unfathomable is at work here: grace.

With his supreme intelligence, God has no trouble calculating an infinite number of billiard balls or an infinite number of kar-mas. This mechanical operation could be as easily performed by a supercomputer. Yet God also loves his creation and wants to be joined with it as intimately as possible, so he throws into his calculation the following special instruction: *Let all of a person's actions bounce and collide any way they have to, but leave a clue that spirit is watching.*

When you feel you have been touched by grace, that is your clue that God exists and cares about what happens to you. I know a middle-aged man, now the owner of his own computer firm, whose entrepre-neurial streak first surfaced when he was twenty. Unfortunately, at that time it took the form of smuggling drugs across the Caribbean in a light plane.

"I only made one trip before I was

detained by the customs officials and almost arrested. As it happens, I didn't have any cargo left on board. But they never found out why, and that is an amazing story," he says. "I was flying out of the Bahamas when we encountered dense cloud cover. I dipped down to escape it, but the fog went down to ground level. Somehow in all this maneuvering, my partner and I lost our bearings. We wasted time trying to get back on course, growing more and more worried. The Caribbean is a great deal of ocean and only a few small places to land.

"We began to run out of fuel and panic set in. My partner started shouting, and we jettisoned all our extra gas cans, then the cargo, and finally our luggage in an attempt to get lighter. The fog didn't lift, and I could tell that my co-pilot was frozen with fear. He was sure that we were going to die. At that moment, I had the unearthly certainty that we weren't.

"I looked to my left, and a hole opened in the fog. I could see a tiny island beneath my wing tip, and on it a short dirt landing strip. I dove the plane through as the clouds closed up again, and we landed, only to have five customs officials converge on us half an hour later. But the whole time of our interrogation, I heard an inner voice that told me my life had been saved for a reason. I didn't become religious in any conventional sense, but this was something I never doubted again."

Whether operating on the level of a saint or a criminal, grace is the ingredient that saves karma from being heartlessly mechanical. Grace is thus linked to free will. A billiard ball must follow its assigned trajectory, and a thief who commits robbery a hundred times would seem to be just as set on his course. But even though his karma is set, at any given moment he has the opportunity to stop and mend his ways. Grace can take the form of a simple thought, "Maybe I should quit," or it can be an overwhelming transformation like the one endured by Saint Paul on the road to Damascus when the divine light blinded him and struck him from his horse. In either case, the impulse to move toward spirit is the result of grace.

What is the nature of good and evil? . . .
Good is a cosmic force.
Evil is another aspect of the same force.

It is so difficult to be good that eventually a person must give up. This is a realization that arrives in stage six. Being good seems easy at first, when it is a simple matter of obeying the rules and staying out of trouble. It becomes harder after conscience enters in, because our conscience is often at odds with desire. This is the phase, familiar to every three-year-old, when one voice inside whispers "Do it!" while another says, "Better not." In Christianity this struggle is predestined to end with the victory of good, since God is more powerful than Satan, but in Hinduism the forces of light and darkness will battle eternally, the balance of power shifting in cycles that last thousands of years.

If Hinduism is right, then trying to resist evil is ultimately pointless. The demons (called *asuras* in Sanskrit) never give up. They can't, in fact, since they are built into the structure of nature, where death and decay are inevitable. As the Indian sages see it, the universe depends as much on death as it does on life. "People fear dying without thinking," one master remarked. "If you got your fantasy of living forever, you would be condemning yourself to eternal senility." Because the body breaks down over time, and even the galaxies are heading toward "heat death" when the stars burn out their supply of energy, the universe must contain a mechanism for renewal. Death is the escape route it has devised.

In stage six a person is visionary enough to see this. He still retains a conception of good. It is the force of evolution that lies behind birth, growth, love, truth, and beauty. He also retains a conception of evil. It is the force that opposes evolution—we would call it entropy—leading to decomposition, dissolution, inertia, and "sin" (in the special sense of any action that doesn't help a person's evolution). However, to the visionary these are two sides of the same force. God created both because both are needed; God is in the evil as much as in the good.

One should emphasize that this isn't an ethical viewpoint. You can't argue against it by saying, "Look at this atrocity and that horror. Don't tell me God is there." Every stage of inner growth is an interpretation, and each interpretation is valid. If you see victims of crimes and heartrending injustice, that is real for you, but the saint, even as he brings untold compassion to such people, may not see victims at all. I am reluctant to go too deeply into this, because the grip of victimization is so powerful. To tell the abused and the abuser that they are locked in the same dance is hard to get across—ask any therapist who works with battered women.

I think there is no doubt, however, that the saint sees the sinner inside himself, just as the saint accepts evil as calmly as any other occurrence. It is reported by eyewitnesses that when Father Maximilian was being injected with poison by the Nazis, he used his last ounce of strength to bare his arm willingly to the needle. During those terrible days when he was trapped in a crypt with other prisoners, the concentration camp guards were astonished by the atmosphere of peace created around the Franciscan monk. This story does not mitigate the evil of Nazism, which has to be countered at its own level. But the working out of the soul stands apart, and at some point the dance of good and evil becomes one.

What is my life challenge? . . .
To attain liberation.

When stage six dawns, the purpose of life changes. Instead of striving for goodness and virtue, the person aims to escape bondage. I don't mean escape by dying and going to heaven, although that interpretation certainly is valid for those who hold it. The real escape of stage six is karmic. Karma is infinite and ongoing. Cause and effect never ends; its entanglement is so overwhelming that you could not end even a portion of your personal karma. But God's force field, as we have been calling it, exerts an attraction to pull the soul out of the range of karma. Cause and effect will not be destroyed. The most enlightened saint still has a physical body subject to decay and death; he still eats, drinks, and sleeps. However, all of this energy gets used in a different way.

"If you spent every moment turning every thought and action to good," an Indian master told his disciples, "you would be just as far from enlightenment as someone who used every moment for evil." Surprising as this sounds, for we all equate goodness and God, the force of goodness is still karmic. Good deeds have their own rewards, just as bad deeds do. What if you don't want any reward at all but just to be free? This is the state Buddhists call nirvana, much misunderstood when it is translated as "oblivion."

Nirvana is the release from karmic influences, the end of the dance of opposites. The visionary response enables you to see that wanting A or B is always going to lead to its opposite. If am born wealthy, I may be delighted at first. I can fulfill any desire and follow any whim. But eventually boredom sets in; I will grow restless, and in many cases my life will be burdened by the heavy responsibility of managing my wealth. So as I toss in bed, worried about all these irksome things, I will begin to think how nice it is to be poor. The poor have little to lose; they are free of duties on corporate boards and charities.

However long it takes, according to Buddhism, my mind will eventually desire the opposite of what I have. The karmic pendulum swings until it reaches the extreme of poverty, and then it will pull me back toward wealth again. Since only God is free from cause and effect, to want nirvana means that you want to attain God-realization. In the earlier stages of growth this ambition would be impossible, and most religions condemn it as blasphemy. Nirvana isn't moral. Good and evil don't count anymore, once they are seen as the two faces of the same duality. For the sake of keeping society together, religions hold it as a duty to respect goodness and abhor evil. Hence a paradox: the person who wants to be liberated is acting against God. Many devout Christians find themselves utterly baffled by Eastern spirituality because they cannot resolve this paradox. How can God want us to be good and yet want us to go beyond good?

The answer takes place entirely in consciousness. Saints in every culture turn out to be exemplars of goodness, shining with virtue. But the *Bhaghavad-Gita* informs us that there are no outward signs of enlightenment, which means that saints do not have to obey any conventional standards of behavior. In India there exists the "left-hand path" to God. On this path a devotee shuns conventional virtue and goodness. Sexual abstinence is often replaced with sexual indulgence (usually in a highly ritualized way). One might give up a loving home to live in a graveyard; some tantric devotees go so far as to sleep with corpses and eat the most repulsive decayed food. In other cases the left-hand path is not so extreme, but it is always different from orthodox religious observance.

The left-hand path may seem like the dark side of spirituality, totally deluded in its barbarity and insanity—certainly Christian missionaries to India had no problem holding that interpretation. They shuddered to look upon Kali with her necklace of skulls and blood dripping from her fangs. What kind of mother was this? But the left-hand way is thousands of years old, its origins in sacred texts that exhibit as much wisdom as any in the world. They state that

God cannot be confined in any way. His infinite grace encompasses death and decay; he is in the corpse as well as the newborn baby. For some (very few) people, to see this truth isn't enough; they want to experience it. And God will not deny them. In the West our abhorrence of the left-hand path doesn't need to be challenged. Cultures each go their own way. I wonder, though, what went through Socrates' mind as he drank the cup of hemlock. It is possible, since he willed his own death by refusing to escape the court's sentence, that the poison was sweet to him. And Father Maximilian may have felt bliss when the fatal needle went into his arm. In stage six the alchemy of turning evil into a blessing is a mystery that is solved by longing for liberation.

> *What is my greatest strength?* . . .
> Holiness.

> *What is my biggest hurdle?* . . .
> False idealism.

Skeptics often point out that gullibility increases the more someone needs a miracle. Since miracles are required to prove that a saint is real (at least in Catholicism), there is a tremendous temptation to make one up. In stage six little room is left for any kind of wrongdoing, but in the tiny crevice that is left, a person could lose the distinction between holiness and false idealism. Let me give an example.

In 1531, a native Indian in Mexico was walking on foot toward the settlement of the Spanish conquerors near Mexico City when a beautiful lady appeared to him on the summit of a hill. She gave him a message to take to the bishop and offered her blessing. In awe, the Indian, whose name comes down to us as Juan Diego, did as he was told. When he recounted his vision, the bishop was skeptical, but then one of the most delicate of Christian miracles occurred. Juan Diego opened his rough-woven cloak and out spilled beautiful red roses. At that moment he and the wonder-struck bishop observed that a painting of the Virgin Mother had appeared inside his cloak, which now hangs in a magnificent basilica in Hidalgo, outside Mexico City, on the spot where the miracle of Guadalupe occurred.

As with the Shroud of Turin, skeptics have wanted to run tests on this miraculous image to see if it was painted by human hands. They point out how conveniently this apparition of the Virgin Mary appeared, just when the Spanish were most zealous to convert Indians. (The miracle did lead to mass conversions.) On the face of it, one might say that any event that helped end the slaughter of the Native Americans was a kind of miracle. Yet lost somewhere in history is this distinction between holiness and false idealism.

Holiness is what makes a miracle miraculous; more is needed than simply defying the laws of nature. Illusionists can do that when they throw knives blindfolded or saw a woman in half. As long as you don't know the secret, the illusion is a miracle. In this section I have been speculating on how miracles work, but the deeper secret is why they are holy. The saint isn't a magician. He transforms more than lead into gold; a saint transforms the stuff of the soul. His attitude is one of simplicity and purity. The first American to be canonized as a saint was Frances Cabrini. When she was still an impoverished nun in Italy, Mother Cabrini was praying when another sister broke into her room without knocking.

To her astonishment, the room was filled with a soft radiance. The sister was speechless, but Mother Cabrini remarked offhandedly, "This isn't anything. Just ignore it and go on with what you were doing." From that day on, the saint made sure that her privacy was securely kept, and the only clue for outsiders was a faint light that occasionally crept out underneath her door. It is a mark of the true miracle worker to be comfortable with God's power. Holiness is marked by a selfless innocence—I would like to think that even if the image at Guadalupe is a forgery, at least the roses were real. Trying to be holy is not innocent. It may be well intentioned, but in stage six idealism has no place; only the real thing will do. J. Krishnamurti, during his more than sixty years of spiritual teaching, used to point out something very interesting about happiness. "If you are feeling very happy," he said, "you don't have to speak about it. Happiness is its own thing and needs no words; it doesn't even need to be thought about. But the instant you start to say, 'I am happy,' this innocence is lost. You have created a gap, however small, between yourself and the genuine feeling. So do not think that when you speak of God, you are near him. Your words have created the gap that you must cross to get back to him, and you will never cross it with your mind."

Idealism is born of the mind. In stage six the saint may sing about God and even speak about him, but the holy relationship is so private that nothing can break in on it.

What is my greatest temptation? . . .
Martyrdom.

Are saints tempted to turn into martyrs? In the third century we are told that there was an epidemic of martyrdom in the Roman empire. At that time Christianity was not recognized as an official religion but seen as a cult, which could be prosecuted under the law. (Oddly, it wasn't the worship of Jesus that offended the courts but the fact that Christianity was too new to be lawful.) Those who would not sacrifice to the emperor as a god were sentenced to death, and eager Christians gave up their lives in the arena as proof of their faith.

Traditionally it is held that the martyrs were legion and that they played a huge part in converting the pagan world. Spectators could not believe their eyes when they saw Christians smiling and singing hymns as the lion tore them to pieces. The spectacle shook their confidence in the old gods and helped pave the way for the final victory of the new religion in 313, when it became the official faith of the empire. But tradition strays from the facts in two ways. First, the number of martyrs was probably much smaller than once believed. Most Christians willingly escaped the death sentence by such stratagems as sending a servant to sacrifice to the emperor in their place. Second, one large segment of the faith did not believe in martyrdom. The so-called Gnostics held that God existed entirely within oneself. Father, Son, and Holy Ghost were all aspects of consciousness. Therefore holiness was everywhere, in every person, and the emperor could be as divine as anyone else.

For this and other heresies, the Gnostics were despised and persecuted as soon as the Christian bishops came to power. By wiping them out, the early church installed martyrdom as one of the highest paths to God. Dying for the faith became exalted as imitation of Christ. It must also have set a symbolic pattern in place, for we find such gentle souls as Saint Francis of Assisi enduring the terrible anguish of stigmata. This is the phenomenon whereby one personally undergoes crucifixion by bleeding from the palms and feet like Christ on the cross.

I am not denigrating martyrdom here, only pointing out that stage six is not the end of the journey, not quite yet. As long as suffering holds any temptation, there is some hint of sin, and in that arises the last tiny separation between God and the devotee. The ego retains enough power to say that "I" am proving my holiness to God. In the next stage there will be nothing left to prove and therefore no "I" at all. Getting to that point is the last struggle of the saint. From the outside, we can't quite imagine what it must be like. The wonder of performing miracles should bring enough happiness; to have God inside you must be the highest joy. Yet it isn't. By the smallest hair there is a distance to go. Amazingly, in that fraction of distance an entire world will be created.

STAGE SEVEN:
GOD OF PURE BEING—"I AM"
(Sacred Response)

There is a God who can only be experienced by going beyond experience.

Down below us, the river was as pure as green crystal. The mountain road was winding, so much that I didn't look at the water despite its beauty, for fear of missing our landmark—a door on the side of the cliff. Unlikely though it was, that's what we were told to look for. But what cliff? The Ganges cuts a roaring gorge a hundred miles from its source in the Himalayas, and cliffs were everywhere.

"Wait, I think that's it!" someone cried from the backseat. The last bend in the road had swung us close to the edge of the canyon. Peering over it, one could just spy a narrow dirt trail leading—it was true— to a door in the cliff. We pulled onto the shoulder of the road and the five of us jumped out, scrambling down the trail to find whoever had the key. We had been told to look for an old saint, a bearded ascetic who had lived here for many years. At the end of the track was a rickety hut but no saint inside it, only a teenage monk who politely said that his master wouldn't be available for hours. What about the key? He shook his head. Then we saw that the door to the holy cave was so rotted that the lock had fallen off. Could we go inside, then? He shrugged. "Why not?"

The door was not only unlocked but falling off its hinges. I pulled it open with a creak; inside was a tunnel. We snaked in a line through the darkness, and the tunnel got lower and narrower, like a mine shaft. It seemed to go on for a hundred yards before opening out into a proper cave where you could stand up straight again. We had no lights with us, and only the faintest glimmer of sunlight still penetrated from the outside world.

The teenage monk had exacted a promise of total silence once we entered the cave. Meditation had taken place here for several thousand years, ever since the great sage Vasishtha had stopped by in legendary times. You could feel it immediately. Vasishtha was the tutor to Prince Rama, an awesome duty considering that Rama was a god.

So here we were, not just in a sacred place but in a holy of holies. I have the misfortune of generally missing out on holiness. Many of India's saints strike me with less than wonder, and I have sat through a number of mystical initiations—such as the one where a woman saint opened the sacred spot on the top of my skull to let a stream of air blow out from the crown—without feeling a thing. In this cave, however, I felt that the world was disappearing. After a moment I could hardly remember the winding road above the Ganges; a few minutes more on the cold stone floor with eyes closed, and our whole holiday trip faded away.

This was a good place to meet the God of stage seven, who is known when all else is forgotten. Each person is tied to the world by a thousand invisible threads of mental activity—time, place, identity, and all past experiences. In the dark I began to lose more of these threads. Could I go far enough to forget myself? "Everything about you is a fragment," a guru told his disciples. "Your mind accumulates these fragments from moment to moment. When you think you know something, you refer only to some scrap of the past. Can such a mind ever know the whole? Obviously not."

The God of stage seven is holistic—he encompasses everything. To know him, you would have to possess a mind to match. One day on a walk the philosopher Jean-Jacques Rousseau was kicked unconscious by a horse, and when he came to he found himself in a strange state; it seemed as if the world had no boundaries and he was a speck of consciousness floating in a vast ocean. This "oceanic feeling"—a phrase also used by Freud—was impersonal; Rousseau felt fused with everything—the earth, the sky, everyone around him. He felt ecstatic and free in that state, which quickly passed and yet left a strong impression that haunted him for the rest of his life.

In Vasishtha's cave, individuals have sought the same feeling for millennia, and so was I. This involved nothing I was consciously doing. It was more like a memory lapse. Everyone's mind is like an automated wake-up device in a hotel, which never stops sending its reminders. Mine churns with a thousand scraps of memory related to who I am. Some are about my family or my job, others are about the car and the house, the plane tickets, the luggage, the half-empty gas tank—the whole tapestry of life that somehow doesn't add up to a whole.

As my mind revolves and buzzes with this data, it keeps assuring me that I am real. Why do I need this assurance? No one asks this question as long as the world is with us. We blend into the scenery and accept its reality. But put anyone in Vasishtha's cave and the bits and pieces of identity will stop coming up so much. The glitter of memory ceases its dazzling flicker and then you cut to the chase . . . which is?

Nothing. A void with no activity. God.

To find God in an empty room—to find the *ultimate* God in an empty room—is the experience that miracle workers sacrifice all their powers for. In place of the highest ecstasy, one gets emptiness. The God of stage seven is so intangible that he can be defined by no qualities. Nothing remains to hold on to. In the ancient Indian tradition, they define this aspect of spirit only by negation. In stage seven God is

Unborn
Undying

Unchanging
Unmoving
Unmanifest
Immeasurable
Invisible
Intangible
Infinite

This God cannot be thought of even as a great light, and therefore to many Westerners he may seem like death. But "lifeless" isn't one of the negatives that describe him. The empty void contains the potential for all life and all experience. The one positive quality that can be attached to God in stage seven is existence, or pure being. No matter how blank the void gets, it still exists, and that is enough to give birth to the universe.

The mystery of stage seven is that nothingness can mask infinity. If we had jumped to this stage at the outset, proving the reality of such a God would not have been possible. You have to climb the spiritual ladder from one rung to the next. Now that we are high enough to view the whole landscape, it's time to kick the ladder away. No support at all, not even the mind, is needed.

For stage seven to be real, there must be a corresponding response in the brain. Subjectively we know that there is, because in every age people report the experience of unity, in which the observer collapses into the observed. In cases of autism a patient may blend so completely into the world that he has to cling to a tree to make sure that it exists; the poet Wordsworth had just this experience as a child. He referred to "spots of time" in which an unearthly sensation made him feel suspended in immortality. In those moments he still existed, but not as a creature of time and place.

Brain researchers have caught epileptic seizures on their scans, another instance where patients report unearthly feelings and losing identity. But such examples do not account for the sacred response, as I will call it. Altered brain waves and subjective reports do not capture the mind's ability to comprehend wholeness. Objectively this state goes beyond miracles in that the person does nothing to affect reality except look at it, yet in that looking the laws of nature shift more profoundly than in miracles.

Let me hasten to give an example. Recently a paranormal investigator named Marilyn Schlitz wanted to test if anything like second sight was real. Schlitz chose the phenomenon of just turning around to discover that you were being watched from behind, which she called "covert observation." She took a group of subjects and looked at them through a video camera in another room. By turning the camera off and on, she could test whether each person was aware of being watched, even with the observer not physically present. Rather than relying upon subjective guesses, she used an instrument resembling a lie detector; it measured even the faintest changes in the skin's response to electrical current.

The experiment was a success—up to two-thirds of the subjects showed changes in skin conductivity while being observed from a distance. Schlitz announced the success of her experiment, only to find that another researcher who tried to duplicate it failed miserably. He used exactly the same methods, but in his laboratory almost no one responded with second sight; they couldn't tell the difference between being watched and not being watched. Schlitz was baffled but confident enough to invite the second researcher to come to her lab. The two of them ran the experiment again, choosing subjects at the last moment to ensure that there was no tampering.

Again Schlitz obtained her results, but when she consulted her colleague, he had obtained nothing. This was an extraordinary moment. How could two people run the same objective test with such dramatically different results? The only viable answer, as Schlitz saw it, must lie in the researcher himself. The outcome depended on *who you are*. As far as I know, this is as close as anyone has come to verifying that observer and observation can collapse into one. This fusion lies at the heart of the sacred response, because in unity all separation ends.

We have other clues to the reality of this response, some negative and some positive. The negative clues center on the "shyness syndrome," in which strange phenomena refuse to be photographed. Everything from ghosts to the bending of keys to UFO abductions are attested to by people who have no trouble passing lie-detector tests, yet when the time comes to photograph these phenomena, they don't show up. Positive clues come from experiments like the classic ones performed at the Princeton engineering department in the 1970s, where subjects were asked to stare at a machine that randomly spit out zeros and ones (known as a random number generator). Their task was to use their minds to sway the machine to generate more ones than zeros, or vice versa. No one touched the machine or changed its software program.

The results were surprising. Using nothing but focused attention, most people could in fact significantly influence the outcome. Instead of spewing out exactly equal numbers of zeros and ones, the machine skewed 5 percent or more away from randomness. The reason that Schlitz's test goes even further is that she *wanted* a random trial in the interest of being unbiased, but she got skewed results anyway, depending on who was running the test.

The sacred response is the last step in this direction. It supports the notion that there is no observer separate from the observation. Everything around us is the product of who we are. In stage seven you no longer project God; you project everything, which is the same as being in the movie, outside the movie, and the movie itself. In unity consciousness no separation is left. We no longer create God in our image, not even the faintest image of a holy ghost.

Who am I? . . .
The source.

A person who reaches stage seven is so free of attachment that if you ask, "Who are you?" the only answer is: "I am." This is the very answer that Jehovah gave Moses in the book of Exodus when he spoke from the burning bush. Moses was herding sheep on the side of a mountain when God appeared. He was awestruck but also troubled that no one would believe him about talking with God. If Moses was going to be a holy messenger, at least he needed God's name, but when asked what it was, God replied, "I am that I am."

To equate God with existence seems to strip him of power and majesty and knowledge. But our quantum model tells us otherwise. At the virtual level there is no energy, time, or space. This apparent void, however, is the source of everything measurable as energy, time, and space, just as a blank mind is the source of all thoughts. Sir Isaac Newton believed that the universe was literally God's blank mind, and all of the stars and galaxies were his thoughts.

If God has a home, it has to be in the void. Otherwise he would be limited. Can we really know such a boundless deity? In stage seven two impossible things must converge. The person has to be reduced to the merest point, a speck of identity closing the last minuscule gap between himself and God. At the same time, just when separation is healed, the tiny point has to expand to infinity. The mystics describe this as "the

One becomes All." To put it into scientific terms, when you cross into the quantum zone, space-time collapses into itself. The tiniest thing in existence merges with the greatest; point and infinity are equal.

If you can get the skeptical mind to believe in this state (which isn't easy) the obvious question is "So what?" The process really does sound like dying, because no matter how you approach it, one must give up the known world to attain stage seven. The miracle worker in stage six is already detached, but he retains inner joy and whatever faint intentions that motivate him to perform his miracles. In stage seven there is no joy, compassion, light, or truth. The end of the chase is the ultimate gamble. You don't play for all or nothing; you play for all *and* nothing.

The problem with models is that they are always inadequate; they select a portion of reality and leave the rest behind. How do you find a model for All and Nothing? The Chinese called it the Tao, meaning the offstage presence that gives the world life, shape, purpose, and flow. Rumi uses the same image:

There is someone who looks after us
From behind the curtain.
In truth we are not here
This is our shadow.

In stage seven you go behind the screen and join whoever is there. This is the source. The spiritual journey takes you to the place where you began as a soul, a mere point of consciousness, naked and undressed of qualities. This source is yourself. "I am" is what you can say to describe it, just as God did. To imagine what it feels like in stage seven, be with me in Vasishtha's cave. As I forgot everything else, I didn't forget to be. In that unattached state there is nothing to hold on to as a label or description:

- You don't think about time. A God of pure being is *unborn* and *undying*.
- You have no desire to pursue anything. A God of pure being is *unchanging*.
- Stillness envelops you. A God of pure being is *unmoving*.
- Nothing in your mind comes to the surface. A God of pure being is *unmanifest*.
- You can't locate yourself with the five senses. A God of pure being is *invisible* and *intangible*.
- You seem to be nowhere and everywhere at once. A God of pure being is *infinite*.

Common sense tells us that if you take away all qualities, nothing is left, and nothing doesn't seem very useful. Even when people can be talked into giving up pleasure because, as the Buddha argued, it is always tied to pain, most Westerners go away and take up pleasure again. The argument for stage seven has to be made in more persuasive ways. First of all, no one forces this final realization upon you. Second, it doesn't wipe out ordinary existence—you still eat, drink, walk, and act out desires. But now the desires do not belong to anyone; they are remnants of who you used to be. So who did you use to be?

The answer is karma. Until you become pure being, your identity is wrapped up in a cycle of desires that lead to actions, every action leaves an impression, and impressions give rise to new desires. (When the potato chip commercial says, "Bet you can't eat just one," the mechanism of desire-action-impression is at work.) This cycle is the classic interpretation of karma. Everyone is caught up in it, for the simple reason that we all desire things. What is wrong with that? The great sages point out that nothing is wrong with karma except that it isn't real. If you watch a puppy chasing its tail, you see pure karma. The puppy is absorbed, but it isn't getting anywhere. The tail is always just out of reach, and even if the animal snaps it in his jaws, the pain will make him let go again, starting the chase all over. Karma means always wanting more of what won't get you anywhere in the first place. In stage seven you realize this and no longer chase after phantoms. Now you end up at the source, which is pure being.

How do I fit in? . . .
I am.

Once the adventure of soul-searching is over, things calm down. The state of "I am" forgoes pain and pleasure. Because all desire is centered on pain and pleasure, it comes as a surprise to find out that what I wanted all along was just to be. There are many kinds of worthwhile lives to lead. Is it worthwhile to lead the life of "I am"? In stage seven you include all the previous stages. Therefore you can live any way you want. By analogy, think of the world as a movie that includes everything; you cannot tell in any way that it is a movie; therefore, everyone behaves as if the scenario is real.

If you suddenly woke up and realized that nothing around you was real, what would you do? First of all, certain things would happen involuntarily. You wouldn't be able to take other people's dramas seriously. The smallest irritants and the greatest tragedies, a pebble in your shoe and World War II, become equally unreal. Your detachment might set you apart, but you could keep it to yourself.

Motivation would also vanish, because there's nothing to achieve in a dreamworld. Poverty is as good as a million dollars when it's all play money. Emotional attachments would also drop away, since no one's personality is real anymore. After you consider all these changes, not much choice is left. The end of illusion is the end of experience as we know it. What do you receive in exchange? Only reality, pure and unvarnished.

In India they tell a fable about this: There was once a great devotee of Vishnu who prayed night and day to see his God. One night his wish was granted and Vishnu appeared to him. Falling on his knees, the devotee cried out, "I will do anything for you, my Lord, just ask."

"How about a drink of water?" Vishnu replied.

Although surprised by the request, the devotee immediately ran to the river as fast as his legs could carry him. When he got there and knelt to dip up some water, he saw a beautiful woman standing on an island in the middle of the river. The devotee fell madly in love on the spot. He grabbed a boat and rowed over to her. She responded to him, and the two were married. They had children in a house on the island; the devotee grew rich and old plying his trade as a merchant. Many years later, a typhoon came along and devastated the island. The merchant was swept away in the storm. He nearly drowned but regained consciousness on the very spot where he had once begged to see God. His whole life, including his house, wife, and children, seemed never to have happened.

Suddenly he looked over his shoulder, only to see Vishnu standing there in all his radiance.

"Well," Vishnu said, "did you find me a glass of water?"

The moral of the story is that you shouldn't pay so much attention to the movie. In stage seven there is a shift of balance; one starts to notice the unchanging much more than the changing. In the Sermon on the Mount Jesus called this "storing up treasure in heaven." But again analogies fail. Stage seven isn't a prize or reward for making right choices; it is the realization of what you always have been. If someone asks

"Who are you?" every answer is misleading except "I am"—which means that we are all misled, even the miracle workers. We are the victims of mistaken identity. Our time has been spent projecting versions of reality, including versions of God, that are inadequate.

How do I find God? . . .
By transcending.

Whatever it takes to get beyond illusion and back to reality, it's a bumpy landing when you get there. In fact, those few yogis and sages who have spoken about entering stage seven report that their first reaction was one of total loss. The comfort of illusion was stripped away. These are people who had reveled in ecstasy, miracles, deep insight, and intimacy with God. Yet those experiences too were misleading. Leaving all of it behind, at a deeper level they now knew that something good had happened. Like sloughing off an old skin, they transcended to a new life and a new level of existence because the old life had simply withered.

Transcending is going beyond. In spiritual terms it also means growing up. "When I was no longer a child, I put aside childish things," writes Saint Paul. By analogy, even karma can be outgrown and put aside. Here is the argument for that: Two ultimate realities vie for our approval. One is karma, the reality of actions and desires. Karma is played out in the material world, forcing us to run on the same treadmill over and over. The other reality that claims to be ultimate has no action in it; it just is. This reality is exemplified by the open, detached, peaceful state of deep meditation. Few people accept it, and those who do generally stay outside society as renunciates and ascetics.

However, to see yourself caught between two choices is false. "Ultimate reality" means the one and only; the winner swallows up the loser. So if you put your money on the loser, you have made a mistake that will cost you dearly. Eventually you will see that you have bought shadow for substance; your desires were ghostly wisps leading you down wrong paths. As one Vedic master put it, "The world of karma is infinite, but you will discover that it is a boring infinity. The other infinity is never boring."

The reason, then, to return to the source derives from self-interest. I don't want to be bored; I don't want to come to the end of the chase and wind up empty-handed. Here all metaphors and analogies end, because just as a dream gets exposed as illusion when you wake up, so Being eventually unmasks karma. Strip away the unreal and by definition all that remains must be real. The soul's journey isn't a game, a chase, or a gamble. It follows a predetermined course toward the moment of waking up.

Along the way tiny moments of waking up foreshadow the final event. I might be able to illustrate this through a story. When I was ten our family lived in the hill station of Shillong, within reach of the Himalayas, and my father had an aide called Baba Sahib who cleaned his shoes and washed his clothes. Baba was a Muslim and a strong believer in the supernatural. Whenever he went down to the *dhobi ghat*, or wash place by the river, he pounded the clothes next to a cemetery. Baba was certain that ghosts inhabited the place and proved it by hanging the wet clothes on the gravestones. If they dried in less than half an hour, Baba knew that a ghost would be seen in the cemetery that night.

To prove it, he sneaked me out of the house and told me a story about a mother and child who were the primary haunters, both dying young under tragic circumstances. The two of us sat among the graves for two hours, I grew sleepy and afraid at the same time, but as we were leaving, Baba pointed in the distance.

"See—see there?" he cried.

And I did see—two pale apparitions floated above one of the gravestones. I rushed home in great excitement and told no one. After a day the secret was too hard to keep, so I told the safest person in the house, my grandmother. "Do you think I just imagined it?" I asked, hoping she would either confirm my vision or be amazed by it.

"What does it matter?" she said with a shrug. "The whole universe is imagined. Your ghosts are just as real as that."

At its source, the cosmos is equally real and unreal. The only way I have of knowing anything is through the neurons firing in my brain, and although they might take me to such a fine degree of perception that I could see every photon inside my cortex, at that point the cortex dissolves into photons as well. So the observer and the thing he is trying to observe merge, which is exactly how the chase after God also ends.

What is the nature of good and evil? . . .
Good is the union of all opposites.
Evil no longer exists.

The shadow of evil stalks behind goodness up to the last moment. Only when it is totally absorbed into unity does the threat

of evil end once and for all. The story of
Jesus reaches its poignant climax in the garden of Gethsemane, when he prays that the
cup be taken from his hands. He knows that
the Romans are going to capture and kill
him, and the prospect gives rise to a terrible
moment of doubt. It is one of the loneliest
and most wrenching moments in the New
Testament—and it is utterly imaginary.

The text itself tells us that Jesus had
walked apart from everyone else and that his
disciples had fallen asleep. Therefore no one
could have overheard what he said, particularly if he was praying. I think that this last
temptation was projected onto him by writers of the gospel. Why? Because they
couldn't conceive of his situation except
through their own. They viewed Christ
across a gap, the same gap that keeps us from
imagining how all fear, temptation, sin, evil,
and imperfection could be transcended. Yet
this is what happens in stage seven.

Religions have a hard time being funny,
and in the Middle Ages people didn't see
much humor in the soul's journey. They
were too aware of death, disease, Satan's
temptations, and the many woes in this vale
of tears. The church underscored these
horrors, and about the only escape was on
holidays when a rough plank stage was

erected outside the cathedral. Upon it miracle plays were performed, and then Satan wasn't so frightening because he could be played as a clown. The same people who trembled at the prospect of sin now witnessed the devil taking pratfalls. In those moments, the church was teaching a new lesson: evil itself must be redeemed. History comes to an end here on earth when Satan is accepted back into heaven; then the triumph of God becomes complete.

On the personal level, you can't afford to have the last laugh until stage seven. As long as the mind is caught up in choices, some are going to turn out worse than others. We all equate pain with evil, and as a sensation, pain doesn't end; it is part of our biological inheritance. The only way to get beyond it is to transcend, and that is accomplished by attaining a higher point of view. In stage seven all versions of the world are seen as projections, and a projection is nothing more than a point of view that has come to life. The highest point of view, then, would encompass anything that happens, without preference and without rejection.

I was starkly confronted by this possibility on two occasions when evil stood on my doorstep. The first occurred in the early 1970s when I was a struggling resident living in a seedy part of Boston. My wife had gone out, leaving me in charge of our infant daughter. It was getting late when the door to our apartment flew open, and a very big, menacing man strode in. He didn't say anything. My head swiveled around, and before I was even aware that he was carrying a baseball bat, I jumped up and grabbed it. Neither of us spoke. In less than a second I had swung the bat and hit him on the head, knocking him unconscious. A few seconds later my heart was pounding with adrenaline, but at the instant I acted, I wasn't myself—the action didn't belong to me.

Naturally a great deal of turmoil resulted, and when the police arrived it was quickly discovered that the man was a released felon with a history of assault and suspected murder. I had acted perfectly correctly, even though at a conscious level I have a strong commitment to nonviolence.

But the story isn't complete. Two years ago I had just finished a lecture in a southern city and happened to exit from the hall by a back door into an alley. This looked like the shortest route back to my hotel, but waiting for me were three gang youths. One pulled a gun and held it to my temple. When he demanded my wallet, I suddenly knew what to say.

"Look, I can give you my bills but not my credit cards," I told him in a calm voice, holding out the money. "You don't want to shoot me over two hundred dollars. That would be murder, and it will follow you the rest of your life. So just drop your weapon and go, okay?"

It amazed me to be saying these words; it was as though I were standing there watching myself. The youth's hand was shaking, and the three of them looked undecided. All at once I shouted, "Go!" at the top of my lungs. The gun fell at my feet, and the three of them ran away.

Two scenes of evil, two different reactions. I offer them as evidence that something inside us already transcends the present situation. Where we see the play of opposites, our inner awareness takes every moment as unique. I haven't told quite the whole story about the second incident. In my bargaining, I also promised the youths that I would not tell the police, and I never did. One act of potential violence was met with violence, the other with pacifism. I can't explain my choices except to say that they weren't chosen. The actions performed themselves. Justice was served in both cases, acted out from beyond my limited point of view. In stage seven a person realizes that it isn't up to us to balance the scales; if we hand our choices over to God, we are free to act as the impulse moves us, knowing its source is divine unity.

What is my life challenge? . . .
To be myself.

Nothing would seem easier than to be yourself, but people complain endlessly about how hard it is. When you are little your parents won't let you be yourself. They have different ideas about eating the whole chocolate cake or drawing on the walls with crayons. Later on teachers keep you from being yourself. Then teenage peer pressure takes over, and finally, once society has imposed its demands, freedom is more restricted still. Alone on a desert island you might be able to be yourself, only guilt and shame would pursue you even there. The inheritance of repression is inescapable.

The whole problem is one of boundaries and resistance. Someone imposes a limit on you, and you resist it in order to break free. Thus "being myself" becomes a relative thing. Unless someone tells me what I can't do, I have nothing to push against. By implication, my life would be shapeless. I would follow one whim after another, which itself is a kind of prison. To have a hundred wives and a feast on the table isn't being yourself, it is being your desires.

In stage seven the problem comes to an end as boundaries and resistance both melt. To be in unity, you cannot have limitations. You are wholeness; that is what fills your perception. Choice A and choice B are equal in your eyes. When this is true, desire can flow where it will. Sometimes you get to eat the whole cake, have the hundred wives, and walk on the grass. But being deprived of these fulfillments is just as good. I am not my desires. Being myself no longer has the slightest outside reference.

Doesn't this deprive me of choice? Both yes and no. In stage seven there are still preferences. A person will want to dress and talk a certain way; there may even be decided likes and dislikes. Yet these are karmic holdovers from the past. Because I speak English and Hindi, come from a doctor's family, do a lot of traveling, and write books, those influences could well persist into stage seven. But they would recede into the background, turning into the wallpaper of my real existence, which is simply to be.

How would I be able to tell that such a state is real? The skeptic who looks at stage seven would claim that unity is just a form of self-deception. All this talk about All and Nothing doesn't erase the necessities of this world, and in fact the greatest mystics do preserve the trappings of ordinary life. The problem of self-deception seems trickier still when you realize that the ego, in its need to continue as the center of all activity, has no trouble pretending to gain enlightenment.

One is reminded of the story of the saffron monk: A young man in India used to attend a discussion group with his friends. They considered themselves to be serious seekers, and their discussions ran to esoteric subjects about the soul, the existence of an afterlife, and so on.

One night the talk grew very heated and the young man stepped outside for some air. When he returned to the room, he saw a monk in saffron robes sitting off to the side. No one else in the room seemed to notice this. The young man took his place, saying nothing. The arguments continued in loud voices, but still the monk sat silently and no one took any notice. It was after midnight when the young man got up to go; to his surprise the saffron monk got up and followed. For the entire walk home in the moonlight the monk kept him company, and when the young man woke up the next morning, the monk was waiting by the bed in the young man's room.

Perhaps because he was so spiritual, this vision didn't frighten the young man or make him fear for his sanity. He was delighted to have the peaceful presence of the monk around him. For the next week they remained constant companions, despite the fact that no one else saw anything. Eventually the young man had to tell his story to someone; he chose the teacher J. Krishnamurti (from whose writings I got the story).

"First of all, this vision means everything to me," the young man began. "But I'm not the kind of person who needs symbols and images to worship. I reject religion—only Buddhism ever interested me because of its purity, but even there I didn't find enough to make me want to follow it."

"I understand," Krishnamurti said. "So what is your question?"

"I want to know if this figure is real or just a figment of my mind. I have to know the truth."

"You said it has brought you a great deal of meaning?"

The young man grew enthusiastic. "I have undergone a profound transformation. I feel joyful and at peace."

"Is the monk with you now?" Krishnamurti asked. The young man nodded, but hesitantly.

"To be quite honest," he said, "the monk is starting to fade. He is not so vivid as at first."

"Are you afraid of losing him?"

Anxiety showed in the young man's face. "What do you mean? I came here wanting the truth, but I don't want you to take him away. Don't you realize how this vision has consumed me? In order to have peace and joy, I think about this vision, and they come to me."

Krishnamurti replied, "Living in the past, however pleasant and uplifting, prevents the experience of *what is*. The mind finds it difficult not to live in a thousand yesterdays. Take this figure you cherish. The memory of it inspires you, delights you, and gives you a sense of release. But it is only the dead inspiring the living."

The young man looked crestfallen and glum. "So it wasn't real after all?"

"The mind is complicated," said Krishnamurti. "It gets conditioned by the past and by how it would like things to be. Does it really matter if this figure is real or projected?"

"No," the young man admitted. "It only matters that it has shown me so much."

"Has it? It didn't reveal to you the working of your own mind, and you became a prisoner of your experience. If I may say so, this vision brought fear into your life because you were afraid to lose it. Greed also came in because you wanted to hoard the experience. Thus you lost the one thing this vision might have brought you: self-knowledge. Without that, every experience is an illusion."

I find this a beautiful and moving tale, worth recounting at length. Before stage seven the full value of being yourself isn't known. Experience can be shaped to bring great inspiration. But in the end this isn't enough. Every divine image remains an image; every vision tempts us to hold on to it. To be really free, there is no option except to be yourself. You are the living center around which every event happens, yet no event is so important that you willingly give yourself up to it. By being yourself you open the door to *what is*, the never-ending play of cosmic intelligence curving back to know itself again and again. In this way life remains fresh and fulfills its need to renew itself at every moment.

What is my greatest strength? . . .
Unity.

What is my biggest hurdle? . . .
Duality.

Like every other stage, this one must ripen. Many people have had flashes of unity, but that isn't the same as living there permanently. A flash of unity can feel like bleeding into the scenery, but unlike autism, which can make a child lose the boundary of identity, the experience is positive—the self expands and achieves a higher vision. Instead of needing to intuit anything, you simply are that thing. Stage seven brings the ultimate form of empathy.

The opposite of unity is duality. Currently two dominant versions of reality are believed by almost everyone. Version one: there is only the material world, and nothing can be real that doesn't obey physical laws. Version two: two realities exist, the earthly and the divine.

Version one is called the secular view, and even religious people adopt it for everyday use. Yet total belief in materialism, as we have seen, has become unacceptable for a host of reasons. It cannot explain credible, witnessed miracles, near-death experiences, out-of-body experiences, the testimony of millions of people who have had answered prayers, and most convincing of all, the discovery of the quantum world, which doesn't obey any ordinary physical laws.

The second version of reality is less rigid. It allows for spiritual experience and miracles, which exist on the fringes of the material world. At this moment someone is hearing the voice of God, witnessing the Virgin Mary, or going into the light. These experiences still leave the material world intact and essentially untouched. You can have God and a Mercedes at the same time, each on its own level. In other words, there is duality.

Many religions, Christianity being a prime example, declare that God sits in heaven, unapproachable except by faith, prayer, death, or the intervention of saints. Yet this dualism falls apart once we heal the divisions between body, mind, and spirit. Duality is another word for separation, and in the state of separation, many illusions crop up. Steam and ice, sunlight and electricity, bone and blood are examples of things that seem totally different until you know the laws of transformation, which turn one form into another. This holds true for body and soul as well. In separation they cannot be more different, until you find the laws that transform invisible, immortal, uncreated spirit into flesh.

In India there has been a strong nondual tradition for thousands of years, known as Vedanta. The word literally means "the end of the Vedas," the point where no sacred texts can help you anymore, where teaching stops and awareness dawns. "How do you know God is real?" a disciple once asked his guru.

The guru replied, "I look around and see the natural order of creation. There is tremendous beauty in the simplest things. One feels alive and awake before the infinite majesty of the cosmos, and the deeper one looks, the more astounding this creation is. What more is needed?"

"But none of that proves anything," the disciple protested.

The guru shook his head. "You only say that because you aren't truly looking. If you could see a mountain or a rain cloud for one minute without your doubts blocking the way, the evidence of God would be revealed instantly."

"Then tell me what is revealed," the disciple insisted. "After all, I have the same eyes as you."

"Something simple, undivided, unborn, eternal, solid as stone, boundless, independent, invulnerable, blissful, and all-knowing," the guru replied.

The disciple felt a rush of despair. "You see all that? Then I will give up, for I can't possibly learn to perceive such a wonder."

"No, you are wrong," the guru said. "We all see eternity in every direction, but we choose to cut it into bits and pieces of time and space. There is one quality of the All that should give you hope. It wants to share."

If the divine mind wants to share itself with us and we are willing to accept, then the stage is set for unity. The main tenet of Vedanta is extremely simple—duality is too weak to stand forever. Take any sin or delusion, and in time it will come to an end. Take any pleasure, and in time it will start to pall. Take any depth of sleep, and in time you have to wake up. In Vedanta they say that the only real thing is eternal bliss consciousness *(sat chit ananda)*. These words promise that the timeless waits for me when the temporary expires, bliss outlives pleasure, and being awake comes after sleep. In that simplicity the whole notion of duality collapses, revealing the unity behind all illusion.

What is my greatest temptation? . . .
Beyond temptation.

You can't be tempted when you have it all. It is even better when they can't take it away from you. Vedanta is expressed in a famous saying, "I am That, You are That, and All this is That." When the ancient sages refer to "That," they are referring to an invisible but quite real power. It is the power of existence. You have it forever when you can say, "I am that power, you are that power, and everything around us is that power." Other words like grace, godhead, the light, alpha and omega work just as well—yet none of them equals the experience, which is very personal and totally universal at the same time.

The sage Vasishtha was one of the first human beings to realize that we experience only the world we filter through our minds. Whatever I can imagine is a product of my life experience so far, and that is the tiniest fragment of what I could know. As Vasishtha himself wrote:

Infinite worlds come and go
in the vast expanse of consciousness,
like motes of dust dancing in a beam of
*   light.*

This is a reminder that if the material world is just a product of my awareness, so is heaven. I have every right, therefore, to try to know the mind of God. A journey that begins in mystery and silence ends with myself.

In the holy cave I visited above the Ganges, only at the last moment did I get a hint that someone else was sharing the place with us. Our group was lost in the vast silence that blossomed there. It had become evident without a doubt that God existed, not as a person but as an infinite intelligence moving at infinite speed through infinite dimensions, a creator modern physics could come to terms with as well. But at that moment none of us had any thoughts. We got up to go, and in the dimness we sensed that we weren't alone. Peering into the gloom, we made out the faint shape of another person who had been there all the time—it was the old saint who couldn't meet us with the key when we arrived. Sitting in lotus position, he hadn't stirred when we entered and didn't stir now.

We left quietly, and as we emerged into the blinding daylight, what we had shared started to fade. My mind began churning again. Words that first sounded like harsh cymbal clashes became normal within a few minutes. The usual distractions grabbed hold. But some flavor of that cave remained with me for weeks in the form of a quiet certainty that nothing was ever going to go wrong again. This is not nearly the same as being unborn, eternal, hard as stone, boundless, invulnerable, blissful, and all-knowing. Yet I am closer to it, nearer to the source. For once my mind jumped off the ledge of everyday life and landed in a good place, where struggle isn't necessary, I opened the door on the side of eternity. Now I can fully appreciate Rumi's words:

> *When I die I shall soar with angels,*
> *And when I die to the angels, what I shall*
>   *become,*
> *You cannot imagine.*

GOD IS AS WE ARE

WHO IS GOD?

Stage One: Fight-or-Flight Response:
God the Protector
  Vengeful
  Capricious
  Quick to anger
  Jealous
  Judgmental—meting out reward and
    punishment
  Unfathomable
  Sometimes merciful
Stage Two: Reactive Response:
God the Almighty
  Sovereign
  Omnipotent
  Just
  Answerer of prayers
  Impartial
  Rational
  Organized into rules

Stage Three: Restful Awareness
Response: God of Peace
    Detached
    Calm
    Offering consolation
    Undemanding
    Conciliatory
    Silent
    Meditative
Stage Four: Intuitive Response:
God the Redeemer
    Understanding
    Tolerant
    Forgiving
    Nonjudgmental
    Inclusive
    Accepting
Stage Five: Creative Response:
God the Creator
    Unlimited creative potential
    Control over space and time
    Abundant
    Open
    Generous
    Willing to be known
    Inspired

Stage Six: Visionary Response:
God of Miracles
  Transformative
  Mystical
  Enlightened
  Beyond all causes
  Existing
  Healing
  Magical
  Alchemist
Stage Seven: Sacred Response:
God of Pure Being—"I Am"
  Unborn
  Undying
  Unchanging
  Unmoving
  Unmanifest
  Immeasurable
  Invisible
  Intangible
  Infinite

WHAT KIND OF WORLD
DID GOD CREATE?

Stage 1: Fight-or-Flight Response:
   World of bare survival
Stage 2: Reactive Response:
   World of competition and ambition
Stage 3: Restful Awareness Response:
   World of inner solitude, self-
   sufficiency
Stage 4: Intuitive Response:
   World of insight, personal growth
Stage 5: Creative Response:
   World of art, invention,
   discovery
Stage 6: Visionary Response:
   World of prophets, sages, and seers
Stage 7: Sacred Response:
   Transcendent world

WHO AM I?

Stage 1: Fight-or-Flight Response:
   A survivor
Stage 2: Reactive Response:
   Ego, personality
Stage 3: Restful Awareness Response:
   Silent witness
Stage 4: Intuitive Response:
   Knower within
Stage 5: Creative Response:
   Co-creator
Stage 6: Visionary Response:
   Enlightened awareness
Stage 7: Sacred Response:
   The source

HOW DO I FIT IN?

Stage 1: Fight-or-Flight Response:
   I cope.
Stage 2: Reactive Response: I win.
Stage 3: Restful Awareness Response:
   I stay centered.
Stage 4: Intuitive Response:
   I understand.
Stage 5: Creative Response: I intend.
Stage 6: Visionary Response: I love.
Stage 7: Sacred Response: I am.

HOW DO I FIND GOD?

Stage 1: Fight-or-Flight Response:
   Fear, loving devotion

Stage 2: Reactive Response:
   Awe, obedience

Stage 3: Restful Awareness Response:
   Meditation, silent contemplation

Stage 4: Intuitive Response:
   Self-acceptance

Stage 5: Creative Response:
   Inspiration

Stage 6: Visionary Response: Grace

Stage 7: Sacred Response:
   By transcending

WHAT IS THE NATURE
OF GOOD AND EVIL?

Stage 1: Fight-or-Flight Response
> Good is safety, comfort, food, shelter and family.
> Evil is physical threat and abandonment.

Stage 2: Reactive Response
> Good is getting what you want.
> Evil is any obstacle to getting what you want.

Stage 3: Restful Awareness Response
> Good is clarity, inner calm, and contact with the self.
> Evil is inner turmoil and chaos.

Stage 4: Intuitive Response
> Good is clarity, seeing the truth.
> Evil is blindness, denying the truth.

Stage 5: Creative Response
> Good is higher consciousness.
> Evil is lower consciousness.

Stage 6: Visionary Response
> Good is a cosmic force.
> Evil is another aspect of the same force.

Stage 7: Sacred Response
> Good is the union of all opposites.
> Evil no longer exists.

WHAT IS MY LIFE CHALLENGE?

Stage 1: Fight-or-Flight Response:
   To survive, protect, and maintain
Stage 2: Reactive Response:
   Maximum achievement
Stage 3: Restful Awareness Response:
   To be engaged and detached
Stage 4: Intuitive Response:
   To go beyond duality
Stage 5: Creative Response:
   To align with the Creator
Stage 6: Visionary Response:
   To attain liberation
Stage 7: Sacred Response:
   To be myself

WHAT IS MY GREATEST STRENGTH?

Stage 1: Fight-or-Flight Response: Courage

Stage 2: Reactive Response: Accomplishment

Stage 3: Restful Awareness Response: Autonomy

Stage 4: Intuitive Response: Insight

Stage 5: Creative Response: Imagination

Stage 6: Visionary Response: Holiness

Stage 7: Sacred Response: Unity

WHAT IS MY BIGGEST HURDLE?

Stage 1: Fight-or-Flight Response: Fear of loss, abandonment

Stage 2: Reactive Response: Guilt, victimization

Stage 3: Restful Awareness Response: Fatalism

Stage 4: Intuitive Response: Delusion

Stage 5: Creative Response: Self-importance

Stage 6: Visionary Response: False idealism

Stage 7: Sacred Response: Duality

WHAT IS MY GREATEST TEMPTATION?

Stage 1: Fight-or-Flight Response:
Tyranny

Stage 2: Reactive Response: Addiction

Stage 3: Restful Awareness Response:
Introversion

Stage 4: Intuitive Response:
Deception

Stage 5: Creative Response: Solipsism

Stage 6: Visionary Response:
Martyrdom

Stage 7: Sacred Response:
Beyond temptation

GETTING WHAT YOU WANT
The Seven Levels of Fulfillment

God is another name for infinite intelligence. To achieve anything in life, a piece of this intelligence must be contacted and used. In other words, *God is always there for you.* The seven responses of the human brain are avenues to attain some aspect of God. Each level of fulfillment proves God's reality *at that level.*

Level 1 (Fight-or-Flight Response)
You fulfill your life through family, community, a sense of belonging, and material comforts.

Level 2 (Reactive Response)
You fulfill your life through success, power, influence, status, and other ego satisfactions.

Level 3 (Restful Awareness Response)
You fulfill your life through peace, centeredness, self-acceptance, and inner silence.

Level 4 (Intuitive Response)
You fulfill your life through insight, empathy, tolerance, and forgiveness.

Level 5 (Creative Response)
You fulfill your life through inspiration, expanded creativity in art or science, and unlimited discovery.

Level 6 (Visionary Response)
You fulfill your life through reverence, compassion, devoted service, and universal love.

Level 7 (Sacred Response)
You fulfill your life through wholeness and unity with the divine.

The Seven Levels of Miracles

A miracle is a display of power from beyond the five senses. Although all miracles take place in the transition zone, they differ from level to level. In general, miracles become more "supernatural" after the fourth or fifth brain response, but any miracle involves direct contact with spirit.

Level 1 (Fight-or-Flight Response)
Miracles involve surviving great danger, impossible rescues, a sense of divine protection.
Example: A mother who runs into a burning house to rescue her child, or lifts a car with a child trapped underneath

Level 2 (Reactive Response)
Miracles involve incredible achievements and success, control over the body or mind.
Example: Extreme feats of martial arts, child prodigies with inexplicable gifts in music or mathematics, the rise of a Napoleon from humble beginnings to immense power (men of destiny)

Level 3 (Restful Awareness Response)
Miracles involve synchronicity, yogic

powers, premonitions, feeling the presence of God or angels.
Example: Yogis who can change body temperature or heart rate at will, being visited by someone from far away who has just died, visitation by a guardian angel

Level 4 (Intuitive Response)
Miracles involve telepathy, ESP, knowledge of past or future lifetimes, prophetic powers.
Example: Reading someone else's thoughts or aura, psychic predictions, astral projection to other locations

Level 5 (Creative Response)
Miracles involve divine inspiration, artistic genius, spontaneous fulfillment of desires (wishes come true).
Example: The ceiling of the Sistine Chapel, having a thought that suddenly manifests, Einstein's insights into time and relativity

Level 6 (Visionary Response)
Miracles involve healing, physical transformations, holy apparitions, highest degree of supernatural feats.
Example: Walking on water, healing

incurable diseases through touch,
direct revelation from the Virgin
Mary

Level 7 (Sacred Response)
    Miracles involve inner evidence of
    enlightenment.
    Example: Lives of the great prophets
    and teachers—Buddha, Jesus,
    Lao-Tze

Four

A MANUAL FOR SAINTS

We are like newborn children,
Our power is the power to grow.
—RABINDRANATH TAGORE

When you read about the seven stages, it becomes clear that religions vary wildly on how to know God. Each has marked out a separate path whose steps are fixed—often rigidly fixed—in dogma. I have steered clear of dogma, knowing full well that Christians do not automatically accept an Eastern belief such as karma, just as Hindus and Buddhists do not accept a Western belief like Judgment Day. If there is one God, there still cannot be one path. Yet no matter which path you walk, two things are necessary. The first is a vision of the goal; the second is trust that you have the inner resources to get there.

To prove that there is a reachable goal, every religious tradition has saints. Saints are spiritual achievers. They exhibit deep love and devotion, but saints are more than saintly. You and I might show forgiveness toward an enemy because we know that it is the right thing to do, or because it raises our sense of inner worth—at the very least we believe God approves of forgiveness. When a saint forgives, she can't help herself; her love is an outflowing of her nature. And since saints begin life the same as the rest of us, developing a natural sense of love, forgiveness, and compassion represents a huge accomplishment. It isn't simply a gift, which is why we are justified in saying that saints must be great achievers. They are the Einsteins of consciousness. Not only have they reached the spiritual goals set forth by their religion, but they prove to the rest of us that the resources exist for getting there ourselves.

This implies that the saint is laying out a map of the future. Mother Teresa and Saint Francis are me, but a me that hasn't yet emerged. The saints of Buddhism, who are called bodhisattvas, are sometimes portrayed looking over their shoulders and beckoning with a smile, as if to say, "I am going over the threshold. Don't you want to follow?"

It makes sense to accept their invitation, not just by showing love and compassion, but by heeding the principles that uphold the soul's journey. These principles would be found in any manual for saints because they hold true from stage one to stage seven. Such a manual doesn't exist, but if it did, the following realizations would be right at its core:

> *Evolution cannot be stopped; spiritual growth is assured.*
>
> *Action is always noticed by God; nothing goes unheeded.*
>
> *There is no reliable guide to behavior outside your own heart and mind.*
>
> *Reality changes at different stages of growth.*
>
> *At some level everyone knows the highest truth.*
>
> *Everyone is doing the best they can from their own level of consciousness.*
>
> *Suffering is temporary, enlightenment is forever.*

Where do these realizations come from? How do we know they are true? They certainly don't come from society or any outward experience. They come from paying attention to the countless clues left by spirit. No two people see God in the same way, because no two people are at the exact same stage of waking up. Yet in those moments when the five senses give way to deeper intuition, each of us gets a glimpse of reality, and as our minds process some remarkable event or insight, reality delivers a scrap of truth.

"Just before college I went to the New York World's Fair," an older friend of mine likes to remember. "And they had this ride I will never forget. It was a long tunnel that had a movie projected inside it. As you rode along, the images of the movie rushed by at high speed, surrounding you with all kinds of futuristic things, but when you got to the end, you realized that the conveyor belt had traveled only fifty feet in real distance. I thought this was fantastically significant, because my life has been like that. On a daily basis I can walk past thousands of people on the street, think myriads of thoughts, go anywhere in my imagination. But how much closer have I gotten to my soul? Maybe an inch, maybe less. The outer show is very different from the inner journey."

To judge by the outer show, everyone's life moves rapidly, if chaotically, through scene after scene. Yet you might never suspect that there even was an inner journey.

Saints prove that there is. Having arrived at the goal, they can look back and say that just beneath the surface, human life has a pattern, a rising arc. In stage one the possibility of knowing God is dim, unlikely, a mere shadow of a possibility. In stage two, as threats and fears subside, the possibilities become more interesting and plausible. In stage three they become intriguing, something you find it worthwhile to contemplate and perhaps even test out. In stage four tentative testing turns more decisive—you actually begin to risk making choices that defy the ego's expectations (to use a wonderful phrase I ran across, you begin to live as if God really matters). In stage five you have done enough testing; now you want to play. You feel assured in your spiritual choices. In stage six you acquire mastery over the spiritual domain, which lets you enjoy incredible freedom in the material domain, a freedom never dreamed of earlier. In stage seven there are no more choices to be made. The saint merges into the God he reveres, and the whole universe operates automatically according to the same principles that were once so irrelevant to the struggle of trying to survive.

If I read in the New Testament that it is right to love your enemy, how does that apply to the thief who tried to rob me in my house or the mugger attacking me in the street? I may pay lip service to forgiving the criminal, but at a deeper level I will react according to my true state of consciousness. I might hate and fear him, or I might want to do everything possible to prevent similar crimes from happening—these are typical reactions in stages one and two. I might pay more attention to my inner agitation and then realize that the crime was born out of the wrongdoer's fear and pain—now we are at stages three and four. As consciousness rises I begin to see that my own inner drama projected the whole scenario in which I played the part of victim, leading to the realization that the criminal and I are two parts of the same karma—insights gained in stages five and six. At this point true forgiveness is available to me. I have linked the teaching of Jesus with my own soul. All that remains is stage seven, where the criminal is an aspect of myself that I can bless and release to God.

Every event in your life falls somewhere on this scale of reactions, and the overall pattern is a rising arc. The road to saint-hood begins in ordinary circumstances with ordinary situations. There is no shorter path to God. Because we all have egos, we fantasize that we will simply leap to the top of the mountain where the halos are handed out, but this never happens. Inner life is too complex, too full of contradictions. An Arctic explorer can tell from his map when he has arrived at the pole, but in spiritual exploration the map shifts with every step you take. "You need to realize that there is no fixed 'me' who is looking for enlightenment," a guru told his disciples. "You have no fixed identity—that is just a fiction made up by your ego. In truth there is a different experiencer for every experience." Because each of us is a lover one moment and a child the next, a seeker stubbornly clinging to old habits, free and yet captive, curious and yet apathetic, secure and frightened at the same time, the spiritual journey is never a straight line. Goals have a way of changing; in fact, they must change, given that stage one melts into stage two just when you think you have arrived at God. In turn stage two will melt away when the time comes.

Which brings us back to the same question, "Where do I go from here?" Let me take the first two principles of a saint and demonstrate how the rising arc applies to you. In each stage I will adopt the voice of someone who is trying to come to terms with the principle.

Evolution cannot be stopped;
spiritual growth is assured.

Stage One (Fight-or-flight response): "This whole idea makes no sense. There are lots of evil people who couldn't care less about their souls. My own life is all ups and downs. I take two steps backward for every step forward. I have no idea why misfortunes and failure occur; I pray to God that they don't and leave it to him."

Stage Two (Reactive response): "My life keeps getting better as long as I work hard and stay up to speed. This makes me optimistic, and I interpret evolution as progress. Since childhood I have increased in confidence and skill, so definitely I am progressing—but I'm not so sure that applies to the people who haven't caught on to how to succeed. They need God more than I do. Inner growth is secondary to success."

Stage Three (Restful awareness response): "I'm not that pulled into outward events anymore, and I think they aren't that real. They are more like symbols of what I hold inside. Since childhood my inner world has grown stabler, more comforting and secure. It seems that evolution takes place near my heart, and I try to obey my inner impulses, even when they don't bring me more money, status, or power. Something deeper is moving forward."

Stage Four (Intuitive response): "I've stopped believing that my ego knows what's good for me. It never made me fulfilled, no matter how often I made choices on behalf of 'I, me, mine.' You have to go deeper inside to make your choices, and I've found that at the intuitive level, I know what is right—or at least I'm getting there. Too many things have happened that can't be explained in the old way. I am part of a mystery, flowing toward an unknown destination. That is what fascinates me now."

Stage Five (Creative response): "Somewhere along the line, I broke free. I am who I want to be, doing what I want to do. How did I get to this place? It didn't happen through struggle and strife. Somehow a deep current swept me along and brought me here. If that is evolution, then I believe in it, although as yet I can't tell you precisely who God is or what my soul looks like. It is enough to trust the process."

Stage Six (Visionary response): "My soul is calling me every hour of every day. I now realize that this has always been true, but only now do I notice it so completely, so clearly. It's unbearable to turn away from the light, which is the source of my ecstasy.

Every time I pray, I am aware that God is with me, because if only I had been awake earlier, I would have seen that any other possibility is false."

Stage Seven (Sacred response): "Evolution is all. Every atom in the universe is guided by a perfection standing outside time and space. Nothing is amiss. Death itself is part of eternal progress, and so is evil. I know, because I am that life force, that endless river. I am its source and its destination, its flow and the obstacles that hinder the flow. I carry a few memories of my old life, most especially this one: I remember the day that God, the Cosmic Mother, embraced me and invited me to join her dance."

In abbreviated form, we've just accounted for many of the spiritual turning points that shake people out of their old beliefs. Truth has many faces, and when you see a new one, your level of consciousness rises. We have also illustrated two more of the saints' principles: Everyone is doing the best they can from their own level of awareness, and reality keeps changing as your consciousness changes. The rising arc of spirit isn't always so obvious. It gets obscured all the time. We don't think about sainthood when corporate downsizing threatens our jobs or when the divorce papers are served. But at dramatic moments the soul drops clues into our laps, and then we have the choice to pay attention or not. Your soul will always be in communication with you, and over time you will heed what it says.

The spiritual journey is 99 percent repetition, because we are all conditioned to obey ego needs, to cling to old habits. We have our ways of doing things, most of them totally dependent on the past. Sheer inertia would defeat the soul were it not for its magnetic pull. That is why it is useful to cooperate in your own awakening—your enemy is not evil but lack of attention. The various practices known as prayer, meditation, contemplation, and yoga have been highly valued over the centuries because they sharpen attention and make it easier not to miss the clues to spiritual reality.

A spiritual person is a good listener for silent voices, a sharp observer of invisible objects. These traits are more important than trying to act in a way that God would reward with a gold star. The second principle of the saints can be dramatized like the first, through the inner voice that plays its beliefs over and over in your head until you move on to a new belief, bringing with it a new voice.

Action is always noticed by God;
nothing goes unheeded.

Stage One (Fight-or-flight response): "Maybe God sees the fall of a sparrow, but you couldn't tell it by me. If I didn't do my part to fit in, I would be alone and forgotten. The cherished feelings I have for my family are what holds my life together, because these few people care that I exist. Events are random, treacherous things that can happen at any moment. I never forget that. After I die, I will just be a memory, or if I am lucky I will then find out if God knows who I am. My faith tells me that he does."

Stage Two (Reactive response): "Everything comes with a price. If you waste your time and energy, life doesn't give you much back. But since I know how to organize my life, I can bring life's rewards my way. Everything I do has a point; my driving ambition is to make each moment count. When the time comes to rest, I will look around with satisfaction at what I've made of myself. I don't have time to think about what comes next, but in scary moments I wonder if God will get me for the bad things I had to do."

Stage Three (Restful awareness response): "I wonder if things are as random as they appear. I've seen evil rewarded and good punished. Yet at other times an underlying purpose seems to raise its head. I need to think about all this because the answers I get from society are too confused and conflicted. It just may be true that someone up there knows everything; I feel it in my bones."

Stage Four (Intuitive response): "I could swear that someone is reading my mind. If I think of something, it seems to happen, or at least there are a lot of unexplained coincidences. I've learned to go with these signals, wherever they come from. I am the master of my own choices. Sometimes I make mistakes, but even those I can witness with calm acceptance."

Stage Five (Creative response): "Things work out because they are meant to. Otherwise the world would be a churning cauldron, and it isn't. Everywhere I look I see patterns and symbols; there is incredible beauty and order. There are times when this complexity intoxicates me. I just can't believe so much potential exists—I have the heart of an artist but the soul of a wizard. Who knows what kind of power I will one day wield."

Stage Six (Visionary response): "The world has a heart, and that heart is love. In the midst of all struggle, I see that God is watching. He doesn't interfere, but he doesn't lose track, either. He brings a solution to fit every problem, a reaction that suits every action. How he does this is a mystery, but nothing is more real. There is grace in the fall of a leaf. Our deeds are weighed in the balance by a loving Creator who never judges or punishes."

Stage Seven (Sacred response): "Action and reaction are one, and always have been. As events spin from the web of time, I see no difference between the action and the one who performs it. The ego used to believe that there was an 'I' who had to oversee and control. This 'I' is only an illusion. No action could ever be lost or overlooked in the fabric of unity."

These viewpoints look very different on the surface, yet the same principle is being unfolded in a rising arc. In other words, a secret spiritual path underlies the apparent randomness of everyday existence. "All of reality is a symbol for spirit," the Sufis say. Or, to recall Rumi's beautiful phrase, "I come from Elsewhere, and though I do not know where that is, I am certain to return there in the end." Only in stage six does the saint realize that his soul's unfolding was always taking place. Until clarity dawns, a certain amount of confusion is always present.

Everyone receives the same signals from God. The impulse to behave in the highest spiritual way comes to us from beyond our five senses. We refuse to believe that we are connected. But in truth when love is called for, each person tries to display perfect love; when compassion is called for, each person tries to display perfect compassion. This holds for the criminal, the saint, the businessman, the dictator, the factory worker. The message is pure; the filter is impure.

The saint sees that we are all hooked into the same level of infinite intelligence, creativity, and love. God and your soul are in perfect communication. The message breaks down for reasons we have been detailing at length: ego needs, distortions of perception, lack of self-worth, and all kinds of traumas and wounds that defeat our best intentions. If lumped together, these impurities are called *avidya* in the Indian tradition, a Sanskrit word that breaks down into two components, the root word for "not" and the root word for "knowing." By not knowing who we are, by not knowing what God is, by not knowing how to connect with the soul, we fall into sin and ignorance. In everyday usage, avidya is sometimes called both sin and ignorance, but these pejorative terms hide the essence of the truth, which is that all such obstacles exist in consciousness and can be cleared away.

What's the one thing you can do today to grow in spirit? Stop defining yourself. Don't accept any thought that begins "I am this or that." You are not this or that. You are beyond definition, and therefore any attempt to say "I am X" is wrong. You are in passage. You are in the process of redefining yourself every day. Aid that process, and you cannot help but leap forward on the path.

If you take a clear look at yourself, you will find that your mind is more like a swarm of bees than like an arrow shooting straight for the goal. A swarm of bees can travel from point A to point B, just like an arrow, but it does so in a vague, swirling, fuzzy way. Thus we hold in our minds all kinds of shifting attitudes, many of which contradict each other. Our love is bound up with hatred, our trust with suspicion, our altruism with selfishness. Because this is so, the only clear path to God is a path of constant self-awareness. You must see through your own mask if you want to take it off.

Avidya is hard to pierce. It takes a lot of attention to look in the mirror, because our masks do not stop looking back at us. But if you take any issue facing you, your present attitudes will be a clue to your deeper beliefs, and belief is where the real change must occur. A belief lies close to the soul. It is like a microchip that keeps sending out the same signal over and over, making the same interpretation of reality until you are ready to pull out the old chip and install a new one. The following pages explore this in greater detail.

MASKING THE SOUL

Our attitudes hide deeper spiritual beliefs, and when we see through them, beliefs can be changed.

Mask: atheist, cynic, or failed seeker
Attitude: Doubt, resistance, ironical detachment, in the habit of mistrust. Fall-back emotion* is anxiety.
Belief: God cannot be proved; if he exists he has no power over the material world; I am alone, my fear of emptiness is my chief reason to keep seeking.

Mask: leader, achiever, or skeptic
Attitude: Certainty, confidence, self-reliance, in the habit of demanding rational explanations. Fall-back emotion is anger or obstinacy.
Belief: I am in control of my life, not God; if he demands surrender I will ignore him; secretly I believe that my own power is greater than his.

Mask: thinker or dreamer
Attitude: Reflective, conciliatory,

---

* A fall-back emotion is a coping response. It arises when you cannot resolve inner tension or a crisis. It also reflects a sense of connection or separation from God.

calm, in the habit of assessing situations emotionally. Fall-back emotion is depression or resignation.

Belief: God hints at his presence inside me; I will get the message once I stop falling into confusion; God favors inward-looking action more than outward action.

Mask: idealist or liberator
Attitude: Self-aware, nonjudgmental, willing to be an iconoclast or to defy normal expectations. Fall-back emotion is detachment.
Belief: God doesn't think I am wrong or sinful; I can only accept him to the degree I accept myself; forgiveness is real.

Mask: artist, adventurer, or explorer
Attitude: Playful, emotionally resilient, eager to try anything new, tendency to be highly sensitive. Fall-back emotion is fantasy (self-absorption).
Belief: God has made a recreational universe; I am safe following my creative impulses; I am approved of by God.

Mask: prophet or redeemer
Attitude: Humble, deeply forgiving and accepting of others, awed by

mystery, able to see to the depth of
any person or situation. Fall-back
emotion is love.
Belief: There are no miracles until
you see that all of life is a miracle;
God works through me, my greatest
joy is service to him.

Mask: no mask
Attitude: Immersion in bliss, wisdom,
and peace, with no personal attitudes—the viewpoint is universal.
Fall-back emotion is compassion.
Belief: No personal beliefs; every
action and word comes directly from
the divine source; a certainty that
being human is a blessed state.

The above serves to show how pervasively
we are influenced by our state of awareness.
Every emotion or attitude has a spiritual
meaning, despite the fact that society doesn't
acknowledge this. In society's eyes, events
become spiritual only in church or during
times of crisis and transition. But the soul
journey is a constant in everyone's life. Your
typical attitudes, along with the emotions
you cannot shake, indicate in a subtle way
that spiritual issues are churning at a deeper

level. Even the saint and the redeemer are wearing a mask, however thin, that doesn't yet let them see the totality of the self.

A set of attitudes may fit you so well that you apply them almost all the time. This is the mark of someone who moves very slowly on the path, such as the confirmed skeptic who remains doubtful about all spiritual issues, from the existence of God to the possibility of an afterlife. People who cling firmly to skepticism are likely to deny that they have any fear of emptiness and abandonment, yet ultimately they have more of these issues than anyone else—the mask is just highly deceptive.

In the same vein, highly successful people who owe their achievements to struggle and competitiveness tend to wear the mask of self-confidence and not to look at the hidden beliefs that would put them in defiance of God. Even if they "believe in" God, they act on personal power, and if seriously confronted with the possibility of surrender, they reject it outright. Between will and surrender, there is no choice for them.

What is the mark of someone who moves very quickly on the path? It may seem to be a paradox, but the more turbulent you are inside, the faster you are moving. Ferment is good. Not buying into your own story is good. Krishnamurti used to say that discontent was the flame of the seeker. Meher Baba, an Indian master aligned with Sufism, taught that the only prerequisite for waking up was total disillusionment. Why? Because the whole notion that you are a fixed entity is a great illusion, and the sooner you see how varied and complex you are, the sooner you will drop the masks of your ego.

There is no standing still in nature; creatures either move forward or die. Seeing how a flower blooms, goes to seed, and sacrifices itself to bring new life, we wonder if our souls fall into the same cycle. Do we rise and fall, going through an endless round of birth and death? Or is there a tendency to keep moving closer to God, despite the many obstacles and setbacks that befall us along the way? Speaking personally, this is an important question for my behavior today, since I can choose to obey my ego drives or my higher ideals. Ninety-nine percent of humanity has a story they believe in, and nothing shakes them from their story. Saints remind us to choose the ideal over the egotistical, and when being selfish, greedy, and ambitious is just too tempting, the saints don't condemn us. "Come to me," Rumi implores, "even if you have broken your vows a thousand times."

The soul can't be hindered by outward action. No one makes the soul journey faster or slower than anyone else. Time doesn't count at the level of the soul. What counts is perception. When you perceive that awakening is inevitable, the magnetic pull of the soul will keep changing you.

You and I are nothing but saints in the making. We can exhibit whatever behavior we want, but life flows upward from the roots, not downward from the branches. On a spiritual basis, being good is never wrong. But in terms of sheer effectiveness—which means trying to wake up with the fewest delays, obstacles, and backsliding—adopting the right belief is much more powerful. As the first principle says, evolution cannot be stopped. With this belief in mind, you have a basis for forgiving any wrongdoing, letting go of the past, and giving yourself a second chance at anything where you failed the first time around. There is no fall from grace, only a very long furlough. In the end there is only one reliable guide: Find your place on the rising arc and keep moving.

SPIRITUAL AWAKENING

If asked what separates a spiritual person from a skeptic, I would not say that the answer is belief in God. It is clarity. Millions of believers still strive to be "saved," whether they are Christians, Muslims, or of any other faith. They actively seek a clear perception of God that will affect them personally. When does this become possible? Do we have to wait for stage six, the stage of the saint, or any particular stage at all? Stripped of religious coloration, being saved is the same as awakening in consciousness, a perceptual leap that makes God real instead of doubtful. Here is a striking example.

A young man in his twenties named Bede Griffiths had been going through a period of deep doubt and depression. Being religious, he sought solace in a church, where he prayed without success. One day during service he heard the line "Open my eyes that I may see the wondrous things of Thy law" from the 113th Psalm. Deeply moved, the young man felt his melancholy lift away, and he had the overwhelming sense that his prayers had been answered by divine intervention. He walked outside onto the London streets, and later described the experience in the following words:

> *When I went outside, I found that the world about me no longer oppressed me as it had done. The hard casing of exterior*

reality seemed to have been broken through, and everything disclosed its inner being. The buses in the streets seemed to have lost their solidity and were glowing with light. I hardly felt the ground as I trod . . . I was like a bird that has broken the shell of its egg and finds itself in a new world; like a child that has forced its way out of the womb and sees the light of day for the first time.[1]

Time and again in such awakenings there is an insistence that outer things have dramatically changed, whereas to other observers they haven't. But this doesn't mean that going into the light, seeing the face of God, or whatever other name we wish to give to the experience is false. The observer isn't separate from outer reality. The photons firing in the brain are exactly the same as photons organized into "real" objects. So inner and outer vision are not separate. The mystical branch of Islam known as Sufism declares that all light, inner and outer, is but one light. This is something people find hard to accept, because the duality of inner versus outer, real versus unreal, objective versus subjective has been drilled into us since birth. To get past this dualism, we have to return to our three levels of existence:

When light is visible and organized into concrete objects, reality is material.

When light contains feeling, thought, and intelligence, reality is quantum.

When light is completely unmanifest, with no qualities anyone can measure, reality is virtual.

In place of the old dualism that insists upon keeping our inner and outer life apart, we can restore the light to its wholeness. One can think of a photon as the archetype of all energy that is blossoming out from nothing and nowhere to something and somewhere: the bridge for mystical awakenings is light as it moves from virtual to material existence.

In this scheme one traditional belief gets reversed. The virtual domain, unlike heaven, is our source rather than our destination after death. When physicists declare that the cosmos once had ten or more dimensions, all but four of which collapsed back where they came from, the virtual state is where they went.

This is so difficult to conceptualize that a simple analogy might help: let's say that you are thinking in words and then shift to humming a tune in your head. This shift to music brings in completely different laws of nature than the laws that govern words. Yet you can move from one dimension to the other quite easily. The musical dimension is always there, even though you may not be contacting it. In the same way, other dimensions exist outside the cosmos, but we do not access their laws, and if we tried, we would have to give up our own. This is why your body and mind could not survive passage through a black hole or travel beyond the speed of light.

In order for a packet of energy to appear, to be seen by the eyes as photons, it doesn't suddenly jump into material existence. Between the void and visible light, between darkness and things you can see and touch, there is the quantum layer. This level is accessible to our brains, which are quantum machines that create thought by manipulating energy into intricate patterns. At this level light dawns as awareness of something, rather than simply being awareness in its pure state. This is the place where Einstein looked for God's mind—he was searching for religious insight without the unscientific subjectivity that would have doomed his theories to rejection by his peers. (It is fascinating to follow the mystical journeys of great physicists like Einstein, Schrödinger, and Pauli, because as they arrived, awestruck before the mystery of creation, they had to cover their trails, so to speak, to avoid any accusation that they were mere mystics and not scientists. In the case of Einstein and Pauli, the taint of being too receptive to religious concepts finally did cast a shadow over their later work.)

To an experimental physicist, a photon is a quantum of light. This might only be of technical interest were it not for the fact that quantum physics holds the key to even greater secrets. We know nothing directly about energy in its virtual state—this is essentially inaccessible to any measuring instrument. But one way to understand the virtual domain is as the space between sub-atomic particles, called the virtual field. A subatomic particle isn't a thing hanging out in space like a baseball drifting over home plate, but a disturbance in the field. The disturbance takes place as a quantum event, sometimes pictured as a wave. There is a spiritual parallel to this in the Vedas, where the sages declare that the undisturbed state of consciousness is bliss, the disturbed state is the world.

Throughout the universe, the photon is the most basic unit of electromagnetic energy. Every single thing you can perceive is actually a swirling cloud of energy. At the moment of the Big Bang the universe exploded with energy that now forms everything in existence, and buried some-where under the skin of every object or event, the primordial light still burns. Being the essence of transformation, primordial light isn't always the same shape or form billions of years later. A granite cliff is solid, hard, flintlike light; an impulse of love is sweet, emotional light; the firing of a neuron is an instant flash of invisible light. Yet as dissimilar as they appear, when broken down to their most basic components, all things derive from the same primal stuff.

Without the quantum level of reality there could be no cosmos, and it is here that order and symmetry, the keys to life, first appeared. But few eminent physicists besides Einstein have ventured to explore the possibility that the quantum level is a transition to God. So it is necessary to con-sider other thinkers. In the last century in India there was a revered saint, Sri Rama-krishna, who held the post of priest in a large, wealthy temple outside Calcutta. It was his duty to place offerings every day before the statue of Kali, one of the guises of the divine mother, the Goddess.

Having done this day after day, Rama-krishna became very devoted to the divine mother. Then one day a change occurred: "It was suddenly revealed to me," he says, "that not just the statue but everything in the room was made of pure spirit. The bowl, the utensils, the floor and ceiling were all manifestations of the same thing. When I realized this, I began to act like someone insane. I began throwing flowers everywhere and worshiping everything. Worship, worship, worship in all directions."

This is what I would call an overlap of levels. Ramakrishna didn't go into a trance or leave his senses behind—the material level of the world was still visible, but something finer suddenly penetrated and permeated it. This permeation came from the virtual level, which can't be registered by the five senses. There is nothing to see, hear, touch, taste, or smell. However, our brains are designed to assign a time and place to everything; therefore the invisible levels get merged into the visible, as if the flower or the statue or the holy water has become infused with spirit before our eyes.

An awakening can be very confusing if the brain suddenly has to make sense of impulses not of this world. New feelings arise. Perhaps the most uncanny feeling is that of pure awareness: one is awake, alive, but without thoughts, and free from the limitations of the body. The closest most of us come to this feeling is the first minute when we wake up in the morning or the last before we fall asleep. There is awareness here, but no content, no rush of thoughts in the brain, and if you pay close enough attention, even the sense of identity is blanked out—you feel yourself being present, yet you aren't aware of any specifics such as your name, address, occupation, age, daily concerns, or relationships. At the instant you wake up, just before all the particulars of your situation flood back once more, you could be a child again and your familiar home could be anyplace in the world.

One would assume that this is just a passing feeling. Yet the experience of pure awareness lies at the heart of religious awakening. The only region of nature that enjoys total freedom is heaven, as religious people might call it. In physics the equivalent would be the virtual level of reality. Not that this is a blessed place where souls enjoy the company of angels—such a concept is totally foreign to physical science, but the resemblance is based on a shift in the rules or laws of nature.

Heaven is imagined as a place free from the bonds of earthly life where gravity no longer holds down the body. In heaven there are no cares or attachments. Eternal joy is the soul's constant state. Without having to imagine them, all these qualities can be traced back to the experience of waking up. The great difference between this experience and heaven is that the virtual domain isn't outside us; one doesn't "go" there either in body or soul. One may look forward to dying and achieving heaven as a reward, but it is more in tune with virtual reality to find it now. How? A famous anecdote in India tells of the ascetic who goes to the mountaintop to become enlightened. He fasts and prays constantly; he gives up all worldly desires in favor of meditation.

His renunciation goes on for many years until the day when he realizes he has finally arrived. No matter where he looks, he senses only the unbounded bliss of pure awareness, without attachment of any kind. Overjoyed, he rushes down into the village below to tell everyone, and as he is going along, he runs into a crowd of drunken revelers. Quietly he tries to thread his way through, but one drunk after another bumps him and makes a crude remark. Finally the ascetic can't stand it and cries, "Get out of my way!" At that instant he stops, turns around, and goes back to the mountain.

This anecdote is about how easily we are

fooled into thinking that we can escape our own anger and frailty, but the larger point is that using the personality to get to the absolute is a contradiction. Certain parts of ourselves are designed to live in this world of time. It takes resolve and purpose to succeed in loosening our bonds enough so that pure awareness feels totally comfortable, and in the face of conflicts we instinctively fall back on anger, as we fall back on stubbornness, self-centeredness, righteous certainty, and so forth. Yet at another level we do not even possess these qualities, much less feel tied to them. Religious seeking, whatever form it takes, tries to regain that unattached level.

Seen in this context, some of the most mysterious writings of saints and sages become very clear. Consider this Chinese poem from Li Po, written in the eighth century:

> You ask why I seclude myself here in my
>   little forest hut?
> I just smile and say nothing, listening to
>   the quiet in my soul.
> This peacefulness lives in another world
> That no one owns.

What we can now see in these words is a change of perspective that is always here, right with us, as a possibility. With the loss of time comes a complete absence of ordinary identity. The personality that I feel myself to be dissolves beyond the material level, and with that, I lose the need for the landmarks that I have gathered since birth.

Awakening is at the root of the world's religions. It unites prophets, messiahs, and saints into a privileged elite. That awakening can be recounted through wondrous stories such as that of the young prince Siddhartha, before he became the Buddha, being transported from his palace on a flying white horse supported by angels at each hoof. Such legends convey the tremendous effect of waking up to a new level of reality. That this reality arose in the mind sounds too abstract and prosaic. There needs to be a more dramatic event, such as a heaven that suddenly opens up, or divine messengers who descend from on high.

Most people outside the faith of Islam are unaware of the moment when the prophet Muhammad was awakened.[2] It took place at night in a cave outside the city of Mecca. Muhammad was forty, a merchant of no memorable distinction; in fact almost nothing is known of his life beforehand. On this night, however, the angel Gabriel appeared in a blaze of light and said, "Recite!"

Amazed and baffled, Muhammad could only ask, "Recite what?" To which the angel replied, "Recite in the name of the Lord the creator" and then delivered the gift of prophecy that enabled Muhammad to know the word of God. This event occurred in the year 610 and is revered in Islam as the Night of Qadr (which means glory or power). But the actual text of the Koran was not assembled until more than thirty years later, after the Prophet's death. Since Muhammad could neither read nor write, his account of events is not recorded. All the *suras*, or chapters, of the Koran, which vary widely in length from three lines to thirty pages, were gathered by a committee that interviewed those remaining devotees who had heard Muhammad speak, as well as from scraps of written text from the same sources.

It is a specific tradition that insists that the angel Gabriel arrived as a physical presence, just as tradition insists that Jesus confronted Satan in the wilderness or that the future Buddha flew from his palace. (Muhammad would also be accorded a flight on a magical horse, when he was granted a tour of all the levels of heaven. Although one can visit the Dome of the Rock in Jerusalem and view the place where the journey began, including the hoofprint left in stone by the horse's heavenward leap, this legend was born from a single line in the Koran that speaks of the Prophet going from his home in Mecca to a far temple.)

These legends are now articles of faith, and for anyone to speculate that Muhammad might not have seen an angel or that Satan did not literally offer Jesus kingship over the earth would be risking blasphemy. However, it isn't necessary to believe or disbelieve the literal version of the Night of Qadr or the forty days in the wilderness. The essential point is that our minds can open to the sudden inrush of light.

THE MIND FIELD

"Light" as used in scriptures always stands for awareness, whether or not physical light is actually seen. Christians regard Jesus as "the light of the world" because of his state of higher consciousness, and the word "light" is a synonym for a whole range of things, from inspiration and holiness to embodied spirit and God's essence. Versions of the same imagery are applied by followers of Buddha and Muhammad, of course, even though each religion makes claims of uniqueness for its founder. The disputes among religions are almost always over exclusive claims that only their founder entered the light, or that his place before God is highest. Awareness, though, is a common heritage, even a cosmic heritage if we accept the existence of mind at the quantum and virtual level. When asked what the experience of God feels like, people's responses, different as they may be, all converge on a shift into higher awareness.

I am proposing that no one is alive who hasn't taken just such a journey. The "way," whether it is used in the Christian sense of a path or the Taoist sense of the hidden stream of life, means following the light. None of us could even be here without having roots where light is born, in the quantum domain. To understand this fully, however, we have to modify our picture of the world from a reality sandwich with three layers into something more dynamic—a flow chart.

Material

———— QUANTUM ————

Virtual

Reality is constantly flowing from the virtual level to the quantum to the material. In mystical terms, this constant movement is called "the river of life," because to the mystic everything begins in the mind of God before it appears on the surface as an event or object. But the river is more than a metaphor. With every thought, memory, and desire we take a journey upriver, from our invisible source to our material destination.

One day I was sitting quietly, preparing for meditation, when I happened to see an old, faintly familiar face in my mind's eye. After a moment I realized who it was, a patient from twenty years ago. He was a diabetic, and every week I would call him at home to adjust his insulin levels.

As I closed my eyes, I had the faint thought, "I wonder what his name was?" No more than that, just a faint thought. I meditated for an hour, and as I opened my eyes again, a name suddenly came to mind, along with a telephone number. It seemed so improbable that I had recalled them that I went directly to the phone and dialed. The voice at the other end was in fact my old patient Raoul.

Raoul's telephone number hadn't changed in all that time, yet my brain had certainly been changing. Therein lies a mystery. Brain cells are not constant. We are born with about half the complement of neurons found in an adult brain; the rest develop between six months and two years of age. Each neuron is connected to every other through billions of threads that branch out into thousands of tendrils per cell, forming a vast network. These tendrils, known as dendrites, sprout at the end of the cell like a tree trunk sprouting branches (the word *dendrite* comes from the Greek word for tree).

Although it sounds fixed and stable, this network is constantly shifting. And even if a neuron could remain the same, growing no new branches, the signals streaming down the dendrites are never the same from moment to moment. Electrical impulses surge everywhere, shifting as we think new thoughts; our brains are like a telephone system with a thousand calls taking place every second. The main difference is that the cable lines of our nervous system are unstable, constantly changing their molecules with every moment of experience— both inner and outer. The wires are notoriously nonstationary, since they are made not of copper but of fluid fats, water, electrolytes, and the electrical charges running through them. Having a single thought is more complex than sorting out one message from all the telephone calls in the world. While we are managing that feat electrically, the brain also surges with chemical messages. One dendrite isn't strung into another; there is always a tiny gap between them. Across this gap, known as a synapse, each message must find a way to cross; otherwise the neurons would be isolated and unable to communicate. Electricity doesn't jump across the gap—the voltages are much too tiny to accomplish this. Instead, certain chemicals are emitted on one side of the synapse and received on the other. These chemicals, called neurotransmitters, include dopamine and serotonin.

Amid these chaotic swirls of chemicals and electrons, no one has ever found a memory. Memories are fixed. For me to recall Raoul's face, I have to retrieve it intact, not in bits and pieces. Where do I go to do that? Certainly not into the firestorm of the brain. No single neuron in my brain has survived intact for twenty years. Like migrating birds, molecules of fat, protein, and sugar have drifted through my neurons, adding to them and leaving again after a time.

Even though we can identify the memory centers of the brain, no one has ever proved that memory is stored there. We assume it is, but how? To store a memory in a neuron is like storing a memory in water. (In fact, the brain is so fluid that if homogenized it would have the same water content as a bowl of oatmeal. Your blood is actually more filled with solid content than your cerebrum.) The notion that we store memory the way a computer stores it, by imprinting microchips with bits of information, is not supported by the evidence; when neurologists try to prove it, they soon hit a wall.

It is the same wall that Einstein and the other founders of quantum physics broke through. A neuron is a poor receptacle for memory because, at bottom, its molecules are not solid; they are patterns of invisible energy grouped into the appearance of particles. These energy packets themselves survive only on the quantum level; go deeper still, into the virtual level, and the patterns dissolve; the energy vanishes into ghostly vibrations and then into nothing. Can memory be stored in nothing?

The answer is yes. When I remembered my old patient's face, I took a journey into nothing, searching for him nowhere. I used my brain to make this journey, or at least to begin it. But it wasn't my brain that recalled his telephone number, any more than my radio contains the music I hear in my car.

I mentioned already that the virtual domain has no time, space, or energy. This turns out to be immensely important when it comes to memory. No one doubts that the brain uses energy. It burns food as calories, subsisting on glucose, a simple sugar that gets broken down to accommodate the brain's complex activities. But as atoms of food are mined for their energy and this energy gets converted into thought, none of it is channeled into memory. It doesn't take food to store the image of where you were ten years ago on your birthday or what you did yesterday after work.

Nor does it seem to take energy to remember these things. Going back to my example, I didn't consciously try to retrieve anything from my memories. I was meditating, and after an hour a name and a telephone number came to me. Was my brain working on the problem all that time? Currently no one has an answer. Our popular belief is that the brain functions like a Macintosh built from organic matter (one researcher has called it "a computer made of meat," a disturbing but unforgettable phrase). It is my belief that the brain is the last stop downriver, the end point of impulses that begin on the virtual level, flow through the quantum level, and wind up as flashes of electricity along the trunks and branches of our neurons.

When you remember anything, you move from world to world, maintaining the illusion that you are still here among familiar sights and sounds. Sometimes the con-

nections are faulty—I might have come up
with the wrong name or telephone number.
Without understanding this journey, however, there is not much hope of undertaking
the spiritual journey back to God, because
both routes are the same.

The advent of CT scans and MRIs has
afforded us a glimpse into the brain as a place
where energy is constantly being generated.
But the brain and the mind are different.
Sometimes brain surgery has to be performed with the patient awake, conscious,
and able to answer questions. If you are talking to such a patient and ask him to lift his
arm, he obeys like anyone else, even though
a section of his skull has been removed,
exposing the cerebral cortex to open air.
Now take an electrode and stimulate part of
the motor cortex so that the same arm suddenly moves. The action is exactly the same
as when you asked the patient to perform
this action. However, there is one huge difference. In the first instance if you ask what
has happened, the patient will respond, "I
moved my arm." In the second instance if
you ask what happened, the patient will
respond, "My arm moved."

Despite the external similarity (the arm
moved), the first act involved will and
desire; a mysterious entity called "I" did the

work, not simply the brain. Such an experiment was actually performed by the pioneering Canadian brain surgeon Wilder Penfield, which led him to conclude that our minds and our brains are not at all the same.[3] Today we can expand on the ways in which the two seem to diverge:

- You ask me my name, and I give it to you with a flash of activity in my cerebral cortex. But it takes no brain activity for me to *know* my name.
- At the store I choose whether to buy vanilla or chocolate ice cream. As I think about the choice, my brain is working, but the chooser—the person who decides between A or B—is nowhere to be found in the brain.
- You and I are looking at a Picasso painting. I say I like it, you say you don't. It takes brain activity for us to express our opinions, but the difference in taste isn't an activity.
- I am sitting on an airplane worrying about what to say in my lecture when we land. I fall asleep and begin to doze. When I wake up, I know exactly what I want to talk about. This shift from worry to certainty was not a measurable brain event,

since in sleep I did no conscious thinking.

- You are sitting on the sofa reading when all at once the name of an old friend pops into your mind. The next instant, you hear the phone ring and it is your friend calling. It took brain activity to recall the name, but no brain mechanism could time the coincidence.

- You meet a stranger at a party and in a moment of instant attraction you know that this is the person you will marry. In time you do, and it is revealed that he had exactly the same feeling for you. The brain may account for all the hormonal attractions, even the mental and emotional impulses that make each of you "right" for the other. It cannot possibly account for your simultaneous certainty, however.

When Penfield began his work in the 1930s, science had not yet firmly decided that the mind was just a ghost created by neurons. By the 1970s it was obvious to him that many experts "would, no doubt, silence me before I began to discuss the mind and the brain, if they could. They declare that since the mind, by its very nature, cannot have a position in space, there is only one phenomenon to be considered, namely, the brain." Nonetheless, Penfield (along with Sir John Eccles, an equally audacious brain researcher in Britain) asked an obvious question. Where in the brain can you find any mechanism that possesses intuition, creativity, insight, imagination, understanding, intent, knowing, will, decision, or spirit? Indeed all the higher functions of the brain still cannot create the qualities that make us most human. Are we supposed to dismiss them as illusion or postpone discussion until someone discovers genes for the soul?

Among his many observations, Penfield noted that the brain retains memory even while dormant. Patients recover from severe states of coma still knowing such things as language, as well as their own life history. Under deep anesthesia, about 1 percent of surgical patients report that they could hear what the surgeons were saying around them and can even recall details of what transpired during the procedure. Therefore, even though he didn't know how it worked, Penfield speculated that the mind must have its own energy source. Somehow it also gets energy from the brain—when the brain dies or loses function, as in a stroke, certain or all mental operations are cut off. But energy inside the brain isn't enough to explain how the mind survives traumas.

A brain totally deprived of oxygen for up to four minutes (longer if the body is very cold) can still recover complete mental functioning. During that interval of deprivation, the machinery of the brain shuts down. Under deep anesthesia, there are practically no higher brain waves at all, making it impossible for the cerebral cortex to accomplish anything so complex as remembering what a surgeon is saying. The fact that the mind can survive brain trauma and function under anesthesia points very strongly to the separate existence of the mind. In simplest terms, Penfield came to the conclusion that "it is the mind which experiences and it is the brain which records the experience." He concluded that the mind must be a kind of invisible energy field that includes the brain, perhaps even controls it. In place of energy field, I believe we should say "information field," because the brain clearly processes information that is flowing and related to all that exists.

As soon as one uses the term *field*, a step has been taken into the realm of quantum reality. The brain is a thing with material structures like a cortex and a limbic system. A field is not a thing. The magnetic field of the earth exerts a pull over every iron particle, causing it to move this way or that, yet nothing visible or tangible is doing the moving. In the same way the mind causes the brain to move this way or that. Think of the word *aardvark*. Then think of the word *Rangoon*. The first word contains its own sound and meaning, paralleled in the brain by a specific pattern of waves. The second word is also defined by its unique patterns. Therefore, to go from one word to the other requires a radical shift involving millions of neurons. Who makes this shift? The first pattern has to be totally dissolved in order to bring up the second; there is no transition between them that serves as a link. Aardvark is wiped out (including your mental picture of a giant anteater) so that Rangoon can take its place (including your image of its place on the map and whatever you know of Burmese history). In between is only an empty gap, like the black space between two images in a movie.

Yet somehow this gap, which has no brain activity at all, manages to organize millions of neurons. It knows the difference between an aardvark and Rangoon without your having to think about the difference—in fact, you don't have to will yourself to organize even one brain cell into the incredibly intricate pattern necessary to produce a word. It all happens automatically, without expenditure of energy—brain energy, that is. Another kind of energy may exist in the gap. Eccles made the famous statement that "God is in the gap." What he meant was that the empty spaces of the brain, the tiny synapses between two nerve endings, must be the home of higher mind because it could not be found in the material stuff of the brain.

Our minds are a vital tool in the search for God. We trust the mind and listen to it; we follow its impulses; we rely on its accuracy. Far more than this, however, the mind interprets the world for us, gives it meaning. To a depressed person the sight of a glowing Tahitian sunset mirrors his sadness, while to someone else the same signals to the retina may invoke wonder and joy. As Penfield would say, the brain is recording the sunset, but only the mind can experience it. As we search for God, we want our interpretations to rise even higher than our minds can take us, so that we might understand birth and death, good and evil, heaven and hell. When this understanding extends to spirit, two invisible fields, mind and soul, need to be connected if we are to have any confidence in them.

God requires the most delicate response of the mind. If the mind is troubled or unrefined, the journey back to God cannot be successfully made. Many factors come into play here, but in terms of the mind/brain connection, Valerie Hunt, a researcher with degrees in both psychology and physiology, has made some important connections, recounted in her 1989 book, *Infinite Mind.*[4] After hooking subjects up to EEGs, she determined that certain brain wave patterns can be associated with higher spiritual experiences. This finding extends earlier research, now three decades old, which established that going into deep meditation alters the patterns of alpha waves in the brain, along with heartbeat, respiration, and blood pressure.

But Dr. Hunt was further interested in why people do *not* have spiritual experiences. In doing so, she took the step of supposing that we should all be naturally connected to the totality of the mind's field of energy and information, just as we are all connected to the parts that involve thinking. It is a simple but profound assumption. Why do we block spirit out?

"The problem is always fear of the

intense emotions that occur at the mystical level," Hunt asserts, "experiences so real and profound that we cannot easily comprehend or accept them. . . . Another way to describe our blocks is to say that we don't want to change our priorities, nor our beliefs about ourselves and God." The mind field, it seems, is a mine field.[5]

This spiritual "stuckness" is not just a limitation of the brain. Researchers before Hunt have documented that if the right temporal lobe is deprived of oxygen for a few moments, its activity begins to heighten, thus creating the illusion of "going into the light." The same floating feeling, the sensation of being outside the body, feelings of ecstasy and otherworldliness, even visions of departed souls and angels beckoning one into the light—all these phenomena can be imitated through oxygen deprivation, or by whirling subjects in a large centrifuge of the kind used to train astronauts for the experience of intense gravitational forces. Yet inducing the experience isn't the same as having it; there is no spiritual meaning to centrifugal force or oxygen loss, while people who have experienced near-death episodes (not to mention yogis and saints who have grown used to living in the light) report profound spiritual changes.

If the brain normally filters out an entire range of experience, as we know it does, perhaps our crudest access to higher dimensions is unfortunately through damage or deprivation. The brain has to adjust itself to any higher experience. It takes brain waves to turn the whirling, chaotic energy of the quantum soup into recognizable images and thoughts. Hunt makes the point that if you measure the brain activity of someone who is willing to have a spiritual experience, who isn't stuck or blocked, the patterns are very different from someone who is blocked. Going beyond her EEG measurements, Hunt has correlated five states of psychological stuckness that shut out spirituality. All are rooted in some initial experience—a brush with God—that the person cannot integrate into the sense of self that already existed. The five blocked experiences are as follows:

1. The experience of a God-like energy or presence.
2. Suddenly comprehending past, present, and future as one.
3. Gaining the power to heal.
4. Unanswered prayers in the midst of a "good" life—the experience of being forsaken by God.

5. Sensory overload to the nervous system when "the light" enters.

Although related, these are distinct experiences, and when any befall a person, there is often a sense of shock and dismay, despite the fact that something positive may be happening.

One could reasonably claim that Christianity itself might not have survived if Saul had not been blinded by the light on the road to Damascus, when Jesus uttered the words "Why do you persecute me?" But this overwhelming experience included some of the obstacles listed above. Saul's entire belief structure was challenged. His sudden exposure to God as a full-blown reality had to be integrated, and this provoked tremendous struggle within. The sensory overload of the experience caused physical blindness for a number of days. The Buddha sitting under the Bodhi tree, determined to break free of the binding influence of the mind, was volunteering for the same inner struggle. What is common to any spiritual breakthrough is that strong opposition is never far away. For example,

Neurotic defenses such as "I am unworthy" or "I have low self-esteem" are triggered.

Anxiety that an evil or satanic force is at work arises; these may be expressed as fear of insanity or the belief that delusions are being caused from the outside.

The self vainly tries to hold together along its old patterns, fearing change as a form of death.

The absence of a sign from God, such as a voice or vision, makes the experience seem unreal, detached from this world.

The habit of being in duality, of seeing past, present, and future as separate states, does not want to be broken down.

All in all, the mind's journey back to God can have serious repercussions just in terms of the brain adapting to a new mode of perception. This was made clear to me by an accident that recently befell a close friend. Unaccustomed to working out at the gym, he strained on one machine and injured his right foot. Over the next few days he began to feel increasing pain whenever he put any weight on that foot, until after a few weeks he could hardly walk a block without having to sit down. On medical examination it was found that he had a common ailment known as planar fascitis, in which the connecting tissue between the heel and the front of the foot have been stretched or torn. The condition can sometimes be improved through specific exercises; severe cases can require surgery, which isn't always successful.

My friend, a stoic type, decided to tough out the pain and made only sporadic attempts to do the required exercises. In time he found it so difficult to walk, however, that in desperation he sought out a Chinese healer. "I went to his office, which was just a small room in the back of a kung fu studio. He was a short man in his fifties who gave no evidence of being mystical or spiritual, or in any way gifted in healing. But his treatment was remarkable," my friend recalls.

"After gently feeling my foot, he stood up and made a few signs in the air behind my spine. He never actually touched me, and when I asked what he was doing, he said simply that he was turning some switches in my energy field. He did this for a minute or so and then asked me to stand up. I did, and there was no sensation of pain, not the slightest. You have to remember that I had limped in, barely able to walk.

"In complete amazement I asked him what he had done. He told me that the body was an image projected by the mind, and in a state of health the mind keeps this image intact and balanced. However, injury and pain can cause us to withdraw our attention from the affected spot. In that case, the body image starts to deteriorate; its energy patterns become impaired, unhealthy. So the healer restores the correct pattern—this is done instantly, on the spot—after which the patient's own mind takes responsibility for maintaining it that way.

"I stood up on the foot and walked around, just to be sure that I wasn't fooling myself. As I was doing this, the healer told me casually that I could be trained to do the same sort of work. 'Really?' I said. What would it take to be able to accomplish something like this? He answered, 'You only have to discard the belief that it is impossible.' "

To this day my friend has had no recurrence of pain, which is remarkable enough. But here is the spiritual moral of the story: This healing did not change my friend's life. His assumptions about his body remained intact—he didn't begin to see it as a ghostly image or a mask for hidden energies. Belief is incredibly powerful; it can imprint the brain so deeply that even the most remarkable experience doesn't bring any breakthrough into a new reality. My friend's old beliefs were nudged aside slightly, but that is all. One impossible event was not enough to overcome spiritual stuckness. (Christ's reluctance to perform miracles seemed to be based on a similar realization.)

As a child I felt left out spiritually because I would never meet Buddha or Krishna, and my eyes would never see someone raised from the dead or water turned to wine. Now I realize that it isn't the miracle that creates the believer. Instead, we are all believers. We believe that the illusion of the material world is completely real. That belief is our only prison. It prevents us from making the journey into the unknown. To date, after many centuries of saints, sages, and seers, only a few individuals can open to radical change in their belief system, while most cannot. Even so, our beliefs must eventually shift to conform to reality, since in the quantum world, belief creates reality. As we will see, our true home is the light, and our true role is to create endlessly from the infinite storehouse of possibilities located at the virtual level.

Five

STRANGE POWERS

. . . for all things are possible with God.
—MARK 10:27

"I'm the kind of person the church would call lost. Growing up, I didn't have much faith in myself or anything else. If anybody had asked whether I believed in God, I would have said, 'Why should I? He doesn't believe in me.' "

A twenty-four-year-old medical technician was talking about his working-class childhood. In his family, the mother was a devout Catholic, the father a casual believer who stayed home on Sunday while the children were dragged off to Mass.

"Once when I was thirteen, my father and I were walking through downtown Boston, and we passed a street beggar. The guy held out his hand without saying anything. I noticed my father give him a dirty look. We kept walking. In a faint voice behind us the beggar mumbled, 'God bless you.' My father got very angry. 'There's faith for you,' he said sarcastically. 'I work for thirty years and that guy doesn't lift a finger to help himself. Every night he leaves it to Providence whether he gets to eat or have a place to sleep. Faith doesn't get much greater than that.' "

The story illustrates how religious faith clashes head-on with the necessities of life. If there are two realities competing for our allegiance, the material and the spiritual, why should we abandon the material? A cynical Arabic saying advises, "Trust in God but tie up your camels." And since God doesn't interfere to bring even the bare necessities to millions of poor people, disbelief makes sense.

Yet disbelief doesn't seem to work, either. There are mysterious phenomena that can be explained only in terms of an invisible domain that is our source in the sacred. It is the home of our intelligence and our sense of order in the universe. To prove that such a place exists, we look to a vast range of anomalies on the fringes of ordinary events. These include religious awakening and "going into the light," which we have already covered, but also the following:

Inspiration and insight
Geniuses, child prodigies, and savants
Memory of former lifetimes
Telepathy and ESP
Alter egos (multiple personality syn-
  drome)
Synchronicity
Clairvoyance and prophecy

Diverse as they are, these fringe phenomena all take us beyond our present knowledge of the brain into the regions of the
"mind field" that are closest to God. The
brain is a receiver of mind, like a radio
receiving signals from a faraway source. If a
battery-operated radio were dropped from
the sky into the midst of a primitive society,
its members might wind up worshiping it,
because there would be no one who would
understand about how music and voices
could be emitted from this mystical box.

Right now the brain also resembles a
mystical box. We utilize it in very chaotic
ways, however, which is why the ultimate
signals—the ones sent by God—often pass
unnoticed. After sixty years of exploring the
paranormal, and many years of experiencing music, genius, insight, and inspiration,
there are still many spiritual connections
yet to be made. We will be working on

those connections in the following sections, and as we do it will become clearer that quantum reality—the zone of miracles—is a place very nearby.

INSPIRATION AND INSIGHT

If the brain produces thoughts, and these are the result of stored information inside our neurons, how does anyone ever have a new idea? Why aren't we constantly combining and recombining old information? New thoughts come to us from the mind, not the brain. The most original new thoughts are called inspired; on the personal level seeing something new about yourself is called an insight. When you feel inspired, more than ordinary thinking is involved. There is a sense of being uplifted, of suddenly breaking through. Old boundaries fall away, and one feels, if only for a moment, a rush of liberation. If the inspiration is powerful enough, one's whole life can be changed. There are insights so potent that years of patterned behavior can change in an instant.

Let's look more closely at how insight works, because it is very revealing about the mind. A woman who was in therapy showed up at her psychiatrist's office in a state of outrage. She declared that her best friend, Maxine, had committed a terrible personal betrayal. When asked how, she told this story: the two of them were in the last year of law school and had belonged to the same study group. A serious and competitive person, the woman had done everything to help Maxine, providing extensive notes, catching lectures that her friend couldn't attend, and even going so far as to bring food to the group if study hours ran late into the night.

In other words, she considered herself a model of support. The time for finals came, and the two friends spent many hours outside the group preparing for all the possible areas to be covered. During the exam the woman was distressed to find that she was unprepared in one key area. She had forgotten to study an important Supreme Court case, and she missed all the questions devoted to it. She consoled herself with the feeling that at least she could share her misery with her best friend. But when grades were posted, Maxine had done much better than she had, and when asked how this happened, the friend casually dropped that she had studied that particular case on her own.

"All right," the therapist said, "I see all that, but why are you so outraged?"

"You have to ask?" the woman protested. "She betrayed me. She was supposed to be my best friend. I've done everything for her, bent over backward to get her through law school. Now look what she has done."

"Did she do it intentionally?" the therapist asked. "Or was she just looking out for herself? Maybe she meant to tell you, but then she forgot."

The woman set her jaw. "That's not the way you treat a best friend," she maintained. "Maxine obviously doesn't care what happens to me."

If you look beneath the surface, you'll find two deeper layers to this incident. The first layer is psychological and was addressed by the therapist. He didn't see a simple falling-out between friends. His patient was exhibiting all the signs of a severe control defense. Being a perfectionist, taking care of other people's needs even when not asked, taking charge of situations on the assumption that others cannot look out for themselves, and implicitly wanting to be thanked for one's trouble—all these are glaring signs. But how could this insight be transferred from therapist to patient?

"You think Maxine betrayed you," the psychiatrist said. "But actually she is the normal one here. It is perfectly normal to look out for oneself. She had no obligation to share every detail of her study habits with you."

The woman was astonished to hear this and very resistant to it. "You are taking her side?" she asked in bewilderment. "But what about me?"

"It is you I am concerned with. What you haven't been able to see is that there is a piece of reality you can't face. All this help and concern you showed toward Maxine is fine, but it serves to keep you defended from what you can't accept."

"And what is that?"

"Listen carefully," the therapist replied. "Other people have a right to reject you, and there is nothing you can do about it."

The woman sat back, perplexed and upset. The words had been heard, but they hadn't really sunk in. She hesitated on the brink of insight. From her perspective, her actions were those of a betrayed saint. The alternative would be to see herself in a new light, as someone who for years had been "taking care" of others in an attempt to make sure that no one, absolutely no one, ever rejected her.

As it happened, she took the leap: the insight was accepted. Ahead lay several months of anguish as pent-up fear and grief poured out. The defense of her old behavior was gone, and now the hidden energies trapped so long inside could find release.

Earlier I mentioned that there was a second layer to this story, which is spiritual. Insight is one thing, but the impulse to find it is another. Must we accept that this was a random event in this woman's life? Or did a deeper layer of her self provide a situation that opened a door? I believe that life events do not unfold randomly; our materialistic worldview may insist that they do, but all of us have reflected on turning points in our lives and seen, sometimes with bafflement or wonder, that lessons came our way at exactly the time we needed them.

In a word, some hidden intelligence seems to know when and how to transform us, often when we least expect it. By its nature, inspiration is transforming—it brings in spirit—and no model of the brain has come close to explaining how a cluster of neurons could transform itself. One school of neurology is predicated on the notion that the human brain is a computer of enormous ability, but computers don't wake up one morning and decide to have a new attitude toward life. Nor do they have moments of spiritual awakening, whereas human beings experience them all the time.

Computers don't find any idea suddenly meaningful. For them every download of data is the same, a collection of zeros and ones arranged in a coded language. Yesterday's E-mail is no less significant than the New Testament, and no more.

Inspiration is the perfect example of how the invisible level of reality works. *Whatever is needed is provided.* A person may not be prepared to accept the insight, and therefore a chance for transformation will be missed. But that isn't the essential point. The mind is greater than any individual. Your mind isn't a computer; it is a living intelligence, and it evolves, which is why fresh insight is needed.

In the primitive stages of evolution, life became more complex physically—green algae made the leap to becoming plants, for example, by developing a more complex ability to use sunlight. Higher evolution takes place in the mind, as when an Einstein is produced, for example. But the leap from algae to plants was a leap of intelligence, a moment of inspiration, just as much as the discovery of relativity. Unlike the brain, the mind can take leaps; it breaks through old limitations and glories in feeling free.

At every level, to be inspired is a step toward greater liberation, and liberation is a choice. Cells that evolved into plants, flowers, and trees moved ahead of blue-green algae, but at the same time, the lower level of evolution continued to exist as long as it served the environment.

At the moment of insight, there is an "aha!" that opens up new possibilities. At the moment the Buddha was enlightened, there was no further reason for any form of violence or suffering among humankind. Buddha saw that suffering and evil are rooted in a mistake about how life works. He saw that the endless struggle to achieve pleasure and avoid pain would never end as long as we were attached to our ego needs. The ego's selfishness and insecurity would never heal by themselves; there would always be another battle to fight.

This insight came to Gautama under the Bodhi tree, just as it came to Jesus in the desert when he struggled with Satan (one could say the same of any great master or teacher). The fact that the mass of humanity still dwells in ignorance, giving rise to all kinds of suffering, goes back to levels of awareness. In the domain of the mind there is both freedom and attachment; we make the choice which to attune to. Each person sets his own boundaries and breaks through them when the evolutionary impulse is felt.

We've all met people whose problems are completely unnecessary, yet they lack the insight to find the solution. Try to give them this insight, hand it to them on a platter, and still they won't take it. Insight and inspiration must be sought and then allowed to dawn. As our spiritual masters indicate, this is the kind of knowledge you must tune in to. Inspiration teaches us that transformation must begin with trust that a higher intelligence exists and knows how to contact us.

GENIUSES, CHILD PRODIGIES, AND SAVANTS

Brain research has little to say about genius that is very convincing. Statistically we know that geniuses are rare and unpredictable; they are predominantly born in ordinary families, and their own offspring are rarely of exceptional intelligence. This leads us to believe that genius derives from a unique combination of genes—it is somehow encoded from birth in a very few children.

Under autopsy the cerebral cortex of geniuses is only rarely found to be exceptional. (In June 1999, headlines were created by the news that Einstein's brain, preserved for almost half a century after his death, was indeed abnormal. A center that is connected to mathematical ability and spatial perception known as the inferior parietal lobe was found to be 15 percent wider than normal in Einstein's case. Is this proof of genius? Hardly, but there is an almost universal craving to think that geniuses are "different." I would argue that our brains are wired by our minds to begin with, and it is the genius of Einstein's mind, not the radio apparatus under the skull that received its signals, that is fascinating.)

If DNA does not endow geniuses with special structures in their gray matter, then how do genes play a part? After all, unless a gene gives rise to a physical expression, it has no way to influence us. You cannot turn an ordinary brain into a genius's brain, either, and in fact the electrical patterns exhibited when a genius is thinking are not dramatically different from my brain waves when I add up my checkbook.

In our new model genius would be defined as something nonphysical: the ability to activate unmanifest levels of the mind much more efficiently than usual. Contrary to the popular assumption that geniuses think all the time, their minds are in fact quieter and clearer than normal. This clarity may be narrow, however. Geniuses can be plagued by the same mental obstacles as the rest of us, only they have achieved one or more open channels back to the mind field.

Mozart, for example, had difficulty managing the simplest financial affairs; his emotional life was torn between two women; feelings about his father filled his unconscious with suppressed anger and resentment. But the channel of music was so open that Mozart could compose freely from the age of four onward, and in his prime had little difficulty seeing whole pages of a score in his head at once.

Genius is beyond ordinary thought and learning—we could call it continuous inspiration. The same process is involved in a burst of inspiration, but a genius has these bursts longer and with more ease than the rest of us. This brings up an important point: you can only access the mind field at your own comfort level. Your brain and nervous system become fine-tuned to who you are. If you are a civil engineer, your brain becomes accustomed to schematic diagrams, tensile stresses, and so forth. Should you suddenly begin to receive musical inspiration on the order of Mozart, your personal world would be thrown into chaos.

In California a stockbroker who had no

interest in art began to paint canvases of bright-colored ellipses, often in yellow or purple. He startled his friends by beginning to wear clothes in the same bright hues. Emotionally distant from his children as they grew up, he suddenly became more affectionate toward them and seemed less stressed than he had been for years. All of these developments were somehow linked to a change in his visual perception, which caused objects to catch his eye as they never had before. At times a color might be intensely pleasurable in a way he had never experienced, while other colors were intensely painful or caused him to feel sick.

His fascination with color led to a deepening desire to paint; this passion grew so dominant that he retired from his profession to devote himself to his art. As events progressed, however, a darker side emerged to his transformation from broker to amateur Picasso: his memory began to fail, accompanied by the onset of compulsive behaviors such as searching obsessively for lost coins on the street. He became erratically angry and had fits of depression. When these symptoms blossomed into impaired speech and further loss of memory, a UCLA neurologist named Bruce Miller diagnosed a specific rare disease, an early dementia or senility brought on by the gradual destruction of the frontal lobes of the brain.

As a rule patients with dementia do not develop anything positive or life-enhancing from their disorder. But Miller found that in frontotemporal dementia (FTD) a significant number of patients gain sudden talent in music, photography, art, and other creative areas. Although FTD had been known for a hundred years, this particular aspect, which remains mysterious, was a new discovery.[1]

The blossoming of talent is always temporary. The brain's deterioration worsens gradually over time until complete mental derangement results. In the stockbroker's case, his art improved for several years. His early fascination with bright colors developed into complex designs—intricately detailed flowers, birds, and animals emerged and were sold at gallery prices. A single-minded obsessive talent was born from the ashes of a declining brain.

This phenomenon is not unprecedented. Famously ill geniuses include Dostoevsky, afflicted with epilepsy, and Van Gogh, who suffered from an undiagnosed disorder that could have been schizophrenia, epilepsy, or the ravages of advanced alcoholism. Although they never gained fame, certain chronic schizophrenics have painted canvases in which faces peer out at us with distorted, horrific, yet fascinating expressions; sometimes these are accompanied by obsessive attention to tiny details, spiderwebs of lines woven by fixated minds. Yet in the vast majority of cases the balancing act between art and madness eventually tips over into chaos; the beautiful patterns become scrambled, frantic jigsaws as the disease overwhelms the art.

Some psychiatrists have concluded that insanity has the power to incite creativity, but in the case of dementia, there is such disastrous deterioration of the cortex itself that one wonders where any gift could be coming from. Somehow genius, and in rare instances disease, produces wonders of art by opening the brain to regions of awareness unknown in "normal" life.

Child prodigies are at the extreme end of genius. Einstein was not a child prodigy, which means that he didn't have fully formed mathematical skill from the age of ten or younger. His genius was more attuned to an overall vision, not to technical details. Yet some genius is totally formed at birth, it seems, and there is no material explanation for it.

All our current models of the brain indicate that it is unformed at birth and needs experience to mature. If you bandage a kitten's eyes as soon as it is born and leave the blindfold on for just a few weeks, its brain will not have the experience of light. Without that, the visual centers cannot develop, and the kitten will be blind for life. If you don't expose a newborn baby to language, it will never learn to speak. There is even evidence that early deprivation of love and nurturing will leave a lifelong void that later experience cannot fill, or only with great difficulty. In all these cases the experience flowing in from the outer environment shapes the so-called hardwiring of the cerebral cortex. The primitive, unformed network of neurons that a newborn brings into this world isn't like a computer's wiring. Neurons need to interact with all kinds of stimuli before they can form the infinitely ordered, flexible, and efficient network of a mature brain.

According to this model, it should be impossible for the Russian pianist Evgeny Kissin, the most famous musical prodigy of the present generation (he is now nearly thirty), to have displayed musical ability almost at birth. And yet his mother, who took her baby to market in Moscow as she stood in line for food, vividly recalls that her one-year-old hummed Bach inventions in perfect pitch as the other mothers stared in disbelief. And as soon as Evgeny could toddle, he made his way to the family piano and began to pick out the same Bach exercises that he had heard his older sister practicing. These were just the first signs exhibited by a child prodigy who was composing music at six and performing both Chopin piano concertos in a single concert at the age of thirteen—a prodigious feat even for an accomplished virtuoso.

A child's unformed brain could not accomplish these feats. Normal development consists of month after month of random experimentation on a child's part, testing one ability after another until the desirable skills (walking, talking, feeding oneself, toilet training) gradually emerge from the undesirable ones (wetting the bed, making mumbling sounds, crawling on hands and knees). There may be a musical gene that might enable one person to carry a tune while another is tone deaf, but a gene alone can't coordinate all the incredible gifts of a child prodigy. It takes a trained mind to decisively develop one ability out of raw experience. We have to remember that the infant brain must somehow take its stock of 100 billion neurons, all intricately layered but not exposed as yet to the first sight, sound, desire, wish, fantasy, dream, frustration, or fulfillment, and with this soup of raw cells make networks and connections that will last a lifetime. It is astonishing to think that prodigies are doing all that while also developing their one, laser-like talent.

And that is where the unmanifest domain helps us, because a prodigy doesn't come out of nowhere; he is formed by invisible intelligence that has somehow (no one knows exactly) decided to speed up the learning process far beyond the normal pace, leaving nothing to chance, not even the environment. Kissin's family happened to own a piano, but musical geniuses have been born in families with no musical background, and math prodigies regularly appear in nonscientific settings. Somehow or other, they still unerringly find their gift. Mind shapes brain, not the other way around. The intelligence that courses through you is turning you into what you are going to be.

Rarely super-prodigies emerge whose abilities are not confined to a single talent but encompass all mental activity; these children are estimated to fall within the top one-quarter of 1 percent of IQs measured worldwide. A current example is a boy who could recite the alphabet before he was a year old; by eighteen months he could read and memorize books. His mind proved to be omnivorous for knowledge, leading him to complete grades one through twelve by the time he was eight. "I knew my child would surpass me intellectually," his mother was quoted as saying. "I just didn't know it would happen when he was six."

Prodigies are not the most inexplicable sort of genius, however; that honor belongs to idiot savants, people with severe mental defects who exhibit extraordinary abilities at the same time. An idiot savant isn't a complete genius. Usually a single clear channel has been opened to a deep level of the mind field, but with corresponding weakness in other areas. A savant may be able to instantly multiply long numbers, to name the day of the week for any date thousands of years forward or backward in time, or even to calculate square roots beyond the ability of mainframe computers. At the same time, however, such a person may not be able to pick out the right change for the bus or to learn simple reading skills.

Among currently living savants there is one who can recall any license plate number, going back a dozen years. Another has mastery of fifteen foreign languages, including good to excellent knowledge of some of the world's most difficult tongues, including Finnish, Welsh, Hindi, and Mandarin Chinese. A native speaker of English, this particular savant once got lost on the streets of Paris and was found hours later cheerfully translating between two groups of tourists, one Greek, the other German. On his own, however, he was not mentally capable of finding his way back to his nearby hotel. This particular savant can also read writing held upside down or sideways.

Only recently has medicine put a name to this mysterious phenomenon, which is now called "autistic savant syndrome." As the name implies, usually savants are autistic, prone to extreme introversion and obsessive-compulsive behavior; the syndrome is five times more likely to strike males than females. Researchers have been able to pinpoint certain brain anomalies, especially left-hemisphere damage, which causes the right hemisphere to compensate with extraordinary abilities. The right brain dominates in music, art, and unconscious calculating abilities, all of which are common among savants. (Why there is no such compensation among other autistic children is not known.)

Yet does this fully account for such a bizarre mixture of genius and mental deficiency?[2] For one thing, mastery of foreign languages would be a left-brain activity, so the theory that the right hemisphere is compensating for left-brain damage doesn't always hold true. More important, there is no known mechanism by which a deficient brain that cannot organize simple reasoning abilities should suddenly develop supernormal ones. Instead we might speculate that the idiot savant is like a reckless explorer. Some impulse has led him to cross certain frontiers far ahead of normal minds, while at the same time not paying attention to basic necessities.

One savant was almost helpless as a child, a victim of severe retardation, cerebral palsy, and blindness. He was kept in an orphanage at birth until his adoption by a compassionate couple. Not until the age of fourteen was it discovered that he was a musical prodigy. One night his parents awoke to hear someone playing the Tchaikovsky first piano concerto downstairs in the middle of the night. They were astonished to find that it was their adopted son, who had never been exposed to a piano and was far too retarded to take music lessons. Once his savantism emerged, however, he could play any piece of piano music, however complex, after hearing it only once, a feat beyond even a trained professional. Yet this same young man could not manage the simple tasks of cooking, buying clothes, or holding a job.

Such wide disparities are examples of imbalance, not just on the material level but on the level where one's inner life gets organized. The unmanifest domain is beyond time, and yet one of its responsibilities is to organize the world over time. When a rose progresses from winter to spring, it could not survive by releasing the chemicals that would make it go dormant when the genes for blossoming are required. A rose is attuned to the rhythm of the seasons, responding to the slightest changes in daylight and temperature, the angle of the sun, and the moisture in the soil.

We are more fortunate than a rose, since we are not a prisoner of the seasons, but in another sense we are much less fortunate, because we can misuse our freedom of choice and turn to self-destructive behavior. The idiot savant has somehow made some drastic choices inside his mind, and although the intelligence of nature does not snatch away the gift of genius, it does not erase the wrong decisions, either. Our own lives obey the same principle—it is common for anyone to have mastered one aspect of life, such as earning money, while being very poor at another, such as maintaining a loving relationship. In all cases of imbalance, events will be organized to bring the weak parts into focus, even though it is still our own choice whether or not to follow where nature wants to lead us. All these examples of genius, even though they have no obvious spiritual lesson to teach, point to the possibility that the mind can organize an infinite number of ingredients. God's mind feels very close at this point. We are not there yet, but genius is like a window into infinite possibilities.

MEMORY OF FORMER LIFETIMES

Who were you before you were you? The possibility of an afterlife is widely argued in the West, but the existence of a before-life is just as likely. If you believe only in an afterlife, you are restricted to a very limited, dualistic view of time. There is only "here" and "after." But if life is continuous, if the soul never stops making its journey, a completely different worldview opens up.

As part of our medical training in India, every young doctor was sent to a village posting, which was the equivalent of doing public health service. Rural India exists exactly as it did in centuries past, and after the urban culture of New Delhi, the shock of village life feels like time travel. One day in my mud dispensary patients began running outside for no reason. I stepped outside to find that a crowd had gathered around a little girl standing barefoot in the dusty road. She was four or five, and apparently she had appeared from nowhere. Her name, she said, was Neela. It's a common enough name in northern India, but after a few moments the little girl began calling one or two of the villagers by name, people she had never met before. She was gathered up in someone's arms and carried into a nearby house; on the way, however, she pointed to this dwelling and that and made remarks as if she knew them.

Within an hour her frantic parents showed up. They had stopped by the side of the main road in their car, and while unpacking for lunch, the mother noticed that Neela had wandered off. There was a tearful reunion with the little girl. Then the questions began: How had Neela walked the long distance, more than a mile, from the roadside stopping point to the village? How had her parents known to look for her there?

The answer was very strange and yet very Indian. Neela, it turned out, was not her real name, but Gita. As soon as she learned to talk, Gita had kept pointing to herself and saying, "Neela, Neela."

Naturally everyone believed that Gita was a reincarnation. The locals considered the matter, and it wasn't long before someone remembered another Neela, a little girl who had died young on one of the surrounding farms. Someone would have run off to fetch the family who lived there, but Gita's parents became quite nervous. Despite protests, they grabbed up their daughter and sped away in the car. Gita cried as they took her away, staring out the back window as the vehicle receded in a cloud of dust. To my knowledge she never returned.

Many similar incidents of overlapping lifetimes crop up, and not just in the East. Some years back it made news when the search for a reincarnated high Tibetan lama took a delegation of priests to Spain. There a small Catholic baby was identified as a likely candidate. How do boundaries of birth and death become so thin? People who spend time with geniuses and prodigies often find them unearthly, somehow preternatural, as if a very old soul has been confined to a new body and yet brings in experience far beyond what that body could have known. It is easy to credit that some kind of former life is casting its influence on the present. Speaking of his own experience, one musical prodigy stated, "It is as if I am playing from outside my own consciousness. The music comes through me. I am the conduit, not the source."

Does the same effect apply to all of us? Reincarnation is a contentious subject; the Eastern world has adopted it for thousands of years, while the Judeo-Christian tradition has only flirted with the concept and for the most part rejected it. During the Middle Ages belief in earlier lives amounted to heresy.

The unmanifest domain allows us to see this issue a different way. We can frame the notion of former lives as one of awareness. To be aware means that you can activate either a small or a large part of your mind. Some people are keenly aware of their deeper motives, their subconscious emotions, or their creative ability, while other people are closed off. Seers and sages activate deep regions, seeing into human nature as it applies far beyond their own lives. A humble monk in a cave in the Himalayas may be capable of peering into my soul far more clearly than I can (I have had this experience, in fact). So it would seem that the mind isn't limited by experience—all of us have had moments when we know much more than we should.

There is much evidence that the mind is not confined by time and space. Because the brain is located inside the head, we assume that the mind is as well, looking out at the world like a prisoner in a tower. When you say, "I've got this idea running through my head," you operate from this assumption. But awareness is more than ideas and much more even than brain function. I can remember sitting on a bed in a cheap motel watching a crime scene on television. I was twenty-four, it was my first night in America, and the violence I saw on the eleven o'clock news was shockingly new to me. I leaned forward, watching the gunshot victims being carted on gurneys into a local hospital. Suddenly my stomach turned over.

They were going to the hospital where I was supposed to report the next day. The emergency room that was scrambling to remove bullets and crack open chests to massage stopped hearts would be my workplace in twelve hours. I had an unreal feeling as I saw myself being swept into all this American mayhem. The blood staining the sidewalk would soon be on my hands; I would be saving patients who might be policemen or murderers.

I was very emotional at that moment, caught between fascination and dread, and emotions create strong memories. I can feel and see the scene vividly anytime I want to. Is the memory inside my head? If so, then how is it that you are experiencing it as you read this page? Some version of my memory, however faint, has transferred itself to you. You saw an image, you felt a feeling. How did an event supposedly trapped inside my skull get inside yours without passing through something in between?

The brilliant British biologist and researcher in evolutionary theory Rupert Sheldrake has devised extremely clever experiments that turn on this very riddle. For example, he gave English-speaking children several groups of Japanese words and asked them which ones were poetry. Even though they knew not a word of Japanese, the children could pick out the verses with remarkable accuracy, as if they heard the difference between ordinary sentences, or even nonsense syllables, and delicate haikus. How did this knowledge get into their heads? Is it floating in the air or available through a planetary mind that we all share?

Just as a quantum of energy can leap between two points without crossing the space in between, so apparently can a thought. A field of awareness flows in, around, and through each of us. Some of this awareness is localized. We say "my" memory and "my" thoughts, but that isn't the whole story. A neuron can't claim "this is my idea" until millions of cells have come together to form each image or thought. Their ability to communicate doesn't require them to touch. Millions of heart cells that keep the same cardiac rhythm do not touch, either. The coordination of brain or heart depends on an invisible electrical field whose minute charges establish patterns among billions of tiny individual cells. A heart in which the electrical field becomes jumbled begins to writhe in agony as each cell loses contact with the others; the effect is like a bag of worms pulsing violently until the heart deprives itself of oxygen to the point of death. (This is known as fibrillation, one symptom of a heart attack.)

Awareness seems to be an even more subtle field, not only invisible but needing no energy. When you picked up my old memory, no electrical or magnetic current passed between us. The simple act of recognizing a friend on the street contains a similar mystery. When you see a familiar face, your brain doesn't run through its catalog of all known faces to arrive at who your friend is. A computer would have to do that, consuming energy as it did so. But your brain doesn't scan its entire memory bank when it sees a strange or a familiar face— what we call recognition takes place instantly, at a deeper level of awareness.

Awareness does need chemical links. In your immune system a T cell floating past an invading virus recognizes it and goes on the attack. It recognizes the enemy according to the chemical coding on the outside of the germ, which has to match another coding on the outside of the T cell before any kind of alert is sent via messenger molecules throughout the body. A few cold viruses or pneumococci are enough to put billions of immune cells on alert. However, such a chemical explanation of immunity fails to solve some basic issues. Why does a T cell let in the AIDS virus without fighting it?

The answer given by virologists focuses on the outside coating of the HIV virus, a deceptive code of molecules that disguises itself in such a way that it can sneak past the corresponding coding on the outside of the T cell—rather like a guerilla warrior using underground tactics instead of a frontal assault. If this is so, how did HIV learn to do this? Chemicals are neutral; they have no awareness built into them. Therefore to a chemical it is insignificant whether the HIV virus or the T cell survives. Yet to the cells that is all-important. This leads us to ask how a cell learns to reproduce in the first place. DNA is composed of simple sugars and bits of protein that never divide or reproduce, no matter how many billions of years they exist. What step caused these simple molecules to get together, arrange themselves in a pattern with billions of tiny segments, and all of a sudden learn to divide?

One plausible answer is that an invisible organizing principle is at work. The need for life to reproduce itself is fundamental; the need for chemicals to reproduce themselves is nil. So even at this most basic level, we see certain qualities of awareness— recognition, memory, self-preservation, and identity—coming into play. Now add the element of time. It isn't enough for DNA just to reproduce itself randomly; that is the behavior of cancer, which reproduces without regard and eventually engulfs its host, leading to its own death.

To form a baby, a single fertilized cell must be a master of timing. Every organ of the body exists in seed form within a single strand of DNA, yet to emerge correctly, they must take their turn. For the first days and weeks, an embryo is called a zygote or seed; it is an undifferentiated mass of similar cells. But very soon one cell starts to give off chemicals unique to itself. Even though the mother cells are identical, some of the off-spring know, for example, that they are meant to be brain cells. As such, they need to specialize, growing into far different shapes than muscle or bone cells. This they do with amazing precision, but in addition they send out signals to attract other proto-brain cells. Like attracts like, and as brain cells float toward each other, they cross paths with proto-heart, proto-kidney, and proto-stomach cells, none of them getting in the way or causing a confusion of identity.

This spectacle is far more astonishing than the eye can see. Visibly there is nothing but a soup of cells swimming around and forming patterns. Yet think of it: a baby brain cell somehow knows who it is going to be in advance. For many weeks a neuron is developing its structure, not yet mature but no longer undifferentiated, either. How does it keep track of its purpose in life with so many billions of signals being sent all around it? This is as mysterious a question

as asking how a T cell first learned to recognize an enemy before meeting one.
Memory, learning, and identity precede
matter; they govern matter. If a cluster of
brain cells misses even one beat, if a cerebral cell floats up to its assigned layer of the
brain but gets slightly clogged in traffic,
bunching up instead of spreading out into
an even layering, the result is that the baby
will be born with dyslexia. How did such a
mishap occur, given that brains have been
evolving for tens of millions of years,
whereas reading a book is at most three
thousand years old? It would have made no
difference to a Neanderthal brain whether
the word *God* looked like the word *dog*, yet
a newborn neuron has been able to avoid
that mistake for eons in advance of the
invention of language.

I conclude that the field of awareness is
our true home, and that awareness contains
the secrets of evolution, not the body or
even DNA. This shared home is "the light"
spoken of by mystics; it is the potential for
life and intelligence, and it is life and intelligence once they appear. Your mind is one
focus of this cosmic awareness, but it
doesn't belong to you like a possession. Just
as your body is held together by inner
awareness, there is a flow of awareness out-

side you. If you consider for a moment, you can catalog many common experiences that require you to be outside your brain. Have you ever felt that someone is watching you behind your back, only to turn around and find that in fact someone is there? We've all finished a friend's sentence or exclaimed, "I was thinking the same thing!" on the heels of another person's thought.

A woman told me about standing on the Pacific shore in Oregon worrying about her dying father. She looked up at the sunset and saw his face in her mind, while his voice distinctly said, "Forgive me." Later that night the woman called her sister, and it turned out that she had had the same vision and heard the same words. As an exercise I sometimes encourage a group of people to try to go beyond their limited perception— I call this "going into your virtual body." Each person sits with eyes closed and gives himself permission to travel anywhere the impulse wants to go. The images that come to mind don't have to be judged, only accepted and allowed to flow. One woman, who was single and living with her boyfriend, saw him cleaning out the closet at home, startling only because he had never done such a thing. The image was vivid, as if she were right there with him, and apparently she was, because when she called home, he had a surprise for her—he had completely cleaned and rearranged her closet so that she could get at her things more easily.

Now let's return to the original question: Who were you before you were you? Even though we all identify with a very limited slice of time and space, equating "me" with one body and one mind, in reality you also live outside yourself in the field of awareness. The Vedic seers say, "The real you cannot be squeezed into the volume of a body or the span of a lifetime." Just as reality flows from the virtual to the quantum to the material level, so do you. Whether we call this reincarnation or not almost doesn't matter. The package of body and mind that came before is a stranger to you now, and the one that might arise after your death is equally alien. But on a deeper level, millions of seeds have already been planted. Some are the thoughts you will have tomorrow or the actions you will follow a decade from now. Time is flexible at the quantum level and nonexistent at the virtual level. As we watch these seeds sprouting in the fertile field of time and space, awareness wakes up to itself. This is how a single fertilized cell learns to become a brain—it wakes up to itself, not on the chemical level but on the level of awareness.

Perhaps you are a single cell among millions too, each cell being a lifetime. It was said that the Buddha closed his eyes for a few minutes and experienced ninety-nine thousand incarnations. If this is not breathtaking enough, we are told that he experienced every minute of them; births, deaths, and time itself expanded in a few minutes of silence. Such an amazing ability to control time lies not only with the enlightened. If you weren't a master of time already, you would be an amorphous glob of cells like the sea cucumber; you might have entered a world where puberty could come at any moment and kidney cells could fuse into spleens, or where the first pollen of hay fever season might kill half the population.

Now imagine that expanded awareness is normal. Time and space could just be convenient concepts that hold true in the material world but dissolve gradually as you approach the quantum level. This is what I believe reincarnation is about. Former lives fall into the unexplored territory of expanded awareness. It isn't absolutely necessary to decide whether they are "real" or not. Concrete verification that I was a Nepalese soldier at the time of the Emperor

Ashoka is never going to come my way. But if I find myself extremely attracted to that period, if I start to read about Ashoka and his conversion to Buddhism, and if my empathy is so strong that I cannot help but adopt some of those principles, we can truthfully say that a wider range of life has influenced my mind. In a very real sense, the terms *former life* and *expanded life* are the same thing.

All of the quantum and virtual levels are open to us all the time. To navigate them completely is impossible; they open up to us according to our own needs and abilities. But no part is intentionally closed off. Although we normally look no deeper than the personal domain, to look deeper is always possible. It is more normal to learn from the past than not to, and people who shut out their former lives—if we want to use that terminology—are shutting out lessons that give this present lifetime its purpose and meaning. For someone who has absorbed these lessons fully, there is no need to go beyond this lifetime, and yet such visitations are still part of the natural order of things.

Finally, the fact that we are not confined to our physical body and mind gives us reason to believe in the existence of a cosmic intelligence that permeates life—and brings us close to the mind of God. But since we are talking about a quantum phenomenon, it isn't correct to say that God has been found, the way you would find a lost book where you forgot to look for it. A woman who had read some of my earlier writings on quantum reality had become excited and then went enthusiastically to her minister. He listened somewhat grimly while she poured out her bubbling happiness over these new spiritual ideas. When she was finished, he said curtly, "Call this man up and ask him if God is inside all of us."

Obediently she tracked down my number and called. In a hesitant voice she asked the question, and I said, "Yes, according to the quantum model, God is inside all of us."

She couldn't disguise her disappointment. "Oh dear, that's exactly what my minister said you would say." And then she hung up, crestfallen that the acceptable God, the one who looks over us from heaven, had been undermined. Only afterward did I realize that I had been carelessly trapped, for my answer wasn't right. In the quantum model there is no inside or outside. God is no more in us than he is anywhere else—he is simply not locatable. To say that we go within to meditate, to pray, or to find God is really just a convention. The timeless place where God exists can't be reduced to an address. Our exploration into former lifetimes indicates that the same may be true of us as well.

TELEPATHY AND ESP

The ability to know what another person is thinking, whether you call it mind reading or extrasensory perception, also occupies a shadowy middle ground between popular belief and science. In the laboratory, psychologists have discovered that some individuals are much more skillful at this than others. Subject A, when placed in a separate room staring at a series of picture cards, can sometimes transmit these mental images with surprising accuracy to another room where subject B is trying to receive them. Yet science has more or less stopped there. Various underground experiments were conducted by defense agencies during the Cold War to see if spies might be able to send messages or images by telepathy to a cohort across the Iron Curtain, but these attempts were never reliable. On the other hand, they were not complete failures, either.

ESP has hindered investigation because it isn't clear that there really is a sender and a receiver. The blurring of two minds or the sharing of one thought is just as likely an explanation. We spoke about the fuzzy boundaries of time and space, and the boundary of personality is just as fuzzy. Are you really separate from me, or is this a convenient illusion we maintain so that life can proceed in a certain predictable way?

Old married couples often seem to merge in both personality and thought. Twins can have uncanny similarities in the way their lives unfold. Extensive studies of identical twins, however, show that no stereotype covers all cases. At one extreme, a pair of identical twins can be so completely merged that they never live apart and, when questioned, speak with one voice and apparently think with one mind. In the unfortunate instance that one twin dies prematurely, the other mourns for life. At the other end of the spectrum, a pair of identical twins can be almost total strangers, sharing no experiences or thoughts. Many studies have been conducted of twins separated at birth and raised apart by totally different sets of parents. Generally in these cases the twins still exhibit about a 50 percent strong resemblance in behavior and thought patterns. When reunited, they also can form strong bonds, and then it is likely that some kind of mental sharing, whether it is ESP or not, will take place. Even when the empathy is intense, though, the twins do not divide into a sender of thought and a receiver.

What this implies is that in the mind field, any boundary can be tenuous. If necessary, your mind can merge and communicate with another mind. A thought that, properly speaking, should belong to one of you becomes a joint experience. Why would such a merging be necessary? No one can really answer that precisely—in general, momentous events will act as a trigger, causing a spouse to intuit her dying partner's last wishes or one twin to know that his brother had suddenly been struck by lightning. The twin to whom this actually happened felt the shock of the lightning passing through his own body at the instant his sibling was killed. (To further underline the point in a bizarre way, after writing this example down, I met a lawyer who was pulled from an afternoon meeting by a wrenching pain in his abdomen. He had never had such an experience and departed home immediately. When he got there the police were waiting with tragic news. His mother had been stabbed and killed by an act of random violence at exactly the moment he had felt the pain. By what mysterious stroke of synchronous timing were mother, son, and murderer tied in a karmic dance?)

But some ESP is totally trivial and inconsequential, too, as when we phone someone and hear, "I was just thinking about you." The real fascination lies deeper. We all assume that we are the authors of our thoughts. They don't simply appear as messages in our heads; we actively think them. But ESP tends to contradict this assumption. If two people vividly share the same thought, it may be that neither one is the author; there is simply the simultaneous reception of an idea. We can cite instances where two philosophers or scientists had the identical inspiration without knowing each other. The simultaneous invention of the calculus by Leibniz and Newton is one famous example.

In Hollywood identical story lines arrive in clusters, so that millions wind up being spent on competing asteroid collision plots or volcano epics. The U.S. Patent Office gets bombarded by nearly identical inventions. We often say that an idea is "in the air," and this may be literally true, in that the unmanifest may unfold certain insights or revelations on a broad scale. This is particularly true on the collective level, where an entire society may be gripped with enthusiasm for revolution or social change. There doesn't have to be a sender or receiver in these cases, even though a prominent speaker of the new thought usually appears. We just say that a society is ripe for change when in fact a much more subtle process—the attunement of millions of individuals to a collective mind field—is taking place.

In a fascinating experiment, mothers who breast-fed their infants were separated from them and given no information about their babies' activities. Even though miles away, many mothers started to lactate at exactly the same moment that their babies began crying and demanding milk. Two intimately connected minds can be united at the level of awareness. You may have cried out for help or solace from someone miles away, and sometimes they respond by showing up or calling. In wartime it is not uncommon for parents to know with certainty the exact moment that a son is killed on the battlefield.

Awareness doesn't have to be human; it seems to pervade all life-forms. In a forest where trees are being heavily foraged by

animals, individual trees can protect themselves with a chemical defense. They start
to exude indigestible tars into their leaves
before they are even touched—having been
warned by neighboring trees via chemical
signals in the air or through their roots. In a
similar act of communal awareness, the
cells of a sea cucumber are arranged to give
a mouth and digestive tract to this primitive
animal, which is little more than a giant
feeding tube. You can puree a sea cucumber
in a blender, pour the solution of brine and
cells into a bucket, and after a while the
entire animal will regroup itself from the
unformed biological sludge.

These are all examples of awareness as a
field beyond the body. These examples help
us to shift away from a strictly private, isolated mind to a universal, shared mind
whose body is the universe. Isolation is a
material fact but not a quantum fact. The
boundaries dividing "me" and "you" are
much thinner than we realize. There is reason to believe that personal identity is just
another convenience, useful for everyday
living but ultimately too flimsy to be taken
as real. I believe this is implied in the scriptural phrases "children of God" and "created in his image." Insofar as we are
children of our parents, personality is sim-

ply continuing itself. One generation teaches the next how to obey the rules of limited identity. But in a multilayered reality, there has to be another father/mother for our extended identity, and this is the role we assign to God. We have not yet proved that there is such a divine parent, but it seems undeniable that our cosmic identity is real.

ALTER EGOS (MULTIPLE PERSONALITY SYNDROME)

In spiritual literature the body is sometimes called the vehicle of the soul, which is another way of saying that the invisible part dresses itself in visible clothing. Actually, the body is just as spiritual as the soul; both are expressions of the same awareness. As it unfolds into manifestation, the field of mind has to assume form, and form isn't simple—it takes thousands of processes to organize a single amoeba, much less a human body. Therefore, the flow of intelligence must obey laws that are set in place at the deepest level.

Where one law ends, another begins, and between them a boundary is set as a division. For example, a skin cell in the middle level of the epidermis lives its life, dividing, breathing, and feeding, but as it is pushed closer to the surface, it begins to harden gradually, and by the time it arrives in contact with the air, its exterior is toughened enough to withstand contact with the environment. However, in this process the cell also dies, to be sloughed off and make way for the next generation of epidermal cells.

The same proteins that will lead to the end of a cell's life serve to protect the body as a whole. How did the body learn this sacrificial act of altruism? When white cells become engorged with invading bacteria, they die in that service as well. An overarching awareness realizes what is good for the whole and can therefore sacrifice a small part.

One law never applies to all; even life and death are apportioned out in small, precise steps. Every cell in your body, as it evolved in the embryo, obeyed a host of different rules as it matured. The original fertilized ovum split into some cells in the stomach that survive only a few days, while others in the brain may last a lifetime. The same DNA that willingly destroys itself in a skin cell fights for survival in a sperm cell, whose frantic rush to fertilize an egg has been evident as long as plants and animals have existed.

Now we are faced with a paradox, for awareness seems to be capable of infinite organization. It is both inside us and outside; it fights to live and yet rushes to die; it organizes itself into an incredibly complex whole yet is subdivided into almost infinite tiny compartments. This organization becomes noticeable mostly when it breaks down, such as when the laws that govern cell division, or mitosis, become deranged and a cancer cell wildly divides without limit. In this case the cell is acting for its own survival, feeling that it must reproduce at maximum rate, much as locusts breed out of control into plagues. Ultimately a plague dies out because it exceeds the amount of food available, and a cancer cell ultimately dies because it kills the host body. This outcome is obvious and would be communicated to the cancer cell if it were in contact with the body's basic intelligence, yet somehow this natural connection has been broken.

In psychological terms, a similar thing happens with alter egos or its clinical extreme, multiple personality syndrome. Alter egos are formed under psychological pressure. The stress that one personality cannot contain spills over into another. If I feel unfairly treated at work, I may have a dream in which I am a lion tamer whipping a big cat to do my will, and these may be symbols of the stress I'm not able to handle when I'm awake. The dream's interpretation may not be open to me, so I may not be aware that the lion is my boss or that my fear of him is being acted out here.

The person suffering from multiple personalities is in much the same situation, but the lion tamer exists in waking state. The negative energies of hatred, fear, child abuse, self-doubt, humiliation, and so forth get played out as if they belonged to someone else. These other personalities are trapped within one body, but they are separate enough to pretend that they aren't.

At the unmanifest level, each of us is many people; you can define this in terms of lifetimes, but that isn't necessary. When you read a novel with a fascinating character in it, you subtly blend into that figure, allowing a boundary of awareness to melt temporarily so that you can have the experience of being inside someone else's skin. If you come from a family where certain striking events are discussed for years, it becomes hard to remember whether these strong memories really belong to you or were piped into your mind. I know a man whose parents lost their home to fire when he was two years old, and he cannot recall if he saw the house burn down or sees it only with secondhand vividness. Emotionally he feels the same trauma as if he had been there, but he could have absorbed his parents' emotions of shock and loss.

Normally our alter egos are shadowy, and the ability to rejoin our "real" personality is overtly ours to control. We know that we aren't Scarlett O'Hara or Ebenezer Scrooge, yet we allow the willing suspension of disbelief to take over for a brief hour or so. Some characters are so overpowering that you may fall under their influence for a much longer time. Neurosis is often marked by this kind of long-range influence, where an inner child with all its weakness and fearfulness continues to preside inside an adult personality.

If your boundaries are too thin, however, you cannot control this act of becoming another character. The extreme state of this is alter egos.

From the perspective of the mind field, if an alter ego is strong enough, it can actually change the body to conform to it. Striking cases are on record in which one personality is menopausal, for example, while the others aren't, or where each of the alter egos has its own menstrual cycle. In other cases a single personality may be diabetic or allergic to pollen while the others show no signs of these disorders. The patient can be in the throes of a severe asthma attack when a new personality enters the scene, and at that instant all evidence of asthma will disappear. The diabetic personality may be insulin dependent and yet revert to normal blood sugar levels during the times when other personalities appear.

This phenomenon, as I see it, cannot be explained as brain function. The brain adapts itself in our childhood, so that what we know, what we have experienced, what we like and dislike are all formative. A person who violently dislikes insects will jump at the sight of a spider without having to think consciously about it. To claim that the brain could form different reactions for a dozen personalities is not credible; it would defy everything we know about childhood development. Alter egos must come from a region beyond personal experience; they are like voluntary incarnations—or partial incarnations—activated from the storehouse of the mind field.

This alone doesn't make an alter ego unnatural. A great actor also activates his portrayal of Hamlet by going to the unmanifest. We say that he is bringing his character to life, as opposed to lesser actors who only imitate. The school of acting known as Method consists of going inward and finding emotional memories powerful enough to convince the audience that they are real, that one is actually feeling Hamlet's guilt on stage before our eyes. Someone afflicted with alter egos is like a master of Method who doesn't realize that he is acting. He has no fixed core, no central perspective that is not acting; he therefore can't see that the illusion is an illusion.

"Why do you insist that my normal self is unreal?" a disciple once complained to his master.

"Why not put it the other way?" the master replied. "What makes you think you are real?"

"It's obvious," said the disciple. "I think and feel and act. I know myself for who I am, with all my habits, my likes and dislikes."

"Yes, but what do you really know?" the master insisted. "Did you have your habits when you were asleep?"

"Of course not. I am unconscious when I am asleep."

"Perhaps you are unconscious now."

"No, right now I am awake."

"Really?" The master smiled. "Can you remember everything that happened to you yesterday? Or even what you were thinking an hour ago? Isn't your self-awareness very selective, amounting to just a partial memory? And then there are your dreams, which you lose as soon as you wake up. Not to mention that your habits and preferences are always changing, and even when you do seem stable, don't your emotions often betray you? An insult from a passing stranger can completely throw you off balance, or the news that someone close to you has died. Isn't there also the problem of being lost in wishes, false hopes, and various mental illusions?"

The disciple looked baffled. "All this may be true, sir, but none of it makes me unreal. Perhaps I am just very confused."

The master shook his head. "If so, then everyone is just as confused. The truth is that what we call a person is constantly in flux. There are long stretches of forgotten time, not to mention our lapse of consciousness when we sleep. Memory is faulty, and only the mind's craving for continuity keeps alive the illusion that 'I' is constant. 'I' is never constant. For every experience there is a different experiencer."

"I am beginning to see what you mean," the disciple said with considerably more humbleness. "Although you make it seem that nothing can be trusted."

"Nothing about the changing personality

can be trusted," said the master. "But there is more to life than experience. Things come and go—feelings, events, achievements. Pleasure is inevitably followed by pain. Success is bound up with failure. Yet behind all this show of change, something remains aware at all times. Find out what that awareness is and you will have what can be trusted. This is the way out of illusion."

In a society where we do not cultivate spiritual relationships, this kind of lesson is hard to learn. We continue to foster our alter egos, the many experiencers who are born with every experience. From the virtual perspective, however, our lives are therefore spent in illusion, because in reality we are not really limited by time and space, nor by this one body and mind. To discover our true nature involves a process of growth, and part of that growth is to deal with conflicts inside boundaries. If you have anxiety, you aren't supposed to shuffle it off onto another ego but deal with it within the limits of yourself. Multiple personality syndrome is therefore a strategy that works in the short run, because the separate egos usually have no idea of what the others are going through, but in the long run the person isn't anybody whole, just a collection of floating, disorganized fragments.

Multiple personality doesn't have to be so disordered. We are all multiple personalities in that we switch from one role to another every day. I shift my identity among personas called father, son, brother, husband, professional. In fact, our inner dialogue is always based on the roles we are playing. If I think about a patient, the role of doctor becomes my internal reference point; if I think about my son, the internal reference point shifts automatically to father. This is not a disordered process; indeed people who cannot shift roles, who always have to be the authority or the boss, for example, even when that is not appropriate, suffer from an inability to express their multiple personalities.

But the real "I" is neither doctor nor father nor any of my roles. "I" exists beyond and then manifests as father or doctor or son with the flicker of intention. To be grounded in this "I" is to be an alert witness to the roles we assume. This alert witness, because it exists in the virtual realm, approaches the mind of God. It may even be a part of God, for we assign to God the role of cosmic witness, the creator who looks on his creation with an all-knowing gaze. We don't yet know what that gaze means. We haven't yet addressed the issue of whether God is judging us. But at least we have gone beyond the illusion of our ever-shifting ego, and any step closer to the witness is moving closer to the divine.

SYNCHRONICITY

Time is not neutral. We say that it flows, and flow implies a direction, as well as a place where the journey ends. To the human mind, time has always flowed toward us. We are the end point of all those billions of years of evolution. God laid out time for us, as he continues to lay out each person's life so that it has a purpose to its unfolding. Such at least was the old belief, but to hold that God, a timeless being, sits outside the universe and plans the ticktock of creation is no longer tenable.

We assume instead that randomness rules. Science has offered chaos theory to demonstrate that disorder lies at the heart of nature. As we have already seen, every object can be reduced to a swirl of energy that has no more pattern than a swirl of tobacco smoke puffed into the air. The scientific worldview tells us that events are not organized by any kind of outside force. A coincidence says otherwise; it is like a momentary reprieve from chaos. When two strangers meet and discover by chance that they have the same name or phone number, when someone decides at the last minute not to board a jet that later crashes, or when any train of events takes place that is exactly what is needed to reach an outcome, it seems as though more than simple coincidence is at work. Jung invented the term *synchronicity* to cover these "meaningful coincidences," and the term has stuck even though it doesn't cast much light on the mystery. What outside force can organize time in such a way that two things meet, like the *Titanic* and the iceberg, with such a sense of fatefulness?

My own life has been touched often by synchronicity, so much so that now I get on an airplane expecting the passenger in the next seat to be surprisingly important to me, either just the voice I need to hear to solve a problem or a missing link in a transaction that needs to come together. (One time a staff consultant called me on the cell phone with enthusiastic plans for manufacturing a new and healthier line of herbal teas. I was running late to a plane, so I couldn't talk, and the proposal at that moment seemed far-fetched and rather impractical. The flight attendant guided me into the last remaining seat on a totally booked flight, and as if by design, the stranger next to me was a wholesaler in herbal teas.)

Therefore my thoughts on this matter are highly personal: I believe that all coincidences are messages from the unmanifest— they are like angels without wings, so to speak, sudden interruptions of superficial life by a deeper layer. On the scientific side, however, I also suspect that there are no coincidences at all. Synchronicity is built into us at the genetic level, but our conscious minds choose to ignore this fact. We do not admit that our lives are balanced on the knife-edge of time.

In a way no one has satisfactorily explained, our DNA is both in time and outside it. It is in time because all bodily processes are subject to cycles and rhythms, yet DNA is much more isolated than other chemicals anywhere in the body. Like a queen bee in her chamber, your DNA remains insulated within the cell's nucleus, and 99 percent of your genetic material lies dormant or inactive until it needs to uncoil and divide to create a mirror image of itself. Inactive DNA is chemically inert, and here is where time becomes more ambiguous. How does an inert chemical decide to wake up, and when?

For a child to lose her baby teeth and replace them with adult ones, DNA has to know a great deal about the passage of time. The same holds true for any process—the maturing of the immune system, learning to walk and talk, the long gestation of a fetus in the womb—that must take place on schedule. Death itself may be a genetic response coded into our cells with a hidden timetable, the theory being that our ancestors could not have afforded to live too long. A tribe of mostly young, child-bearing members would be able to fight and gather food better than one burdened by excessive numbers of old people. DNA could take care of that dilemma by programming its own decline and demise, as grass does with the first frost, guaranteeing the survival of the species at the cost of the individual.

Such speculation, however fascinating, begs the main question. How does DNA have *any* sense of time? It lives in a purely chemical world, surrounded by molecules that float by. It is certainly true that every cell maintains incredibly complex sequencing of chemical reactions—the marvel is that a cell can breathe, feed itself, excrete wastes, divide, and heal while living on death row, since a sentence of death is hanging over each cell all the time. This sentence is imposed by the fact that a cell cannot store reserves of oxygen and nutrients. It depends entirely on what flows into it. Cells stand at the forefront of life, storing no more than three seconds' worth of food and air; they cannot wait on late deliveries; lapses in efficiency would be instantly fatal.

Researchers can isolate those enzymes or peptides that carry the messages needed to trigger any given process in a cell, or to end it. This doesn't really tell us who decided to send the messages in the first place or how thousands of signals manage to stay so precisely coordinated. Ultimately, all messages are sent by DNA to itself.

Looking outside our bodies, one can assume that DNA had to evolve in a random world. Even at this very moment the assault on your body from the environment remains unpredictable. Cosmic rays penetrate your cells randomly, a bombardment that can potentially damage your genes. Random cell mutations occur as the result of mischance or accident, and your DNA has no guarantee that food, water, and temperature will be predictable, not to mention the sudden inrush of new toxins and pollutants of every kind.

Imagine ancestral strands of DNA trying to survive in conditions far worse, as a young Earth convulsed through extremes of hot and cold in an atmosphere electrically charged with storms and filled with methane gas. Somehow DNA not only survived conditions that would have killed us in a matter of days or hours, but it evolved in such a way that when this hostile environment changed to a more benign one, our genes were prepared for that as well.

Except for the rotation of the planet and the change of seasons, DNA wasn't exposed to a world of precise timing. Yet one has to conclude that when DNA took the immense step of learning to reproduce itself, a mastery of time came along. As strange as it sounds, bits of nucleic acid learned to read a watch down to thousandths of a second, and no amount of trauma from the outside world has made a dent in that ability. DNA's mastery of time is woven into the texture of life itself.

Having seen this, the leap into synchronicity is not far. We only need to add the subjective ingredient: time has been ordered to benefit me, not just for my genes. Have you ever been stuck on some problem and turned on the television, only to have the next words coming out of it suddenly offer you a solution? A friend of mine was stepping onto a bus one day, wondering if he should heed the advice of a certain spiritual teacher, when the man ahead of him in line turned around and without any prompting said, "Trust him."

These messages come from a level of mind that knows life as a whole, and ultimately we would have to say that we are really communicating with ourselves—the whole is talking to its parts. Synchronicity steps outside the brain and works from a larger perspective.

Eliminating mind from the equation won't work because the only alternative is chance. In the mid-1980s, a man in Canada won the national lottery two years in a row. Since we know how many tickets were sold, the odds against this happening by chance can be precisely computed, and the answer is trillions and trillions to one—the exact number was said to be greater than the known stars in the universe. One reason Jung invented a new word for these meaningful coincidences is that the normal rational way of explaining them turned out to be too unwieldy. If I sit next to a stranger on a plane who is looking for a certain book idea to publish and that happens to be the very idea I am working on, the explanation of statistical probability does not apply.

Although not easy to calculate, the odds of most synchronous events are preposterous. Anytime two people meet and discover that they have the same name or phone number, the odds are millions to one against their encounter. Yet this occasionally happens, and the simple explanation—that they were meant to meet—makes more sense than random numbers, but it isn't scientific. In spiritual reality, however, literally everything happens because it is meant to. The world is a meaningful place; everyone is working out their own lives' purpose. At synchronous moments, you get a peek at just how connected your life is, how completely woven into the infinite tapestry of existence.

In the future, as spirit is given more credibility, I think the term *synchronicity* will become outmoded; our descendants will take for granted that all events are organized into patterns. Like our DNA, we have always flowed with the river of time and sat on the banks observing it simultaneously. It is only outside time that we can view our own deepest intelligence, because in the thick of things, time captures our attention and pulls us into its web. When we consider that we might be weaving the web, but from another level of reality, the possibility opens that God is sharing this task with us. We are building the argument that every aspect of creation requires us to be a co-creator, and this notion makes intimacy with God more and more likely.

CLAIRVOYANCE AND PROPHECY

The quantum world is a place of blurry edges and uncertain outcomes. As we have seen, the things that seem so well defined in the material world turn into shadowy phantoms the deeper we go into the unmanifest domain. Time is no exception, and at a certain level of reality it hardly exists. When the boundary of time dissolves completely, it is possible to experience a kind of mental time travel called clairvoyance, or the ability to see into the future.

The brain cannot construct the clairvoyant state, as far as we know, since its visual centers are preoccupied with present sensations. Dreams are a kind of false vision, in that they are not really happening before our eyes yet appear to be. The clairvoyant is also experiencing an "unreal" visual state, yet the inner vision happens to come true. How, then, can a purely internal firing of neurons match events that have not come to pass?

In my experience those who consider themselves clairvoyant are not all gifted with the same abilities. Inner vision can be clear or blurred; it can come and go, which makes it often unreliable; and its accuracy is always open to question, since no one knows to what extent the future is predetermined or open to change. A young friend of mine fell in love with a woman who, though fond of him, did not return his strong feelings. He became convinced, however, that she was his soul mate. He despaired of ever turning her feelings around and went to a psychic to find out if his soul-mate theory was true. The psychic came up with a startling number of accurate details. She assured him that she saw a woman named Tara with long brown hair who was going to art school. She further saw that the two of them would soon be living together; Tara's feelings would change, and as she recognized their deep spiritual bond it would become possible for the two to marry. This future vision, which included two children and a move to Los Angeles, delighted my friend, because it precisely fit his own vision of what the future *should* be.

And that was the problem. Even though the psychic had tuned in to something deep in my friend's awareness, the pictures in her vision didn't come true. Far from being reassured, Tara was made very uncomfortable by the revelation that she was destined to wed a man whom she considered no more than a good friend. She withdrew from him, eventually finding her own boyfriend and moving in with him during summer vacation. The connection of two soul mates was never realized.

Yet I know of other clairvoyants who do not seem to be misled by the hopes of their clients. They seem able to divide the wishful image from the actual event that will transpire, giving accurate images of a future mate or the outcome of a lawsuit, down to the exact timing of a judge's rulings. This accuracy gives serious pause, because as much as we might want to know the future, a preordained outcome renders all our striving insignificant. (To a skeptic who discredits clairvoyance, the problem is moot, naturally.)

What would make us believe that clairvoyance is genuine? How is it different from other subjective illusions like dreams and hallucinations? For one thing, dreams typically contain material that was already present inside the person's memory. The symbols of a dream may be mysterious at first glance, but since dreams are wholly drawn from past experience, like old wine in new bottles, they are subject to interpretation. A clairvoyant, however, sees something new. But dreams and clairvoyance do have one strong link: they seem to depend on a person's belief or the belief system of a whole society.

This implies that there is more than one way for the future to flow into the present. It can send messages ahead or keep itself completely veiled; it can choose those who will see and those who will be blind. Much more than we realize, our own awareness may be creating the boundaries of past, present, and future. In other words, we may be choosing not to be clairvoyant so that our belief in a hidden future is confirmed. When Cassandra foresaw the fall of Troy in the *Iliad*, her vision might have been believed, since the belief system of the ancient world included clairvoyant knowledge. (As it happened, the gods had cursed her always to be right and yet never to be believed; we call such a person a Cassandra to this day.)

In quantum terms, one cannot be certain about the line between hallucinations and reality. There are no definite events, no river of time that flows from past to present to future. What exists in its place is a rich matrix of possible outcomes. There are infinite choices within every event, and we determine which select few are going to manifest. At the depths of the mind field, where all things exist in seed form as virtual events, it hardly matters which ones eventually sprout. They are no more real than the seeds that didn't.

The most famous expression of this concept is the paradox of Schrödinger's cat, named after one of the founders of quantum physics. Schrödinger was trying to imagine how matter behaves when it begins to disappear into energy. He imagined a clever and rather sadistic mechanism, a box that holds a cat inside, hidden from view. A trigger in the box will release a poison to kill the cat if it is hit by a single electron. An electron is shot at the box in such a way that it can only go through two slits—if it takes a path through the left slit, the cat will survive; through the right, the cat will be killed. But since this is the quantum world, things are not well defined, and there is no way to tell which slit the electron chooses. Until the observer looks, the electron has chosen both slits equally.

In this paradox the observer will know what path the electron took only by opening the box and seeing if the cat is alive or dead. Until that moment, both choices are valid, which means—and here is the star-tling part—that the cat is alive and dead at the same time. Opening the box determines its fate, because it takes an observer to cause the electron to have a defined place in space and time. Without the observer's act, there is no defined outcome.

For decades the paradox of Schrödinger's cat has been taken to be a clever mental trick, since physicists do not believe that quantum uncertainty exists beyond the level of electrons and photons. But the clairvoyant seems to indicate otherwise. In his vision, the future has two locations—here and later. He can choose which one to participate in simply by using the same power of observation that the physicist uses with an electron.

Those of us who accept a simpler world, in which the future has only one location—later—are showing a personal preference; we are not obeying an iron law. The useful-ness of time is that it keeps all the seeds of future events from sprouting at once. Time dictates that first one thing happens and then the next, without overlap. You cannot be a child and an adult simultaneously—except through clairvoyance. Then the leaking of one event into the next is allowed. All of us have had "gut feelings" that tell us when some situation will not turn out well. In these instances we have called upon a diluted form of clairvoyance that affords a clue to what will happen next.

Is clairvoyance useful or not? Should one try to develop it or ignore it out of respect for the boundaries of time? Here no fixed answer can be given. Our DNA has to be clairvoyant; we could not survive if our genes did not know the future; the unfolding of an embryo in the womb, as it evolves from a single cell to billions, requires that DNA precisely foresees when neurons, heart cells, muscle tissue, and every other specialized mutation needs to develop. If neurons grew on the wrong day, the day when fingers needed to emerge, for example, havoc would result. So that first fertilized ovum contains a map of the future imprinted in invisible ink.

Other situations are not so clear. In general, the highest purpose of clairvoyance may be to give us a glimpse into the mind of God, because a divine mind could not be constrained by time and does not recognize past, present, or future. If you decide to soften the boundary of time, you must take responsibility for all that comes with such a decision. Science fiction is rife with stories of reckless time travelers who found disaster when they broke into the future or the past. At the very least, one runs the risk of getting present time and vision time hopelessly confused. The spiritual masters keep teaching us that living in the present moment is the ideal, if only we can reach it. The Jewish philosopher Philo, who was a follower of Plato, writes: " 'Today' means boundless and inexhaustible eternity. Periods of months and years and of time in general are ideas of man, who calculates by number; but the true name of eternity is Today." This is the ultimate mystery of clairvoyance—any moment, whether now or later, is a doorway into the same eternity.

I believe that prophets live in this expanded space as well, and although we tend to fixate on their ability to foresee events, their truly spiritual function is to see *beyond* time. An ability to transcend time isn't mystical; every culture has specific beliefs about this. In India, prophecy has been organized into a detailed system of astrology called Jyotish (the name is rooted in the Sanskrit word *jyoti*, which means "light"). Prediction of the future literally means examining what the light has to say, and the ultimate astrologer is a visionary who bypasses all charts to peer directly into the light of the future.

We can begin to understand how this works only by our knowledge of quantum reality, for there all light is born. Time and space are interchangeable at the quantum level. Where a particle will be and when it will be there are bound up together. In this way energy is not separate from space-time. They form one tapestry. The astrologer goes a step further. He breaks the entire cosmos down into specific kinds of energy as they apply to human existence. In Jyotish certain planets are generally beneficial in their energies (such as Jupiter and Venus), while others are generally harmful (such as Mars and the Sun).

As these energies interact, enormously complex patterns emerge. Jyotish can generate sixteen separate charts for each person, involving the most minute motions of planets; time can be subdivided into fractions of a second to arrive at specific predictions about a person's future. And since each degree of change in the heavenly bodies creates a new frequency of energy, the astrologer must memorize several thousand individual patterns between any two or three planets—these arrangements are called *yogas*, literally the "yoking" of stars.

To its proponents Jyotish is a quantum science, because what is seen on the material level—the rotation of planets in their orbits—disguises a deeper scheme. In the deeper scheme, every atom and molecule is connected. By exchanging energy, each point in the universe is whispering to every other point. In this case, however, energy contains information. Imagine a line of people passing a secret by whispering it from person to person down the line. If each person whispered gibberish, there would be no information being passed along, only raw energy. But if there is a secret being spoken, the same energy becomes meaningful. It binds the group together through shared knowledge, and this invisible bond, even when unspoken, can be extremely powerful. Jyotish considers the universe to be secretly bound in just this way; every exchange of energy contains some clue to future events.

The concept of information embedded in energy isn't totally alien outside astrology. To a physicist information is pervasive throughout nature. The specific frequencies that make infrared light different from ultraviolet, or gamma rays different from radio waves, all form a kind of cosmic code. Human beings tune in to this code and use it for our own purposes—it is the information embedded in energy that allows us to build electrical generators, infrared lamps, radio beacons, and so forth. Without that coded information, the universe would be a random vibration, a quantum soup of alphabet letters but no words.

Jyotish asserts that the information coded into energy has human significance. In other words, the future is spelled out in light. Photons actually speak to the astrologer, forming exact patterns that will emerge eventually as events in time. An ancient master of astrology named Brighu gave startling proof of this. Thousands of years ago he sat down to write charts that would predict the lives of people in the future, those not yet born. But even more amazing, he set down only the charts of people who would actually show up in the future to get a reading. If I were to go to Benares and visit a Brighu reader, as one is called, the test of his authenticity would be that my chart would be waiting for me, detailed down to the minute that I crossed the doorstep.

Boundaries are all made in consciousness and dissolved in consciousness. To be able to cross the boundary of time or to speak the language of light tells us that even our most basic assumptions are open to choice. Awareness is all. The present moment is so valued by spiritual masters because it is the place where awareness can be focused. The past and the future are distractions, pulling us into an abstract mental state that will never be alive. You cannot dive deep into an illusion, but it may turn out, once awareness is willing to expand, that you can dive infinitely into this moment. The present has been called "the eternal now" because it refreshes itself without end. With this realization, the door to wisdom is opened, despite all our current fears that wisdom has withered or is somehow a thing of the past. The past is actually the enemy of wisdom. Any kind of linear thinking is doomed to remain trapped on the surface of life. But if we experience our minds as multidimensional, we get closer to God's mind, which is all-dimensional.

Six

CONTACTING GOD

Ask, and it will be given to you;
seek, and you will find; knock,
and it will be opened to you.
—MATTHEW 7:7

Knowing God would be impossible if he
didn't want to be known. There is nothing
to prevent every stage of spirituality from
being a delusion. The saint who speaks to
God may be suffering from a lesion of the
right temporal lobe. On the other hand, a
convinced atheist may be shutting out messages from God every day.

Our quantum model tells us three ways
that God is already contacting us:

1. He exists at a level of reality
   beyond the five senses that is the
   source of our being. Since we are
   quantum creatures, we participate
   in God all the time without
   acknowledging it.

2. He is sending us messages or clues into the physical world. We've called this the flow of reality.
3. He is attracting notice through "second attention," the deepest intuitive part of our brains, which most people ignore.

These three ways to know God are based on the facts accumulated in our search so far. We've built the plane and we know the theory of flight—what remains is to take off.

God seems to be sending us messages from outside time and space. Some of these spiritual clues are faint, but some are very dramatic. One of the most recent healings at Lourdes happened to a young Irishman afflicted with multiple sclerosis. He arrived late at the shrine, after the holy waters were closed to the public for the day. His only access to Lourdes was to wait outside the walls and listen to the vesper services before sunset.

Disappointed, he was taken back to his hotel in a wheelchair. Sitting alone in his room, he suddenly felt a change. His body grew warm and as he lay down on the bed, a bolt of light shot up his spine, causing him to writhe from its intensity; he lost consciousness. But when he awoke, he could walk, and all signs of his MS had vanished. He returned home healed. I think there is no doubt, given the thousands of people who have had such experiences, that this is the "light of God," revered in every sacred tradition. The light fascinates us because God enters our world in few other ways that are as tangible.

In research polls, up to half of Americans say that they have experienced some form of light that they couldn't explain, either internally or as an external aura or halo. About a third of Americans say that they are "born again," which we can interpret as a spiritual awakening of some kind. One of the most famous of modern Indian saints was Sri Aurobindo, a Bengali who attended Cambridge around the turn of the century before entering the holy life back in India. Aurobindo's own awakening began the instant he set foot on native soil, when an almost electric shock awakened him to the truth of higher consciousness. He later speculated that all human beings are on the road to enlightenment via a process of mental evolution. (The late Jonas Salk devoted many years to a similar theory that human beings were about to make the transition from biological evolution, which perfected our physical structure, to "meta-biological" evolution, which would perfect our spirit.)

A form of "supra-consciousness," as Aurobindo termed it, is gradually descending upon us, beginning with the higher centers of awareness, those that cause us to intuit God's existence, then making its way down until our very cells are transformed. According to Aurobindo, God can send "arrows of light" into our world, but these go in only one direction. We can receive them as impulses of inspiration, yet our thoughts cannot retrace their path.

To get back to the source of God's messages, we would have to use second attention, our ability to know something without any physical information. Intuition and prophecy involve second attention. So does the saint's insight into God and the controlled experiment in which people know that they are being watched from another room. Jesus speaks about his Father as if possessing intimate knowledge, and this too derives from second attention at its most developed level. Significantly, when we hear the sayings of Jesus, such as "Know the truth and the truth shall set you free," our minds respond. It is as if second attention in us is sleepy but willing to wake up. This accounts for much of the fascination that all sages and seers hold for ordinary people.

For the moment I am going to set aside the conventional ways to find God, such as prayer, contemplation, faith, good works, and virtue. This isn't to discount them, but certain stark facts have to be recognized. Many believers use all these means to know God and come up empty-handed. When they seem to work, they are inconsistent— some prayers are answered while others go completely unheeded, faith can work miracles but sometimes it can't. Most important, the conventional paths to God have not abolished atheism. However powerful a subjective experience may be, since it cannot be shared, person A is outside the inner world of person B. The process is shut in a private, self-enclosed cocoon.

Before describing how second attention—the key to picking up the spiritual messages sent by God—can be developed, we have to rid ourselves of self-delusion. Stripped down to its essentials, by seeking to know God we run into the same problem we do when we seek to know what lies outside the universe. It is the problem of defining objective reality. By definition the universe contains everything, so the rational mind might assume that nothing lies outside it. The rational mind would be wrong. Theorists can construct perfectly plausible versions of other dimensions. In one model our universe is just a bubble on the outside of an expanding super-universe with ten or more dimensions that our senses can't perceive. Perhaps one of them is the home of angels? Reason can neither prove nor disprove the possibility, but it can get tantalizingly close.

Without ever seeing into this other world, we can observe black holes and quasars, which are the nearest thing to windows on the edge of infinity. As light and energy get sucked into a black hole, they disappear from our cosmos. This implies that they are going somewhere; therefore they might also return to us via "white holes" or acts of creation like the Big Bang. God is not this knowable, however. There is no black hole that sucks you into his world, unless it is death. The great fascination of near-death experiences is that people return convinced that they have entered the divine presence, but the information they bring back is limited. Most report a white light that bathed them in love and peace, but a small minority say it burns with the torment of hell rather than the rapture of heaven and that the being who beckons at the end of the tunnel isn't benign but evil. Moreover, near-death experiences can be duplicated artificially through oxygen deprivation to the brain, as we mentioned before. In these cases the same white light often appears, so perhaps it is just an artifact of the cerebrum as it begins to suffocate.

We need better proof that God wants to be found in his cosmic hiding place. Then the whole development of second attention will fall into place as the truest approach to the domain of spirit.

To know God personally, you must penetrate a boundary that physicists call "the event horizon," a line that divides reality sharply in half. On this side lies anything that remains within the speed of light; on the other side is anything faster than the speed of light. Einstein was among the first theorists to propose that the speed of light is connected to space-time in a crucial way. The speed of light is absolute; it is like a wall that no object can crash through. As we approach the wall, time slows down, mass increases, and space becomes curved. If you try to crash through, weird things happen to prevent you from doing so.

For example, any light that passes too near a black hole gets pulled into its field of gravity. Black holes are the remnants of old stars that collapsed onto themselves when they ran out of fuel. Aging stars are already too dense for us to imagine—a single tea-spoon of matter inside one may be millions of times heavier than the whole earth. As this stellar fuel collapses it can get out of control, like a runaway train. In some instances the momentum is irreversible, and even light cannot escape from the star's force field. In that case there is only black-ness—a black hole—that engulfs any pass-ing object. If a photon of light tries to go around a black hole, it will start to curve in the hole's direction until it falls in.

This is where Einstein's absolute wall meets its match. The photon is traveling as fast as anything can go, so it isn't possible for a black hole to make it go any faster. On the other hand, a photon has to go faster if it wants to escape the clutches of the black hole's immense gravity. At the exact meet-ing point where the photon and the black hole are equal, everything becomes weird. To an outside observer, the photon falls into the back hole forever, frozen in time. Inside the black hole, however, the photon has already been devoured, in less than a hun-dred microseconds. Both versions are true. One is seen from the world of light, the other from the world beyond light. To use Heisenberg's phrase, an "uncertainty prin-ciple" holds true at this level of nature—

event A and event B both exist together, even though they are opposites. This borderline of uncertainty is the event horizon, the exact margin dividing reality in half between the certain and the uncertain, the known and the unknown.

Any place where knowledge stops there is also an event horizon. The brain can't explore beyond where photons go. There is no perception without juggling photons around. If my cat or dog was staring right at God, it would do me no good because I don't share their nervous systems. A nervous system is just a machine for sensing photons. Depending on what model you have, your pattern of photons is different from that produced by other models. The mind may cross the event horizon in theory, using intellectual speculation and advanced mathematics, but this is like Alice jumping down the rabbit hole. When Kierkegaard made his famous remark that God is known only through a leap of faith, he was referring to a spiritual rabbit hole. What lies beyond the event horizon? It could be a new universe with intelligent life in it; it could be a tea party of gods and goddesses; or it could be a chaos of squashed dimensions tumbling like twisted sheets in a dryer.

Thus ends the whole search for God. Or

does it? Strangely enough, lots of things lie beyond the event horizon that turn out to be useful. Quantum physics dips across the border all the time, only it can't stay there very long. When a particle accelerator bombards two atoms, causing a subatomic particle to jump out of its hiding place for a few millionths of a second, the event horizon has been crossed. Something that was unknowable by the five senses suddenly jumps into our world. Combining this with various "thought experiments," science inched its way toward nuclear power, transistors, and (if we look into the future) advanced computer memory and time travel. Already a beam of light has been made to move from one location to another in a Cal Tech laboratory without crossing the space in between, which is a form of primitive time travel. We are learning little by little to be at home across the event horizon.

A skeptic may argue (quite fiercely) that I am distorting the event horizon beyond its literal meaning. If you throw a pebble into a black hole, it will seem to freeze in place forever, utterly defying physical laws of motion, but does that mean God is eternal? No—the event horizon is not accepted by science as the limit of mind. It is intriguing that the Buddha once shut his eyes for a moment and upon opening them declared that he had experienced ninety-nine thousand past incarnations, but this example of time travel could be imaginary. What we do know is that God can't be on this side of the event horizon. Since the Big Bang, light has been traveling for about ten to fifteen billion years. If a telescope is pointed in any direction, it cannot receive light older than that; therefore an entity farther away must remain invisible. This doesn't mean there is no existence beyond fifteen billion years. Strangely enough, certain faraway objects appear to be emitting radiation that is older than the universe, a fact cosmologists are unable to comprehend. If the human brain contains its own event horizon (the limit of photons to organize themselves as thought) and so does the cosmos, we must cross over to find the home of spirit.

A MAP OF THE SOUL

In the dead of night I was awakened by the sound of screaming. Groggy as I was, I knew it must be coming from somewhere in the house, and my heart was pounding before I could sit up. Then someone flicked on the light above my bed.

"Come, get dressed, we have to leave," a

half-familiar voice said. I didn't move. It took a moment before I had enough presence of mind to realize that it wasn't a scream I had heard but a wail.

"Come on," the voice repeated, this time more urgently. Strong arms picked me up and carried me out of the room. I was seven, and our neighbor in Bombay had come for me, but he didn't tell me why. Instead the warm dampness of tropical air caressed over my face until we reached his house, where I was put to bed again.

This was the night my grandfather died. We called him Bauji, and he was famous for getting on the rooftop with his old military bugle, blasting the neighbors awake on the morning I was born. He died without warning at 3 A.M. The wailing came from the servants and women of the house. It was their way of beginning the long process that makes death acceptable, but that wasn't a help to me. I had a reaction common to young children; I refused to believe what had happened. Just that day my grandfather had been jubilant. His son, my father, had been admitted into the Royal College of Physicians in London, a rare achievement for a native-born Indian in those days just after World War II. The minute he got the telegram, Grandfather swept me and my younger brother into his old black sedan and rushed us to not one but two movies (a Jerry Lewis movie and then *Ali Baba and the Forty Thieves*). He had heaped so much candy and toys on us that my brother, Sanjiv, started to cry from sheer stress.

Yet within a day my grandfather was a cloud of ashes thrown into the river at the holy city of Hardwar—I refused to accept that. How could he be gone, who hardly a day before was sitting next to me in the dark laughing at Ali Baba's antics?

A new and painful act in the family drama then ensued. My parents, who had left us out of their care during my father's last phase of medical study, rushed back to India. There was lingering guilt that Grandfather had died of a heart attack, because ironically cardiology was my father's specialization. And my brother Sanjiv got very ill, suffering from a skin malady that seemed to have no origin except the shock of recent events.

Now I understand that we were all worrying about my grandfather's soul. We wondered where it had gone; we worried if it had suffered; deep down we might have been wondering if such a thing as the soul even existed. Such questions, in one form or another, have been hard for me to escape. The soul is the carrier that takes us beyond; it is the essence connecting us to God. But what do these words really mean?

In the ancient Vedas it says that the part of us that doesn't believe in death will never die. This simple definition of the soul is not a bad one. It accurately describes everyone's secret belief that death may be real for some but not for us. Psychologists are impatient with this feeling of personal immortality. They claim that we use it to defend ourselves against the inescapable fact that one day we will die. But what if the opposite is true? What if feeling immortal and beyond death is the most real thing about us?

To prove this point one way or another, we need facts, just as we needed them about God. The soul is as mysterious as God, and we have just as few reliable facts about it. I would offer that the first fact about the soul is that it is not really as personal as people believe. The soul doesn't feel or move; it doesn't travel with you as you go about your life, nor does it endure birth, decay, and death. This is just a way of saying that the soul stands apart from ordinary experience. Since it also has no shape, getting a mental picture of the soul isn't possible.

Instead, the soul is really a junction point between time and the timeless.[1] It faces in both directions. When I experience myself in the world, I am not experiencing my soul, yet it is somewhere on the periphery. There is no doubt that we sense its presence, however vaguely. But it would be a mistake to think that the soul and the person are the same. My grandfather was an old man with thinning hair, prone to enthusiasm and fierce in his love for us. I have powerful memories of him, yet all his qualities and all my memories have nothing to do with his soul. Those qualities died with him; his soul did not. So the soul is like a carrier of the essence, but what is that essence like? If I can't experience my soul as an emotion, if everything I know about myself since birth is separate from my soul, it must not be a material thing.

In other words, the soul begins at the quantum level, which makes sense since the quantum level is also our doorway to God. To go through this door isn't something we choose; participation is mandatory. In India the soul has two parts. One is called *Jiva*, which corresponds to the individual soul making its long journey through many lifetimes until it reaches full realization of God. When a child is taught that being good means your soul will go to heaven, it is Jiva that we are talking about. Jiva is involved in action. It is affected by our good and bad acts; it rules our conscience, and all the seeds of karma are planted inside it. The kind of person you turn out to be is rooted in Jiva, and the kind of life you make for yourself will change Jiva day by day.

The second half of the soul, called *Atman*, does not accompany us on any journey. It is pure spirit, made of the same essence as God. Atman cannot change in any way. It never reaches God because it never left in the first place. No matter how good or bad your life, your Atman remains constant; in fact, the worst criminal and the holiest saint have the same quality of soul when it is this aspect that is in question. There is no good approximation for Atman in the West, and many people might wonder why the soul has to be divided in this way.

The answer lies at the virtual level, for we have seen that all the familiar qualities of life, such as time, space, energy, and matter, gradually fade into a shadowy existence until they disappear. But this disappearance leaves something intact—spirit itself. Jiva lives at the quantum level, Atman at the virtual. So the faintest, subtlest trace of "me" that can be detected at the quantum level is Jiva, and once it disappears, pure spirit remains—that is Atman. The distinction between them is absolutely necessary, for otherwise the path back to God would break down.

> *You need Jiva to remember who you are personally. You need Atman to remember yourself as pure spirit.*
>
> *You need Jiva to have a reason to act, think, wish, and dream. You need Atman for the peace beyond all action.*
>
> *You need Jiva to journey through time and space. You need Atman to live in the timeless.*
>
> *You need Jiva to preserve personality and identity. You need Atman to become universal, beyond identity.*

As you can see, even though they are melded together as "soul," these two aspects are exact opposites in many ways. Such is the paradox of the soul that it manages to accommodate itself to our world of time, thought, and action while dwelling eternally in the spiritual world. The soul must be half-human, half-divine in order to give us a way to retain our identity during all the prayer, meditation, seeking, and other spiritual work that is involved in finding God, and yet the soul must have a divine aspect that embodies the goal of all seeking.

On the material level I am not aware of my Atman. I walk and talk and think without any consciousness that my source lies much deeper. But at the soul level I am totally aware of who I am. The soul level is a very strange place, because it gives rise to all activity without being active itself. Think about that carefully. As I travel around from here to there, my soul doesn't move, because at the quantum level the field just ripples and vibrates—it doesn't change location from A to B. I am born, grow old, and die—these events have tremendous significance for my body and mind. Yet at the quantum level nothing is born, grows old, or dies. There is no such thing as an old photon. We can get some clues to this riddle from a common device, a television set. When you see a TV character walking from left to right on the screen, your brain registers a false impression. Nothing on that screen, not a single electron, has actually moved from left to right. With a magnifying glass you would see that the only activity taking place is the flickering of phosphors on the surface of the cathode-ray tube. If phosphor A is to the left of phosphor B, its flicker can be timed so that just as it goes off, phosphor B lights up. This trick makes it look as if something has moved from left to right, just as twinkling Christmas lights seem to circle around the tree.

Now let's apply the same trick to ourselves. When I get out of my chair and walk across the room, my body seems to be moving, but in fact nothing of the sort is happening at the quantum level. Instead, a series of virtual particles is flickering in and out to create the illusion of motion. This is such an important point that I want to give several more examples. Go to the beach where ocean waves are crashing on the shore. If you wade out and put a cork on the water, your senses tell you that it will be carried along by the waves—but it isn't. The cork stays in place, bobbing up and down as the waves pass along. The water is also just moving up and down. It is the same water that hits the shore, not new water carried from miles away. The wave motion takes place only at the energy level, creating the illusion that the water is getting nearer to the shore.

Now the examples get more mysterious: When two magnets are drawn to each other, what pulls them together is the magnetic field. But the field itself doesn't move. All over the world compass needles are wiggling, but the earth's magnetic poles aren't.

How does a nonmoving field make a needle or two heavy pieces of iron move? Again it is an illusion—at the quantum level, virtual photons, acting as carriers of the magnetic force, flicker in and out, and because they do this in sequence, the appearance of motion is created.

Let's assume that we can accept the fact that you and I are not moving, either. To a quantum physicist, our bodies are just objects, like any other. A ball thrown across the room isn't moving, only winking in and out of existence at an incredibly fast speed at different locations, and we are no different. But here the mystery deepens. When the ball disappears for a nanosecond, only to reappear just the tiniest bit to the left or right, why didn't it disintegrate? After all, it was completely absent for a while, and there is no reason why its old shape and size and color shouldn't simply dissolve. Quantum physics can even calculate the odds that it won't reappear, that instead of a ball flying across the room, a bowl of pink Jell-O will suddenly appear. What keeps things together?

If we go back to the television, the answer is obvious. The characters walking across the screen are just phantoms, but they are organized phantoms. Their image is fixed on film or videotape, their motions are planned and worked out. In other words, there is intelligence behind the illusion. This presiding intelligence keeps the random flickers of photons from being truly random; it creates forms from formless electrical charges. For it turns out that not just the motion of a TV image is illusion, so is its color and shape. So is its voice, if the character happens to speak. No matter what quality you look for, it can be broken down to pulses of energy, and these pulsations have meaning only because a hidden director has created it.

This is essentially the argument for the soul. It holds reality together; it is my off-screen director, my presiding intelligence. I can think, talk, work, love, and dream, all because of the soul, yet the soul doesn't do any of these things. It is me, yet I would never recognize it if we came face-to-face. Everything that makes the difference between life and death must cross into this world via the soul.

Today I sat down to see if I could list all the invisible events happening at the soul level, and the results inspire a deep awe at the "soul work" (which the medieval church called *psychomachia*) going on with every breath:

Infinity is becoming finite.
The unmoving is starting to move.
The universe is shrinking to a location
   inside you.
Eternity is taking on the appearance of
   time.
Uncertainty is becoming certain.
The undefined is becoming definite.
That which has no cause is starting the
   chain of cause and effect.
Transcendence is coming down to
   earth.
The divine is taking on a body.
Randomness is turning into patterns.
The immortal is pretending to be born.
Reality is putting on the mask of
   illusion.

You share this soul work with God. He can be defined in infinite ways, but one version of God is that he is a process. The process involves bringing life into being. Science has its story about how life originated two billion years ago from a soup of organic chemicals. This soup, probably contained in the earth's ancient oceans, was struck by lightning and began to boil into primitive self-reproducing nucleic acids, from which the long chain of evolution proceeded. But from the spiritual viewpoint, life is being created all the time through the kind of soul work just listed.

There is more to life than raw creation. The soul, as every religious tradition has insisted, exists to bring an end to suffering. The same cannot be said about any other aspect of ourselves. The mind, ego, and emotions cause as much pain as pleasure; they can throw us into turmoil and confusion despite all our efforts to reach clarity and peace. The soul has been assigned the unique function of working only for what is most evolutionary in each person's life. It couldn't accomplish this end by turning the infinite into the finite, the timeless into time, and so forth—these processes have no human value until we add another ingredient, the dispelling of suffering.

Someone who is attuned to the soul begins to perceive that a subtle guidance is at work. The soul is silent; therefore it cannot compete with the contentious voices heard in the mind. You can spend years overshadowed by anger, fear, greed, ambition, and all the other distractions of inner life, but none of that activity touches Atman. The soul has its own project in mind. The Vedas describe this project in terms of the five *kleshas*, or causes of human suffering. They are:

1. Ignorance about the nature of reality
2. Identification with the ego
3. Attraction toward objects of desire
4. Repulsion from objects of desire
5. Fear of death

The great sages and seers who laid out this scheme of suffering all emphasize that all five causes boil down to one—the very first. When a person forgets that he has a soul, that his source is rooted in eternal Being, separation results, and from separation all other pain and suffering follows.

But for these ancient formulations to have any usefulness today, we have to update them. I think a modern restatement would go something like this:

1. A person thinks that only material existence is real and thus becomes totally ignorant of the source, which is quantum and virtual. He accepts the illusion of time and space. When this happens, contact with the source is lost. The voice of the soul begins to grow fainter and fainter.
2. Drifting in separation, the person seeks desperately for something to cling to. Life cannot abide Being

without a foundation; therefore the mind creates an entity known as the ego. This "I" is the same as the personality. It is constructed from all kinds of experiences, and as these become all-important, the "I" and its needs have to be defended at all costs.

3. The ego has many needs, and so it begins to value the fulfillment of those needs. The whole world becomes a means to make the ego stronger, more important, and more secure. To that end, it pulls all kinds of objects toward itself: food, shelter, clothing, money, etc.

4. For a time this strategy seems to work. Although it never becomes truly secure, the ego finds that life can be filled up by acquiring more and more. No one can gain complete control over the environment, however; therefore the ego has to spend a great deal of time avoiding pain and danger. As attractive as certain things are, others are equally repulsive.

5. Caught in a whirlwind of seeking pleasure and avoiding pain, the person achieves many goals. The years pass, and separation does not even seem to

be a problem anymore. However, there is an end to all this acquiring, all this experience for the sake of experience. Over it all looms the certainty that life will end. Fear of death becomes a source of suffering because death is the undeniable reminder that the ego's strategy for survival never solved the original problem—ignorance about how things really work.

If it is true that the five kleshas are still at work—and who could deny that they are?—then the influence of the soul is crucial. Each klesha has its own momentum. We all know the powerful addiction of money, power, career, and ego needs of every type. This momentum has kept suffering alive despite the enormous changes in human existence from age to age. Against this momentum the soul provides a means of solving every cause of pain:

1. Ignorance of reality is solved by delving deeper into the mind. Awareness dives deeper than the material level to find its roots.
2. Identification with ego is solved by learning to identify with these deeper levels.

3 and 4. Attraction to outside objects—and repulsion from them—is solved by valuing the inner life above all.

5. Fear of death is solved when the soul is experienced directly, since the soul is never born and never dies.

As with the five causes of suffering, the five solutions all grow from the first one. *If you explore the true nature of reality, all pain will eventually come to an end.* In some form or other, religious teachings state this truth over and over. There is no way around the fact that it sounds abstract, yet this is the reality of how the soul operates. Your soul deals in abstractions like eternity and infinity so that you won't have to. It converts an inconceivable world into one that we can grasp and understand. Like a car's transmission, which takes the whirling motion of the engine and transforms it into the forward velocity that gets you where you want to go, the soul makes it possible for your life to move forward. Eternity doesn't need to breathe; infinity doesn't need to find a job. But you need those things and more—you need to eat, work, love, and raise children— and these are made possible through the soul. Without it, there would only be quantum soup, a formless swirl of energy and particles.

Now let's see if we can test this new conception of the soul against tradition. Even though we are accustomed to using religious language about the soul, its duties are useful, not poetic. This fact has been hard to realize because the word *soul* has been used loosely to mean a person's deepest emotions, his heart, his highest aspirations, as well as more arcane things like the Holy Ghost. In the Bible, where the word *soul* is used hundreds of times, we find that it goes through every struggle of life. In the Old Testament we hear a lot about the peril of the soul. Satan wants to grab it, the enemies of Israel want to destroy it, famine and illness make the soul heavy, and always there is the plea—this is heard over and over in the Psalms—for God to give balm and solace to the soul. Jehovah is fickle, however, and he can seem to betray even those souls offered up to him: the Book of Job begins with God and the devil gambling with the soul of a righteous man "who feared God and set his face against wrongdoing." For no other reason than to test him, God allows Satan to inflict any harm he wishes against Job except to "touch his person." Job's travails with sickness, poverty, family misfortune, and social rejection describe a condition of suffering that was familiar to the Hebrews and later to the Christians; the fact that God never again speaks in the Bible is an ominous after-note: the soul has been left to survive its tests alone.

The New Testament continues the same drama but more in terms of salvation and redemption. Since Jesus offers an explicit promise of an afterlife, going to heaven is the goal of the soul, and escaping damnation is its greatest challenge. In all this turmoil, one senses that the soul travels through life undergoing every anxiety felt by the person. It isn't aloof or apart but very much down here in the mud of battle. The paradox is that throughout this highly emotional involvement, no biblical writer ever defines what the soul is. As a result, the word remains as diffuse in the end as it was at the outset. If I say to you, "My soul was touched" or "I mean this from the bottom of my soul" or "That person has a lot of soul," nothing specific is being conveyed.

I would venture that the sacred masters, whatever religion they are associated with, were trying to be quite specific. In their awareness the soul meant something much like what we have been describing—a connection between the world of the five senses and a world of inconceivable things like eternity, infinity, omniscience, grace, and every other quality of the unmanifest.

Parables are basically coded stories about the soul and its function. In other words, they take an abstraction like "the unmoving starts to move" or "the immortal pretends to be born" and expresses it in language that is more understandable. Some parables are so simple that we hardly realize their spiritual meaning—every child has heard about the six blind men and the elephant. Each blind man grabs a different part of the beast. The blind man who grabs the leg says, "An elephant is very like a tree." The one who grabs the trunk says, "An elephant is very like a snake." The one who grabs the tail says, "An elephant is very like a rope," and so forth. Originally the story had to do with the five senses and the mind being unable to grasp the nature of God, the moral being that divine reality was too vast to be understood by thought, sight, sound, touch, or taste. Other interpretations hold that the blind men are the branches of Vedic philosophy, which in all their specialized learning cannot grasp the wholeness of Brahman, the One and All.

Jesus told thirty-nine parables, and these are easier to connect with the soul, largely because he delivered the morals himself. The first one is in the fifth book of Matthew:

You are light for all the world. A town that stands on a hill cannot be hidden. When a lamp is lit, it isn't put under a bushel basket but on the stand, where it gives light to everyone in the house. And you, like the lamp, must shed light among all men, so that when they see the good you do, they may give praise to your Father in heaven.

On the surface this parable is so simple that it hardly needs to be interpreted. The phrase "don't hide your light under a bushel basket" means that virtue should be seen so it can have a good effect. But the word *light* has a deeper meaning spiritually, in the sense of awakened awareness, and therefore this is also a parable about the soul. Jesus is saying that like a lamp hidden under a basket, the body hides the soul. He tells the disciples not to let this happen but to allow the soul's awareness to manifest itself. In other words, live from the soul level if you expect other people to believe that you are connected to God, for when they see that you are, they will believe it of themselves as well.

Any of the other famous parables, whether about the mustard seed or the prodigal son or the servant who buries his talents, are equally multidimensional. The actors in them can be seen as aspects of the soul. In fact, these vignettes are so effective and colorful that the soul gets overlooked. The same happens in real life. It is very hard to realize that our origin, our source, is not of this world. Here I am with all my qualities. People see me and hear me; they believe in my existence. Yet my reality is paper-thin at the quantum level, where there is no sound, sight, texture, color, or anything else recognizable. The soul is the junction point between my virtual self and my physical self. It is the organizing intelligence that keeps me intact. This is an exceptional feat, given that every atom of my body is pure empty space with flashes of energy passing through it for no more than a few millionths of a second.

Reality is truly sneaking up on us from nowhere and catching us off guard at every second. (In a beautiful aphorism the great Bengali poet Tagore says, "Life is only the perpetual surprise that I exist.") It is unsettling to confront the fact that none of my cherished qualities are real, yet it is a fact. Let us say that I like the color blue, feel happy, and value my personal freedom. These are three disparate qualities about me. But when I get in my car and drive across town, does the color blue move with me? When I take a bath, does my happiness get wet? When I go to bed, does my personal freedom go to sleep?

It was just this sort of questioning that made the ancient sages realize that we must possess a soul. There is something intangible and undefined about us that yet gets born into this world as a visible, defined creation. In the *Bhagavad-Gita* this aspect is called the "inward dweller" and it is said that fire cannot burn it, water cannot make it wet, wind cannot blow it away, and a sword cannot cut it in two. For all the poetry in that expression, the fact of the soul appears to be undeniable, for stripped of all religious connotations, the essence of each person cannot be reduced to matter or thoughts or any fixed quality.

If you try to do without the soul, you wind up with a handful of nothing. To underscore this, I need to bring back the concept of the field. A magnet attracts iron because it creates a magnetic field around itself. As we saw before, the field doesn't move, yet the iron does. If you tried to locate the exact point where the unmoving field touches the moving iron, where would you be? The answer is that you would be at the point of uncertainty. A very definite object, a piece of iron, is interacting with a completely undefined thing, a field. The two get closer and closer. The iron starts out as a solid lump of matter with weight and motion. The field starts out with no solidity or motion, or any other material qualities. They approach, and of course neither one wants to give up its nature. The field wants to remain boundless, timeless, and undefined. The iron wants to remain exactly the opposite. Inevitably, they meet as strangers, barely shaking hands, suspicious of each other. This is the famous region of uncertainty defined by Heisenberg, where the defined world meets the undefined field. What can you say about it? Only that it connects two very different worlds without living in either.

At this point of uncertainty, a photon may shoot out of a star to travel across the universe, yet nothing really travels. Only a certain charge flickers into existence, passes its energy to another charge, and disappears again. It's the same trick as the television seeming to be populated by living people. Only in this case the trick isn't just a trick. It is as real as anything gets. Or to put it another way, as unreal as anything gets. There is a Zen story about two disciples who are looking at a flag fluttering in the breeze. "See that?" one says. "No one can doubt that the flag is moving." The other disagrees, "No, it is the wind moving. The flag has no motion of its own."

They continue this debate until the master comes along, and he says, "You are both wrong. Only consciousness is moving." This is the kind of tale that often gets repeated as the answer to a Zen riddle, but which no one really understands. Now we are in a position to see the point. The flag stands for any material object that seems to move, the wind is the invisible field or force that creates that motion, but in the deeper reality, neither is moving. Only consciousness—which means intelligence—is at work, here and in all things.

It is profound to realize that my true self is not rooted in time and space. Virtual reality is my source, and like a light wave my body flows out of it, but the source doesn't go anywhere. Therefore my connection to that source doesn't go anywhere, either. Thus the soul is part of me, but not any part my senses will ever detect. No religious claim is being made here; these are stubborn quantum facts. I have never left my source; it is always with me. The famous detachment of great sages comes from knowing full well that they are not confined by any fixed definition. Tagore has a beautiful way of expressing this:

> *When I was born and saw the light*
> *I was no stranger in this world—*
> *Something inscrutable, shapeless, and*
> *   without words*
> *Appeared in the form of my mother.*
> *So when I die, the same unknown will*
> *   appear again*
> *As ever known to me. . . .*
>   GATANJALI

The metaphor of birth is totally appropriate, because the timeless doesn't just turn into time. Something entirely new is born. Infinity doesn't merely shrink until it becomes small and manageable—numberless dimensions give birth to just three or four. What you call your soul manages this birth, not once but thousands of times per second. I call this concept "genesis now." There can never be a single genesis, since virtual reality would just swallow everything back up again.

Super-gravity, like an immense yawning black hole, has an insatiable appetite. It wants to devour time and make it timeless; it wants to engulf matter and energy to return them to virtual photons.

Why isn't the whole world swallowed up? Because creation insists on happening. Life can't be stopped, even by the infinite forces arrayed against it. Genesis now is the ongoing project that is behind all your actions. Soul work never stops. Attempting to put yourself in a box, defining yourself by labels and qualities until you are a finished product once and for all, is as false as trying to put God in a box. The great spiritual traditions have been trying to tell us this with all their teachings. We otherwise would forget that the constant churning of eternity, infinity, and immortality is all that is happening.

There is nothing else. This alone makes us real.

THE STATE OF UNION

Believe it or not, we find ourselves very close to the soul now. We have whittled away the scientific objections to God by placing him outside the reach of measurement. This means that a person's subjective experience of God can't be challenged—at the quantum level, objectivity and subjectivity merge into each other. The point of merger is the soul; therefore knowing God comes down to this: like a photon nearing a black hole, your mind hits a wall as it tries to think about the soul. The soul is comfortable with uncertainty; it accepts that you can be two places at once (time and eternity); it observes cosmic intelligence at work and is not bothered that the creative force is outside the universe. We have a simple picture of the situation, then:

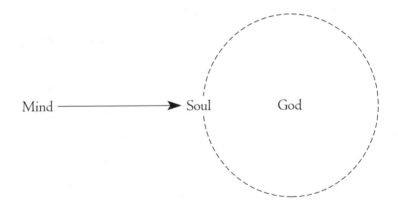

The mind is creeping closer and closer to the soul, which sits on the edge of God's world, at the event horizon. The gap of separation is wide when there is no perception of spirit; it grows smaller as the mind figures out what is happening. Eventually the two will get so close that mind and soul have no choice but to merge. When that happens, the resemblance to a black hole is striking. To the mind, it will be as if falling into God's world lasts forever, an eternity in bliss consciousness. From God's side, the merging takes place in a split second; indeed, if we stand completely in God's world, where time has no meaning, the whole process never even occurred. The mind was part of the soul all along, only without knowing it.

One could rightfully claim that the words of Jesus, "Ask and you will receive, knock and the door will open," are an iron law. The instant that your mind pays any attention to the soul, it is pulled toward it, with the inevitable result that all separation will close. Subjectively this journey toward the soul (a better phrase than journey of the soul) is perceived as the seven stages that we have already covered. But objectively, the process is much more like a particle of light crossing the event horizon.

The fact that our minds can register this journey is astonishing, because the whole time that it is happening, ordinary thought and perception continue. Two shoppers pushing grocery carts are doing the same thing in the material world, but one could be having an epiphany. The word *ecstasy* derives from Greek roots that mean to stand apart or outside—this is the role of second attention, to stand outside material life and witness the dawn of ecstasy. If you regard the soul as a kind of force field steadily pulling the mind toward it, every one of the seven stages can be described as the closing of separation:

Stage One: *I am in such separation that I sense deep fear inside.*

Stage Two: *I don't feel so separate; I am gaining a sense of power.*

Stage Three: *Something larger than me is drawing near; I feel much more peaceful.*

Stage Four: *I am beginning to intuit what that larger thing is—it must be God.*

Stage Five: *My actions and thoughts are drawing on God's force field, as if we are both involved in everything.*

Stage Six: *God and I are almost together now. I feel no separation; my mind is God's mind.*

Stage Seven: *I see no difference between myself and God.*

In ancient India this closing of the gap was described as *yoga* or union (the same

Sanskrit root gave us the verb "to yoke"). Because the Indian sages had thousands of years to analyze it, the entire process of joining with the soul was turned into a science. Yoga precedes Hinduism, which is a particular religion, and at its inception, the practices of Yoga were intended to be universal. The ancient sages had at their disposal the power to witness their own spiritual evolution, which boiled down to watching the mind approach the soul. What they discovered can be stated in a few cardinal points:

- *Evolution takes place inside.* It isn't a matter of pilgrimages, observances, and obeying religious rules. No codes of conduct can alter the fact that every mind is on a soul journey.
- *Evolution is automatic.* In the larger view, the soul is always pulling at us. Its force field is inescapable.
- *A person is required to pay attention.* Since the journey to the soul happens only in awareness, if you block out awareness you impede your progress; if you pay attention, you build up momentum.
- *The final goal is inevitable.* No one can resist the soul forever. Saints and sinners are on the same road.

- *It is better to cooperate than to resist.* The soul is the source of truth and love. If you try to avoid it, those things will not increase in your life. If you cooperate, your life will be organized with the help of infinite power and intelligence as it flows from God.
- *External action still counts.* Action is a physical process linked to the mind; the two cannot be separated, so even though this is a journey of the mind, outer activity either helps or detracts.

None of these statements is startling (or particularly Indian). The fact that Yoga was later identified with extremely esoteric practices is secondary. Because it started out as a neutral way of describing the reality of spiritual awakening, Yoga is no less and no more objective than our quantum model; in both cases one is concerned with how ordinary reality alters the closer one gets to the event horizon. This might be a good place to mention, for those who do not already know, that the physical exercises gathered under the name of Hatha Yoga constitute the smallest part of a huge body of understanding; they are not necessary on the spiritual journey, yet they are highly useful to those who feel attracted in that direction.

If you accept that Yoga is accurate in its description, then any aspect of life can be filtered through it. Let me take the issue of identity and view it in terms of initial separation that gradually becomes a state of union:

IDENTITY

Stage One: *I am small and insignificant, stranded on the vast expanse of Nature. I hope I can survive.*

Stage Two: *I can do more than survive; I can compete and fulfill more of my needs.*

Stage Three: *I am peaceful inside. My inner world is beginning to satisfy me more than outward things.*

Stage Four: *I am self-sufficient. Things may not always go my way, but that doesn't shake me anymore.*

Stage Five: *I have discovered how to manifest my desires from within. My inner world turned out to have power.*

Stage Six: *I am at the center of an immense scheme of Power and intelligence that emanates from God.*

Stage Seven: *I am.*

You can accurately graph a person's spiritual growth on this scale alone. The ego moves from an isolated, helpless state to a realization that it might have power; then it looks for where the power comes from, at first deciding that it must be external, in the form of money and status, but in time realizing that the source of power is internal. More time passes and the difference between inner and outer power dissolves. All of reality is perceived as having one source; in the end, you are that source. Let's try another issue, that of faith:

FAITH

Stage One: *Faith is a matter of survival. If I don't pray to God, he can destroy me.*

Stage Two: *I'm beginning to have faith in myself. I pray to God to help me get what I want.*

Stage Three: *Faith brings me peace. I pray that life should be free from turmoil and distress.*

Stage Four: *I have faith that inner knowledge will uphold me. I pray for more insight into God's ways.*

Stage Five: *Faith tells me that God will support my every desire. I pray*

Stage Six: *that I am worthy of his faith
                in me.*
Stage Six: *Faith can move mountains. I
                pray to be God's instrument of
                transformation.*
Stage Seven: *Faith melts into universal
                being. When I pray, I find
                that I am praying to myself.*

Notice how strikingly different the same word is in each stage. When people say that they have faith or that they believe in prayer, you cannot be certain what they mean without more understanding. This accounts for why there is such wild divergence of opinion about whether God listens to prayers and answers them. In relative terms, it all depends on your level of consciousness. At lower levels the thoughts behind a prayer may be too diffuse to create a result. As separation closes, the gap between prayer and result is closed, too; every prayer is answered. At the level of miracles prayer has the power to alter outward events. Finally, in the state of unity consciousness, there is no need for prayer. Your every thought comes from the soul; therefore you would only be praying to yourself.

A boundary is the same as a horizon. If

you attempt to walk around the world, the horizon is the farthest boundary of your sight, yet it keeps advancing ahead of you as you move. The spiritual equivalent is stated eloquently in a verse from the mystical Catholic monk Thomas Merton:

> *The Lord travels in all directions at once.*
> *The Lord arrives from all directions at once.*
> *Wherever we are, we find that He has just departed.*
> *Wherever we go, we find that He has just arrived before us.*

In literal terms this verse states two things. One we already know: God is elusive because he exists in the domain of uncertainty, where time and space aren't fixed. The other is that God is always perceived within boundaries. We get only a limited idea of him, and that limited idea keeps shifting. There is no cure for this misperception until the final stage of unity; until then, the gap of separation keeps causing the mind to think it knows God when only partial knowledge is available. In shorthand form, here are the horizons that limit our vision in the seven stages:

Stage One: Horizon of Fear

I provide for the necessities and look out for myself. But when I get anxious, I feel lost. Only God knows why bad things happen in this world.

Bounded by anxiety, insecurity, dependency.

Stage Two: Horizon of Control

I exert power and relish competition as a way of fulfilling my ambitions. But when things get beyond my control, I am totally frustrated. Only God knows why things don't work out the way I plan.

Bounded by guilt, duty, victimization.

Stage Three: Horizon of Fatalism

I'm at peace with myself and know what is happening with me inside. But I lose my center when nothing makes sense anymore. Only God knows why destiny can be so cruel and capricious.

Bounded by karma, introversion, lack of power.

Stage Four: Horizon of Self-deception

I navigate through the world with

much more intuition and insight than most people. But I can be misled by my inner voice at times. Only God knows why my intuition deceives me just when I need it most.

Bounded by hidden secrets, past conditioning, ego needs.

Stage Five: Horizon of Fantasy

My inner world is rich with new discoveries, and I have enough awareness to see that my thoughts come true. But some of my deepest wishes stay on the level of unreachable fantasies. Only God knows why this happens.

Bounded by self-absorption, grandiosity, playing God.

Stage Six: Horizon of Identity

My whole life is devoted to service, and I can be selfless in the face of great demands from others. But sometimes the suffering of humanity makes me want to escape this world. Only God knows why I can't lose myself in him all the time.

Bounded by thought, personal ego, traces of old conditioning.

Stage Seven: Infinity—No Horizon

I see no difference between my mind and the mind in all things. My identity is one with all people. Only God knows that I am merged into him in all dimensions at all times.

Boundless.

Perhaps this is the most telling "chart" of all, because we identify so completely with our boundaries. The horizon is fluid, however. Each stage breaks the boundaries of the one that came before. To someone in stage two, where guilt serves to keep the ego from going mad with power, the absence of guilt doesn't seem possible. It would be a sure sign that stage three is looming should the person successfully find real forgiveness. Forgiveness is a mark of stage three, and those who arrive there have pushed their projection of God just a little further.

Society tends to cluster, like seeking like. At a party of psychiatrists, everyone believes in insight; at a party of entrepreneurs, everybody believes in success. This makes it hard to accept that God's values are any different. We all know marriages where both spouses are sure that the world is a certain way, whether it be dangerous, unsafe, abundant, benign, or blessed. Is this a form of organized deception? Yes and no. Although your boundaries define you, that shouldn't be taken as negative; every stage of inner growth allows you the opportunity to see things that are hard to see. Projection is inevitable and very powerful.

The boundaries of belief are true event horizons, because the mind can't go beyond them, even though to an outsider the boundaries don't exist. A fundamentalist Christian may be unable to conceive of divorce without believing that he will be thrown outside God's grace, just as an Orthodox Jew would find it inconceivable to break kosher laws or a Muslim to allow his wife to walk outside with her face uncovered. A stage one interpretation of Christ, if it reflects fear, would center on the times he warns of sinners "cast into the outer darkness with wailing and gnashing of teeth." A stage one interpretation of Allah centers on the Koran's promise that one sin against God's laws is enough to deserve eternal damnation.

These beliefs defy reason, and that is their purpose. Religions have always feared the end of faith. (Recently some Protestant sects attempted to remove all references in the liturgy to original sin and human imperfection, but they failed, even among liberal theologians. The winning argument was that only God is perfect and we should never forget it.) Obedience holds the religious world together and makes redemption possible. For God to have his place, human beings must know theirs.

In every stage the essential point is the same: You believe that God is holding you back for some reason. As long as you are in that stage, you will wrestle with what the reason is; this forms the core of your personal drama. In truth you are projecting all boundaries; this becomes obvious when you see that other people have boundaries totally different from yours.

The end of separation is preordained. Eventually there is no more need for boundaries. The event horizon gets pushed as far as the mind will go, and after that God must take over. The word *mystical* is used carelessly to describe many different things, but I would say that in any stage of inner growth, whatever lies outside your boundaries is mystical to you. The famous cargo cult among the Trobrian islanders in the Pacific derived their religion when Allied planes dropped supplies from the sky during World War II. Being unable to comprehend what an airplane is, the islanders built straw effigies of them and prayed for their return. What was ordinary technology to us was across the event horizon for them.

Even when you find yourself stagnated in fixed beliefs, the possibility of closing the gap is always present. Every morning you have a new opportunity to know God. Your starting point may be one of fear and guilt, or it may be one of expanded awareness—that is all relative. According to our three ways of finding God, no one is ever trapped without hope:

1. We can always cross the horizon to a new reality.
2. Clues are left to tell us how to grow.
3. Second attention enables us to read these clues.

The saint is equal to the sinner in this regard. Both are guided by God from across the gap.

THE POWER OF INTENTION

The aim of spirituality is to learn to cooperate with God. Most of us have been raised to do the opposite. Our skills and abilities come from first attention and not second.

As a result, our issues tend to center on the lower stages, where fear and neediness, however much we deny them, take their toll. In these early stages the ego asserts its needs with great force—money, security, sex, and power make huge claims on everyone in society. It is important to realize that God doesn't judge against these things—when people feel that they owe their success to God, they are right. When wrongdoing goes unpunished and good deeds are ignored, God smiles on both. There is only one reality, which is spiritual, and nothing lies outside God's mind. We tap into the source of creativity and intelligence with every thought.

What makes a life spiritual, then?

The difference is entirely one of intention. I began this book by saying that two people could be followed around from birth to death with a camera, and there would be no external way to show which one believed in God. This fact remains true. Unless you become a recluse or enter a monastery, your social role is irrelevant to how spiritual you are. Everything depends on intention. If someone uses kind words but intends to snub you, the intention cuts through. The most expensive gift cannot make up for lack of love. We know instinctively when intentions come from an honest place or a place of deception.

In spiritual life, intention includes will and purpose, aspiration and highest vision. If you set your intention toward God, spirit grows. If you set your intention toward material existence, that will grow instead. Once you plant the seed of an intention, your soul's journey unfolds automatically. Here are the basic intentions that mark a spiritual life, stated in terms of what a person wants to achieve:

- *I want to feel God's presence.* This intention is rooted in the discomfort of being isolated and separate. When God is absent, the underlying feeling of loneliness cannot be escaped. You can mask it by developing friendships and family ties. Ultimately, however, each of us needs to feel a sense of inner fullness and peace. We want to be satisfied within ourselves, no matter if we are alone or in a crowd.

- *I want God to aid and support me.* God's presence brings with it the qualities of spirit. At the source, every quality— love, intelligence, truth, organizing ability, creativity—becomes infinite. The growth of these things in your life is a sign that you are approaching closer to your soul.

- *I want to feel connected to the whole.* The soul's journey takes a person from a fragmented state to a state of wholeness. This is felt as being more connected. Events around you start to weave into a pattern. Small details fit together instead of being scattered and random.

- *I want my life to have meaning.* Existence feels empty in separation, and this gets healed only by moving into unity with God. Instead of turning outward to find your purpose, you feel that just being here, as you are, fulfills the highest purpose in creation.

- *I want to be free of restrictions.* Inner freedom is greatly compromised when fear is present, and fear is a natural outcome of separation. As you move closer to your soul, the old boundaries and defenses start to melt away. Instead of being wary about the future, you flow with the river of life, awaiting the day when no boundaries of any kind hold you back.

If these basic intentions are present inside you, God takes the responsibility for carrying them out. Everything else you do is secondary. Someone who is in the grip of fear, for example, cannot move beyond stage one, despite good deeds, a secure home life, and positive thinking. We all attempt to mask our limitations with false attitudes; it is only human nature to try to appear better than we are, especially in our own eyes. But once you set your intention in the right direction, self-deception is rendered irrelevant. You will still have to face your ego needs; you will still continue to play out your personal dramas. This activity takes place on the stage of first attention; offstage, spirit has its own devices—your intention is like a blueprint handed to God, which he carries to completion in his own fashion. Sometimes he uses a miracle; sometimes he just makes sure you don't miss the plane to New York. The fact that anything can happen is the beauty and surprise of the spiritual life.

Strangely, people who feel extremely powerful and successful often set the worst intentions in motion, as far as spiritual growth is concerned. Here are some typical intentions that have nothing to do with finding God:

I want to win.
I want to prove myself by taking risks.

I want to have power over others.
I want to make the rules.
I want to be in control.
I want to do it all my way.

These intentions should sound very familiar since they are repeated ad nauseam in popular fiction, advertising, and the media. They all center on ego needs, and as long as your real intentions come from that level, your life will follow suit. Such is the fate of living in a mirror universe. One meets hundreds of people who mistake their own intentions because their egos have taken complete control. Some of the most powerful figures in the world are spiritually quite naive. If intention is left to the ego, great things can be accomplished, but these are minuscule compared to what can be achieved with infinite intelligence and organizing power at your disposal.

God is on the side of abundance. It is a great misfortune that the spiritual life has earned a reputation for being poor, reclusive, and ascetic. God is also on the side of increased happiness. The shadow of the martyr has fallen over spirituality with dire results. In general, to be spiritual in these times means going it alone, far more than in the past. In a society with misguided conceptions of God and no tradition of masters, you are responsible for setting your own intentions.

Here are the ground rules that have proved effective for me personally and which I feel will work for many people:

1. **Know your intentions.** Look at the list of spiritual intentions above and make sure that you understand how important they are. Your destiny is to move in the direction of your soul, but the fuel that makes destiny move is intention. Intend for yourself that the gap of separation gets closed just a little more each day. Don't let your false intentions remain masked. Root them out and work on the anger and fear that keep you attached to them. False intentions take the form of guilty desires: I want someone else to fail, I want to get even, I want to see bad people punished, I want to take away something not my own. False intentions can be elusive; you will notice their existence by the feeling tone connected with them, a feeling of fear, greed, rage, hopelessness, and weakness. Sense the feeling first, refuse to buy into it, and then remain

aware until you find the intention lurking beneath.

2. **Set your intentions high.** Aim to be a saint and a miracle worker. Why not? The same laws of nature operate for everyone. If you know that the goal of inner growth is to acquire mastery, then ask for that mastery as soon as possible. Once you ask, don't strain to work wonders, but don't deny them to yourself, either. The beginning of mastery is vision; see the miracles around you and that will make it easier for greater miracles to grow.

3. **See yourself in the light.** The ego keeps its grip by making us feel needy and powerless. From this sense of lack grows the enormous hunger to acquire everything in sight. Money, power, sex, and pleasure are supposed to fill up the lack, but they never do. You can escape this whole package of illusion if you see yourself not in a shadow fighting to get to God but as in the light from the first moment. The only difference between you and a saint is that your light is small and a saint's is great. This difference pales in comparison to the similarity: you

are both of the light. The irony of near-death experiences is that when people come back to report how rapturously they felt bathed in a blinding light, they overlook that the light was there all along. It is the self.

4. **See everyone else in the light.** The cheapest way to feel good about yourself is by feeling superior to others. From this dark seed grows every manner of judgment. Getting out of judgment is vital, and to plant that seed, you have to stop dividing others into categories of good and bad. Everyone lives in the same light. A simple formula may help here. When you are tempted to judge another person, no matter how obviously they deserve it, remind yourself that everyone is doing the best he can from his own level of consciousness.

5. **Reinforce your intentions every day.** On the surface, the obstacles against spirit are enormous. Everyday life is a kind of swirling chaos, and the ego is entrenched in its demands. You cannot rely on one good intention to carry you through. It takes discipline to remind yourself, day in and day out, of your own spiritual purpose.

For some people it helps to write down their intentions; for others periods of regular meditation and prayer are useful. It isn't good enough to repeat your intentions to yourself on the run. Find your center, look closely at yourself, and do not let go of your intention until it feels centered inside yourself.

6. **Learn to forgive yourself.** The ego has a way of co-opting spirit and pretending that everything is going well. Thus we all fall into traps of selfishness and delusion when least expected. The chance remark that wounds someone else, the careless lie, the irresistible urge to cheat are universal. Forgive yourself for being where you are. To be honestly a creature of stage two, driven by ambition and haunted by guilt, is more spiritual than pretending to be a saint. Apply to yourself the same dictum as to others: You are doing the best you can from your own level of consciousness. (I like to remember one master's definition of the perfect disciple: "One who is always stumbling but never falls.")

7. **Learn to let go.** The paradox of being spiritual is that you are always wrong

and always right at the same time. You are right to try to know God in every way you can, but you are wrong to think that things won't change tomorrow. Life is change; you must be prepared to let go of today's beliefs, thoughts, and actions no matter how spiritual they make you feel. Every stage of inner growth is a good life. Each is nurtured by God. Only your second attention will know when it is time to move on, and when you know, don't hesitate to let go of the past.

8. **Revere what is holy.** Our society teaches us to be skeptical of the sacred. The usual attitude toward miracles is a bemused caution; few people spend much time delving into the world's great wealth of scriptures. But every saint is your future, and every master is reaching over his shoulder to look at you, waiting for you to join him. The human representatives of God constitute an infinite treasure. Dipping into this treasure will help to open your heart. At just the moment when your soul wants to blossom, the words of a saint or sage may be the right fertilizer.

9. **Allow God to take over.** When all is said and done, either spirit has power

or it doesn't. If there is only one reality, nothing in the material world stands outside God; this means that if you want something, spirit can provide it. Deciding what part you need to do and what part God will do is delicate. It also changes from stage to stage. You have to know yourself in this regard; no one else can tell you what to do. Most people are addicted to worry, control, overmanagement, and lack of faith. On a daily basis, resist the temptation to follow these tendencies. Don't listen to the voice that says you have to be in charge, that things aren't going to work out, that constant vigilance is the only way to get anything done. This voice is right because you listen to it too much. It won't be right if you let spirit try a new way. Be willing to experiment. Your intention is the most powerful tool at your disposal. Intend that everything will work out as it should, then let go and see if clues come your way. Let opportunities and openings come your way. Your deepest intelligence knows much more about what is good for you than you do. See if its voice is speaking to you. Maybe the outcome you are trying to force so hard isn't ultimately as good for you as the outcome that naturally comes your way. If you could give 1 percent of your life over to God every day, you would be the most enlightened person in the world in three months—keep that in mind and surrender something, anything, on a daily basis.

10. **Embrace the unknown.** You are not who you think you are. Since birth your identity has depended on very limited experience. Over the years you formed likes and dislikes; you learned to accept certain limits. A hoard of objects acquired over time serves to prop up a fragile sense of fulfillment. None of this is the real you. Yet no one can instantly substitute the real for the false. It takes a process of discovery. Because it is painful to strip away so many layers of illusion, you have to let the unwinding of the soul take place according to its own rhythm and timing. Your overall attitude should be that the unknown is awaiting you, an unknown that has nothing to do with the "I" you already know. Some people reach the edge of illusion only at the moment of death,

and then with a long look backward, one lifetime seems incredibly short and transient.

Around 1890 a Blackfoot Indian chief was dying. His name was Isapwo Muksika Crowfoot, and he whispered these words into the ear of a missionary father:

What is life?
It is the flash of a firefly in the night,
It is the breath of a buffalo in the winter time,
It is the little shadow that runs across the grass
And loses itself in the sunset.

The part of us that we know already is the part that flickers out all too fast. Far better to seize this time and become timeless. When you feel a new impulse, an uplifting thought, an insight that you have never acted upon before, embrace the unknown. Cherish it as tenderly as a newborn baby. The unknown is the only thing that truly cares about the fate of your soul; therefore it would be good to revere it as much as you revere holiness. God lives in the unknown, and when you can embrace it fully, you will be home free.

ENDNOTES AND
FURTHER READING

I drew from three vast areas of material for this book: religion, quantum physics, and neuroscience. Each contains its own mysteries and complexity. As I wove them together, I realized that many new doors were opening. The following notes are intended as a guide to readers who might wish to walk through some of these doors. I have favored imaginative readings here in the belief that there is more adventure in speculation than in conventional thinking. But I also feel that today's speculation will become accepted wisdom in the near future, and I invite the reader to join me in that belief.

If any one thinker inspired me to write this book, it was the noted Dutch neuroscientist Herms Romijn, who has offered a beautiful synthesis of spiritual and scientific thought in his long article "About the Origins of Consciousness: A New Multidisciplinary Perspective on the Relationship Between Brain and Mind" (Amsterdam: Akademie van Weterschapen, June 23, 1997, 100: 1–2, pp. 181–267). In this remarkable work, Romijn argues that conventional models for the brain fall far short of explaining the mind's basic operations, particularly memory. After testing the leading theories of mind against one another, Romijn favors a combination of quantum theory and ancient Vedanta, which together are the only way we can conceive of a universal mind that serves as the source for our own thoughts. With deep gratitude to him for his breakthrough speculations, I must also point out that Romijn does not make any religious arguments—the expansion of his ideas into the domain of God are purely my own.

ONE. A REAL AND USEFUL GOD

1.   A number of short answers to the question "What does the experience of God feel like?" can be found in Jonathan Robinson,

Bridges to Heaven (Walpole, N.H.: Stillpoint Publishing, 1994), pp. 54–62. Responses were all provided by spiritual writers and teachers.

2. The beginning of "spiritual physics" is complex, and because quantum theory has now expanded into at least forty different and often conflicting interpretations, the whole subject remains extremely thorny. I first attempted to unravel the basic ideas in *Quantum Healing* (New York: Bantam Books, 1989), but for more technical resources, I can lead the reader to several books that have made a deep impression on me over the past decade. They are all classics in one way or another and recognized as starting points into the quantum maze.

David Bohm, *Wholeness and the Implicate Order* (London: Routledge and Kegan Paul, 1980).

Fritjof Capra, *The Tao of Physics* (Boston: Shambhala Press, 1991).

Roger Penrose, *The Emperor's New Mind* (New York: Penguin USA, 1991).

Michael Talbot, *The Holographic Universe* (New York: HarperCollins, 1991).

Fred Alan Wolf, *Star Wave: Mind Consciousness and Quantum Physics* (New York: Macmillan, 1984).

Gary Zukav, *The Dancing Wu Li Masters* (New York: Bantam Books, 1980).

The best collection of original writings from great physicists on metaphysical matters was edited by Ken Wilber, *Quantum Questions* (Boston: Shambhala Press, 1984). Wilber went on to publish authoritative books about mysticism and physics that combine compassion and great depth of knowledge. A good appreciation of his insights can be gained from one of his earliest books and one of his most recent: *Eye to Eye* (Garden City, N.Y.: Anchor Books, 1983) and *Eye of the Spirit* (Boston: Shambhala Press, 1997).

3. The Duke project, formally known as the Monitoring and Actualization of Noetic Training, presented its findings in fall 1998 to the American Heart Association.

4. Readers will vary widely in how much quantum theory they'll wish to read about. For an introduction to the paradox of how light behaves, nothing is wittier or more palatable for the layman than a series of freshman physics lectures given by the late Nobel laureate Richard P. Feynman: *Six Easy Pieces* (New York: Addison-Wesley, 1995). Big Bang theory changes so rapidly that it is difficult to find an up-to-date treatment outside the pages of the journals

Nature and *Scientific American.* I have relied upon Stephen Hawking, *A Brief History of Time* (New York: Bantam Doubleday Dell, 1988), now ten years old but still reliable in the essentials on how time and space came into existence.

5. An eye-opening book on the many conflicting aspects of Jehovah, as he careens through the turmoil of the Old Testament, is Jack Miles, *God: A Biography* (New York: Vintage Books, 1995). For a large compendium of modern spiritual writings, the reader is referred to Lucinda Vardey, ed., *God in All Worlds* (New York: Vintage Books, 1995).

6. I am referring to students and devotees of Kabbalah. An introductory explanation of *Shekhinah* can be found in David S. Ariel, *What Do Jews Believe?* (New York: Shocken Books, 1995), pp. 22–23ff.

TWO. MYSTERY OF MYSTERIES

1. Although there are thousands of written scriptures in the Indian tradition, much of the wisdom is passed down from master to

disciple. The most inspiring modern example of this relationship, in my experience, can be found in Sudhakar S. Dikshit, *I Am That* (Durham: Acorn Press, 1973). But the reader is also referred to the many books centering on other notable voices of Vedanta, such as Sri Ramakrishna, Sri Aurobindo, Ramana Maharishi, Paramahansa Yogananda, J. Krishnamurti, and Maharishi Mahesh Yogi, to name some of the best-known exponents in the West of a five-thousand-year-old tradition.

2. For the most literal translation of Christ's words I have relied upon the New English Bible translation, except for some instances where the King James version was inescapable, having become part of our language. For scriptural quotations outside the recognized gospels, see Ricky Alan Mayotte, *The Complete Jesus* (South Royalton, Vt.: Steerforth Press, 1997). I should also point out that all interpretations of Christ's words in this book are my own and not derived from any sect or authority.

3. Hawking himself does not deal in the connections between spirituality and quantum physics. The latest and best summary of those connections is made in Paul

Davies, *The Mind of God* (New York: Simon and Schuster, 1992). In this follow-up to his classic *God and the New Physics*, Davies deals with the central issue of whether an intelligent creator is consistent with modern cosmology.

THREE. SEVEN STAGES OF GOD

1. An excellent discussion of addictions from the social and personality level can be found in Angelus Arrien, *The Four-Fold Way: Walking the Paths of the Warrior, Teacher, Healer and Visionary* (San Francisco: Harper San Francisco: 1993), which I have adapted to fit my spiritual argument.

2. Sister Marie's miraculous feats are recounted in Patricia Treece, *The Sanctified Body* (Liguori, Mo.: Triumph Books, 1993), pp. 276–80. This is the most reliable, detailed account of miracle-working in the Catholic church over the past century.

3. The deeply moving story of Father Maximilian is in Treece, *Sanctified Body*, pp. 140–43. She has also written a complete biography, *A Man for Others* (San Francisco: Harper and Row, 1982).

FOUR. A MANUAL FOR SAINTS

1. Griffith's experience is recounted in full in Vardey, ed., *God in All Worlds*, p. 88.

2. My version of the night of Qadr is derived from Thomas W. Lippman, *Understanding Islam* (New York: Penguin/Meridian, 1995), pp. 38–39.

3. Some of the first and best arguments for the "mind field" were made in Penfield's *The Mystery of the Mind* (Princeton, N.J.: Princeton University Press, 1975).

4. Fascinating connections are made between brain function and spiritual experiences in Valerie V. Hunt, *Infinite Mind* (Malibu, Calif.: Malibu Publishing, 1996).

5. I am making a strong argument for the notion that mind is not localized in the brain but extends like a force field beyond space and time. To make this argument, I have relied upon the most eloquent thinker on nonlocalized mind, Rupert Sheldrake. His major work to date is *The Presence of the Past* (New York: Times Books, 1988), but readers will be drawn to his more informal conversations on science and spirituality in

Michael Fox and Rupert Sheldrake, *Natural Grace* (New York: Doubleday, 1996).

Sheldrake is unique in offering ingenious experiments that would prove the existence of the mind field (he refers to it as the field of morphogenesis). The most recent proposals, which invite the reader to participate, appear in his book *Seven Experiments That Could Change the World* (New York: Riverhead Books, 1995).

FIVE. STRANGE POWERS

1. Dr. Bruce L. Miller reported his findings in the April 1998 issue of the journal *Neurology*.

2. The best popular writing on this mystery is still found in Oliver Sacks, *The Man Who Mistook His Wife for a Hat* (New York: Simon and Schuster, 1987). Connections between spiritual awakening and brain disease have been speculated about for a long time but never proven. A striking modern example, however, can be found in Suzanne Segal, *Collision With the Infinite* (San Diego: Blue Dove Press, 1996).

SIX. CONTACTING GOD

1. Credible attempts to explain the soul in scientific terms are rare. The best is found in Gary Zukav, *The Seat of the Soul* (New York: Simon and Schuster, 1989).

INDEX

153–60
Memory, 358–60,
    363–65, 441
Memory of former
    lifetimes,
    399–415
Mentors, 172–74
Merton, Thomas,
    496
Miller, 390
Mind, *see* Quantum
    domain
Mind field, 354–75,
    417
Miracles, 7, 228–31
    belief and, 2–3
    defined, 316
    healing touch and,
    242
    mystery of, 54–56,
    58–62
    prayer and, 495
    in quantum
    domain, 204,
    235–37, 242
    search for, 52
    seven levels of,
    32–34, 316–18
    in visionary
    response, 34,
    238–45, 262–63,
    307, 317–18

Mother, darshan of,
    243–46
Mozart, Wolfgang
    Amadeus, 388
Muhammad, 352–53
Multiple personality
    syndrome,
    421–31
Murray, Gilbert, 165
Mystery, 44–65
    of creation, 50–52
    material reality vs.,
    64–65
    of miracles, 54–56,
    58–61
    at quantum level,
    48–49, 53, 56,
    64
    reality sandwich
    of, 44–46
    in virtual domain,
    49–50, 53, 56,
    63–64
Mystical, use of
    term, 502
Mystics, 8–10, 20

N
Near-death experi-
    ences, 456
Newton, Sir Isaac,
    276

S

Sacred response, 30, 74, 76
about experiencing God, 266–70
action in, 332
choice of, 42
duality as hurdle in, 297–300, 312
evolution of journey in, 330
faith and, 494–95
fulfillment in, 26–27, 314
God of Pure Being ("I Am"), 266, 306
God response in, 13, 16
good and evil in, 287–90, 310
How do I find God?, 283–87, 309
How do I fit in?, 280–82, 309
identity and, 78–79
infinity (no horizon) in, 499
life challenge in, 291–96, 311

masking the soul in, 337–38
miracles and, 34, 317
self-perception in, 15
separation and union in, 490
Spirit revealed in, 25
temptation in, 301–3, 312
transcendence in, 283–87, 308
unity as strength in, 296–302, 311
Who am I? in, 275–78, 308, 492
Saints, 319–75
action and, 330–31
core of manual for, 321–22
and experience of God, 9, 20
masking the soul, 336–38
mind field and, 354–75
spiritual awakening of, 341–53
spiritual journey